MW00760739

Dean of Umpires

Dean of Umpires

A Biography of
Bill McGowan, 1896–1954

Bob Luke

FOREWORD BY JIM EVANS

McFarland & Company, Inc., Publishers
Jefferson, North Carolina, and London

Library of Congress Cataloguing-in-Publication Data

Luke, Bob, 1941–
    Dean of umpires : a biography of Bill McGowan, 1896–1954
/ Bob Luke ; foreword by Jim Evans.
        p.   cm.
    Includes bibliographical references and index.

    ISBN 0-7864-2136-3 (softcover : 50# alkaline paper)

    1. McGowan, Bill, 1896–1954.   2. Baseball umpires—
United States—Biography.   I. Title
    GV865.M296L84   2005
    796.357'092 — dc22   2005010596

British Library cataloguing data are available

©2005 Bob Luke. All rights reserved

*No part of this book may be reproduced or transmitted in any form
or by any means, electronic or mechanical, including photocopying
or recording, or by any information storage and retrieval system,
without permission in writing from the publisher.*

On the cover: Students practicing their "out" signals; Bill
McGowan's autographed photograph

Manufactured in the United States of America

*McFarland & Company, Inc., Publishers
Box 611, Jefferson, North Carolina 28640
www.mcfarlandpub.com*

For the Future:
Ella, Grace, Jacob, Skylar

Acknowledgments

I owe a debt of thanks and gratitude to many people whose help has been invaluable in the preparation of this book. Paul Dickson, noted author and baseball expert, has provided much-appreciated coaching on how to write a book and where to find information. He has also offered his friendship on trips to flea markets, yard sales, and book auctions where the search for baseball memorabilia of all stripes goes on unabated, and encouragement to keep at it. Dave Kelly at the Library of Congress was generous with his assistance in locating hard-to-find books and articles and introducing me to electronic databases. The staff at the National Baseball Hall of Fame and Museum in Cooperstown, New York, was prompt and courteous in responding to my many requests for information. In particular I'd like to thank Claudette Burke and Freddy Berowski for their prompt answers to questions and making player files available to review and W.C. Burdick for help in identifying players in old photos.

I spent many a pleasant hour with Bill McGowan's son, William A. McGowan, Jr., who shared stories about his father, provided me with access to the scrapbook he kept on his father's career, made photographs from the family album available, and read an earlier draft of the book. Bill McGowan, Sr.'s grandniece, Mary Martelli, provided me with a copy of the McGowan family tree that she had compiled and a copy of a 1900 photograph of the McGowan family. Margaret McGowan Rentz, Bill, Sr.'s niece, and her daughter Margaret C. Harrison provided several helpful letters and documents. Steve Steinberg took time from his baseball research to periodically send copies of newspaper articles and several scarce photographs of McGowan. Steve Gietschier of *The Sporting News* made the newspaper's clipping file on McGowan available to me. Sportswriters Bill Gilbert and Bob Broeg were generous with their stories about McGowan. Former major league umpire Jim Evans filled me in on the differences in umpiring in McGowan's day and today and wrote the foreword. Syl Sobel, a colleague of mine, and his ten-year-old daughter, Izzy, read an early draft and provided insightful suggestions and encouragement to keep going. John Rice, who was appointed to fill the American League umpiring vacancy created by McGowan's death, described his recollections of the two McGowan umpire school sessions that he attended.

I spoke with the following former major league players by telephone about their remembrances of McGowan: Sid Hudson, Gil Coan, Irv Noren, Phil Rizzuto, Walt Masterson, Charlie "Broadway" Wagner, Bob Feller, Buddy Lewis, Matt Batts, Mickey Vernon, Eddie Robinson, Bobby Doerr, Jim Hannen, and (thanks to the efforts of Chandra Tracy of the Major League Baseball Players Alumni Association), Mel Parnell and Jimmy Piersall. Thomas Altherr, who, with Charlie Metro, wrote the book about Metro's career, *Safe by a Mile*, introduced me to Metro, who recounted several stories about McGowan, as did 96-year-old Billy Werber, a one-time teammate of Babe Ruth and the last surviving member of the Ruth-Gehrig-Dickey-Werber bridge foursome who played cards to while away the hours during long train rides. I'd also like to thank Gregory J. Egner, Jr., for his helpful suggestions and Chris Wagenseller for typing McGowan's textbook into an electronic file. Brandon Light provided me with a copy of a letter McGowan had written to Roman Bentz encouraging Bentz to attend his umpiring school. Terry Carlson provided a hard-to-find copy of an article about McGowan's school in *Sports World*. Robert "Skip" McAfee brought his expertise in baseball history to bear by fact-checking the book and compiling the index. Susan Beal, through her considerable editorial and proofreading skills, improved the flow, organization, and readability of the original manuscript.

I am deeply indebted to one and all. Any errors and shortcomings in the book are mine alone.

Contents

Acknowledgments   vii

Foreword by Jim Evans   1

Preface   5

Bill McGowan Timeline   11

Introduction   13

1: Big Shot   21

2: When a Ball Was a Ball and a Strike Was a Strike   48

3: Not Born to Blush Unseen   58

4: Why Don't You Umpire?   78

5: The School   87

6: No. 1   101

7: That's a Sure-Fire Way to Lose Your Job   114

Epilogue   129

Appendix: The Textbook Used at McGowan's Umpiring School   135

Chapter Notes   189

Bibliography   203

Index   207

Foreword by Jim Evans

Thirty-six years ago I stepped off an airplane in Tampa, Florida, into 100 degree heat. I had just completed my first commercial flight, a thousand-mile trip that would be the first leg of a million-mile journey. Tampa was a long way from my home in Austin, Texas. My first game as a professional umpire was only hours away. Family members and friends questioned my decision to make that trip. Right up till the last second as the cabin door was being slammed shut, friends were asking "are you sure?" After all, who in his right mind would want to be that one guy on the field who everyone loved to hate? To many, giving up the semisecurity of a high school teaching offer and a $15,000 salary for a part-time umpiring job that paid $250 a month did not compute. For me, it was a no-brainer. Having umpired since I was 14 and having paid my way through the University of Texas with umpiring proceeds, I had no doubts about what I wanted to do upon graduation. I wanted to be a professional umpire. With true umpire decisiveness, I also knew exactly what I did not want. I did not want to be one of those timid souls who went to his grave with his song unsung.

Leaving Texas and my established reputation behind, I was off and running. All the good ratings, all the accolades, all the pats on the back that inspired me to shoot for the big time were gone. I was starting over. This was pro ball, and it was going to be a whole new ballgame. I was a rookie, but even I could tell. The intensity of play was different. Each pitch and each play seemed to mean so much more. These guys were playing for money. They were playing for fame and fortune. More than anything else, they wanted a shot at the Show and they didn't want some incompetent umpire stopping them. Every player envisioned himself as the next Mickey Mantle or Sandy Koufax. Many of the managers were being groomed for potential jobs in the majors. It was easy to get caught up in the fantasy. Often, I would watch the televised Saturday Game of the Week and fantasize that it was I behind that plate making those calls in Yankee Stadium or Fenway Park. One Saturday while my partner was out sightseeing with his family, I rearranged the furniture in the small, musty motel room and crouched on every pitch and rendered a call that coincided with the plate umpire's. The game went extra innings and lasted about four hours. I was hoping it would end and I could get the room reorganized before my partner returned. It finally ended and I was relieved to know that I had the stamina to work under such grueling conditions. The actual game I worked that night in Lakeland lasted only an hour and 45 minutes. It was a piece of cake compared to my earlier plate job. My partner never knew I worked a doubleheader that day.

Why would anyone want to be an umpire? As I crisscrossed the country for over 30 years practicing my craft, I was asked that question at least a thousand times. In true umpire resolve, I always offered the same answer: "I dunno!" There is no rational answer. No father has ever walked into a maternity ward and proudly announced to the world that his strapping young son there in crib number four was going to be a major league umpire someday. Great military general? Okay. President? Maybe. But an umpire? Get serious. All I can assure you is this: That special feeling one derives from performing a very difficult task under the most challenging conditions is exceptionally rewarding. Words cannot describe the personal satisfaction one gets from making a great call, working a perfect game behind the plate, or handling a tricky rule situation with confidence. And the more pressure there is the greater the potential for enjoyment.

This book is the story of a man who did it as well as anyone in the history of the game. There is no doubt that he enjoyed it. Having faced many of the same challenges as Bill McGowan, I have a genuine appreciation and respect for his consummate skills and even his shortcomings. I began hearing Bill McGowan stories in 1968, my first year in the minor leagues, and was still hearing them my last in 1999 as my own 28-year major league career came to a close. Baseball is conducive to storytelling. Unlike other sports, there are more opportunities for interaction between participants and officials due to the pace of play. And baseball is the only major sport where participants are allowed to engage the officials in heated nose-to-nose confrontations without automatic penalty. This phenomenon definitely leads to some interesting interactions. Many of the stories in this book are first-person accounts of incidents that defined Bill McGowan as an umpire, and, more importantly, as a person.

I was eight years old when McGowan died in 1954, yet I worked in the major leagues with many who had been mentored by him. Hank Soar, John Flaherty, Nestor Chylak, Larry Napp, and John Rice were all senior umpires in the American League when I came up in 1971. Each had his stories and memories of McGowan. There always seemed to be a nugget of wisdom to be gleaned from each account. As this biography reveals, McGowan was by no means cherubic or always right but his heart and soul were always in the right place. He was not averse to offering advice to a superstar and he felt just as comfortable chastising the same individual when he got out of line. Bill McGowan umpired with conviction.

Though the game is still the same in many ways, it is so drastically different in others. The culture of playing and umpiring has changed dramatically since McGowan's career ended in 1954. In McGowan's era, umpires used their authority to control the game. If a player misbehaved or was unfair with his complaint, most umpires did not hesitate to widen the strike zone, narrow it, or tongue-lash the irascible player. There was no instant replay or strong players' union to challenge the umpire's actions. Occasionally, a hostile hack would grab an incident from the field and milk it for a couple stories. Generally speaking, however, the press knew how the game was played and silenced their typewriters. Players respected the stronger umpires. They knew that there were certain umpires you did not mess with. Bill McGowan was one such umpire. As you are going to see as you read Bob Luke's account, the most lavish praise for McGowan came from the players themselves.

McGowan was the perfect umpire for his era. Some of the antics he perpetrated during his brilliant career, however, would get an umpire fired today. McGowan would have probably spared Curt Schilling the task of destroying the QuesTec cameras monitoring umpire decisions on balls and strikes in Arizona in 2003. He would have most likely beat him to it. He threw his indicator at a disgruntled pitcher once and emptied his ball bag for another who complained about how the baseballs were rubbed. Suspended twice by his league president, McGowan was known to curse players occasionally. He bet horses and he suffered from diabetes. Bill McGowan was a normal human being just like you and me, but he had an extraordinary ability to umpire and control a baseball game. He demonstrated an uncanny ability to say the right thing in a heated argument. His first ejection was Babe Ruth. He backed down from no one, yet he showed compassion and leniency as he saw fit. He was not always beloved by the younger umpires he mentored. Though his approach often lacked diplomacy and he was criticized for being brusque, no one questioned the sincerity or value of his tutelage. He was so committed to teaching and helping others that he started his own umpire school in 1938. Most of his instruction has withstood the test of time and is just as applicable today as it was five decades ago.

I was ecstatic when I heard that Bob Luke was going to write a biography about Bill McGowan. Finally, someone was taking the time to tell

McGowan's story. It seems that the shelves of our bookstores are overflowing with accounts of the latest flash-in-the-pan superstar. Yet the tremendous contributions of a person of Bill's stature are buried with the man. The magnitude of McGowan's impact on the game was evidenced by his 1992 Hall of Fame induction, an embarrassing 38 years after his death. For a man's name to still be spoken and his stories recounted 38 years after his death speaks volumes about his significance and contributions to the game. Bob Luke does an excellent job of taking you back into an era when baseball seemed to be a lot more fun.

Preface

Propped up in bed with three pillows under his head, Bill McGowan said to me, "Someday you can sell this for a hundred bucks at a church bazaar." He handed me a snow-white Reach baseball that he'd signed, along with Ted Williams, Nelson Fox, Mickey Mantle, Bob Feller, Joe Coleman, Phil Rizzuto, Eddie Yost, and Yogi Berra. It was November of 1954. He was dean of the American League umpires with eight World Series and four All-Star games, including the first one in 1933, to his credit, and my next-door neighbor. He died a month later of a heart attack brought on by diabetes, which had afflicted him most of his life.

I was 13 years old, center fielder for the after-school pick-up games on the playing fields of Highland View Elementary School in Silver Spring, Maryland, and thrilled to be living next door to an American League umpire. For the six months that we were neighbors, he indulged my hero worship by inviting my younger brother, Don, and me over to his house to watch an occasional Washington Senators game on TV. He hadn't been able to work a game since late July due to his long-standing diabetes taking a sudden turn for the worse.

Whenever I had the chance, I'd ride my red, balloon-tired J.C. Higgins bike (which I bought from Sears and Roebuck with proceeds from odd jobs and allowance payments) to Griffith Stadium to see the Senators play. For other games, my dad would drive my brother and me to the stadium where an enterprising teenager would greet my dad with, "Hey, mister — watch your car for 50 cents?" My father always paid it. Maybe he was being generous, but I remember thinking that it was odd; the car never required watching elsewhere. No one offered to watch it in the Giant supermarket parking lot while my mother and I shopped for groceries. I had a hunch the payment was protection money. Yet, the car was always where we left it, and in the same condition as we had left it, so I figured it was 50 cents well spent. We usually re-entered the car gingerly due to sunburns acquired in the inexpensive center field bleacher seats during a Sunday doubleheader. At the end of every game at Griffith Stadium my dad, brother and I walked across the field, and my brother and I ran the bases if the groundskeepers were in a good mood.

Not only were the center field bleachers affordable seats, they also gave me a close-up look at my favorite player, Jim Busby, the Senators' center fielder, after whose play I modeled my own. If Busby could race full tilt with his back to the plate and spear a ball in the webbing of his glove that would otherwise have been a double or a triple, I could, I figured, do the same. I did get so I could catch those balls once in a while — not including the time I was folded in half by a waist-high chain link fence that bordered our high-school diamond.

I never made a catch as dramatic as Willie Mays' back-to-the-infield, cap-flying, on-the-dead-run catch of Vic Wertz's smash in the 1954 World Series, but my outstretched mitt snared more than one ball out of the air while I was looking over my shoulder into the afternoon sky.

Occasionally Busby, who also lived in Silver Spring, would give us a ride to Griffith Stadium. Not only was it cool riding to a game with my favorite player, but since we arrived a couple of hours before the game started, we took our gloves into the area between the stands and the left field foul line. There we'd field batting practice grounders hit into foul territory, while Senators left fielder Jim Lemon took the ones in fair territory.

You could venture into the dugout before game time in those days without being chased away by security guards. During warm-ups before an exhibition game between the Senators and the Brooklyn Dodgers, I took a baseball into the Dodger dugout and talked with Jackie Robinson, Roy Campanella, Don Newcombe, Gil Hodges, Carl Furillo, and Pee Wee Reese while they signed the ball. I remember asking Newcombe if it was true, as I'd read in the paper, that his fast ball was losing a little zip, and him saying to me, "Son, you can't believe everything you read in the paper."

I had visions of signing baseballs myself someday, but that never came to pass. I got as far as being the starting center fielder for my Montgomery Blair High School team in my junior and senior years. I had more than my share of extra base hits off meaty fastballs down the middle of the plate, but the mysteries of the curve and the slider eluded me.

The wrecking ball demolished Griffith Stadium in 1965 to make room for Howard University's Medical Center. Jim Busby went on to the White Sox, Indians, Red Sox, and Orioles, before retiring with the Astros in 1962. I graduated from Colgate University in 1963 and went on to raising a family and making a living.

Why This Book

I occasionally came across a reference to McGowan in a baseball book and took particular notice when he was inducted into the Hall of Fame in 1992. My curiosity about McGowan's career led me to interview several players who had known him and to do some library research for articles about him in *Baseball Digest* and *The Diamond Angle Quarterly*.[1] In the process I learned there was much more to say about McGowan than would fit in an article, and so was born the idea for a book.

"Do people write books about umpires?" my boss asked somewhat quizzically.

"Not very often," I told her. Information on umpires, particularly those who have been dead for half a century, can be hard to come by. Larry Gerlach, author of *The Men in Blue: Conversations with Umpires*, a collection of interviews he conducted with major-league umpires, told me, "Umpires are tough research topics because they're mostly written up only when some incident occurs."[2]

Still, books on umpires are written. In addition to *The Men in Blue*, other books have tackled the topic, including James Kahn's *The Umpire Story*, Lee Gutkind's *The Best Seat in Baseball*, and John Skipper's *Umpires: Classic Baseball Stories from the Men Who Made the Calls*, to note but a few.

A number of umpires have penned their life stories, too, including Tom Gorman's *Three and Two*, Ron Luciano's *The Umpire Strikes Back* and *The Fall of the Roman Umpire*, Durwood Merrill's *You're Out and You're Ugly Too!*, Ralph Pinelli's *Mr. Ump*, and more recently, Dave Phillips' *Center Field on Fire*. A fair number of books exist about how to umpire, including Billy Evans' classics *Umpiring from the Inside* and *How to Umpire, Including Knotty Problems*, Mark Ambrosius' *Baseball Umpire's Guidebook: Communication and Mechanics*, and C.F. "Skip" Millelbuscher's *Call 'Em Right*. But even with these and other books on umpiring and the fact that there would be no game without them, umpires get nowhere near the ink devoted to players and managers.

Walt Masterson (right-handed pitcher for the Washington Senators, Red Sox and Tigers from 1939 to 1956) told me that if I wanted to sell the book I'd have to do a pretty good job because "umpires don't have a lot of fans." McGowan, as I was to learn in the course of my research, was an exception to this conventional wisdom about umpires. As a prelude to what I'd learn from many sources about the esteem in which McGowan was held, Masterson added, "You're really doing a great thing, honoring a great man."[3]

I was able to find more information on McGowan than I had first thought would be possible. In addition to consulting newspapers, magazines, and books of the day, I interviewed by telephone many former players who knew McGowan's work firsthand. I also interviewed his son, William A. McGowan, Jr., and his son's wife, Henrietta (or "Hetsy," as she is known to friends). In this age of electronic databases, I was able to read everything written about McGowan in *The New York Times*, *The Sporting News*, and *The Washington Post* throughout his 30-year major league career. The textbook that McGowan wrote for his students has been a resource for this book and is included as an appendix. In it McGowan gives advice on the techniques and mechanics of umpiring as well as on the abilities and attitudes that — in his opinion — are likely to ensure an umpire's success.

McGowan is one of the few at Cooperstown whose story hasn't been told. An article in *Sports Collectors Digest* on May 1, 1992, noted that there was little press coverage of McGowan's Hall of Fame induction. The Associated Press wire story had only a few sentences, *The Sporting News* said almost nothing, and not even *The New York Times* had much to say.

So, for those who'd like to know more about a Hall of Famer whose influence on the game was considerable during his lifetime and continues to this day, and for those men and women arbiters at all levels of organized ball looking for tips on how to umpire from one of the acknowledged masters, here's some ink on one of the game's best and most colorful umpires, who "called 'em as he saw 'em" in the days before instant replays, television, player and umpire unions, and computerized scrutiny of the accuracy of an umpire's calls through a system called QuesTec.[4]

The Bill McGowan Story

In considering how to tell his story, I was reminded of my fondness for oral histories such as Lawrence Ritter's classic *The Glory of Their Times: The Story of the Early Days of Baseball Told by the Men Who Played It* and Larry Gerlach's *Men in Blue: Conversations with Umpires.*[5] Oral histories always give me a more immediate and personal feel for the person, the situation, and how that person saw the events he was describing than do third person accounts. It's one thing to say that McGowan wouldn't listen to a player's complaints about being called out. It's another to recount his line in such a situation, which was, "If you don't think you're out, check the morning paper."

Since a literal oral history wasn't possible, as McGowan and many of his contemporaries have died, I have quoted from published primary sources and statements from interviews. I have tried to make connections between the quotations and statements to give the reader a sense of context and continuity, while letting the stories and comments speak for themselves whenever possible.

The reader should also know that this is a book primarily about McGowan's umpiring style and personality and the impact of his style and personality on the games he worked and on the players, managers, and sportswriters who worked with him. This is not a book about his umpiring methods and techniques. Those with an interest in umpiring techniques will find a limited discussion of his system for calling balls and strikes and his methods of signaling his calls. I have also included, as an appendix, the textbook that he wrote and distributed to students at his school. Here you will find his thinking about such techniques as proper stance behind the plate, calling balls hit near the foul lines, a test on "everyday problems," umpiring in the single and double umpire system, positioning yourself for various calls, and a section on the proper attitude for umpiring. You will also find references in the bibliography that describe the accepted methods and techniques for umpiring.

Bill McGowan Timeline

1896: Born in Wilmington, Delaware

1912: Umpired first game in New Castle, Delaware

1915: Umpired first professional game for the Virginia League

1916: Umpired in International and Sally League

1917: Umpired in Blue Ridge League

1918: Married Magdaline Ferry

1919: Returned to International League;
William McGowan, Jr., born

1920: William McGowan joins family

1922: Fired from International League

1923: Umpired in Southern Association

1925: Ejected Babe Ruth from exhibition game;
umpired first American League game

1928: Umpired his first World Series;
byline first appears in *The Sporting News*

1933: Selected to umpire first All-Star Game

1935: Selected best American League umpire by players' votes

1938: Opened umpire school in College Park, Maryland

1940: Missed first game since 1925

1944: Awarded plaque by Touchdown Club for work in World Series

1948: Suspended for 10 days;
selected to umpire Indians–Red Sox playoff game

1952: Suspended for four days

1954:   Conducted first umpire school outside the
          United States, in Montreal, Canada;
          selected by Touchdown Club as Baseball's Man of the Year;
          died December 9 in Silver Spring, Maryland

Introduction

Traditionally regarded as villains by fans, adversarial autocrats by players, and invisible men by the press, umpires have been, as Furman Bisher put it, "submerged in the history of baseball like idiot children in a family album."[1]

One reason that the press may see umpires as invisible is that fans don't pay to see them. Hall of Fame umpire Billy Evans noted that most fans consider the umpire a necessary evil and rarely inquire, "Who will umpire the game today?" "They don't," Evans continued, "go to the park to see the umpire perform as they do the great stars like Tyrus Cobb, Hans Wagner, Napoleon Lajoie, or Tris Speaker."[2] George Will has said of umpires: "Umpires are carved from granite and stuffed with microchips. They are supposed to be dispassionate dispensers of Pure Justice, icy islands of emotionless calculation."[3]

In a similar vein, sportswriter Ed Pollock, commenting about the virtue of umpires being little noticed, wrote: "My idea of a good sports official is one who's inconspicuous at all times. To be inconspicuous, his decisions must be satisfactory.... If he has any color it should be entirely white. He should have no red or purple moments. Neither should he look green at any time. Whatever color a baseball umpire has should be in his ability to render good decisions and not in fanciful methods of making such decisions known."[4]

Bill McGowan

William Aloysius McGowan was a rainbow on and off the field. He was a master of the one-line retort, be it a zinger or a joke; was admired by fans, players, and sportswriters for his on-field dramatics; wrote letters to club owners promoting such players as Goose Goslin, Moe Berg, Stanley "Bucky" Harris, and Jimmy Dykes; was generous with tips to players; was regarded by players, managers, and league presidents as "the best ball and strikes man there is"; wrote articles for such magazines as *Liberty* and *Esquire*; authored, at different times, two newspaper columns titled *Three and Tuh* and *M'Gowan Says*; and wrote numerous articles for *The Washington Times-Herald*, *The Sporting News*, and *The New Orleans Item*. He was suspended twice, not for poor performance or bad judgment, but for his conduct on the field.

Those who knew McGowan remember him for many things, not the least of which was his sense of humor. "He could keep you laughing for hours," said Joe Reeves, brother of Bill McGowan, Jr.'s wife, Henrietta. "It helped," Reeves said, "that you at least had heard of the people he was talking about. It was not a put-down kind of humor, just an animated retelling of funny situations. I remember one story in particular that McGowan told about Leo Durocher in 'The Lip's' managerial days. Mr. McGowan was telling my wife and me and some friends about tossing Durocher from an exhibition game for arguing too long and kicking dirt at McGowan. Well, he didn't just tell us the story. He got up off the couch, got face-to-face with each of us like Durocher did with him, and gave us a sample of their conversation — though he probably edited it a bit. He even went through the motions of kicking dirt. And of course he ended the story by showing off his famous sweeping motion of his right hand that he used when inviting people to leave the field. We always looked forward to his visits."[5]

He was also given to the use of puns as evidenced by his characterization of fellow umpire Red Ormsby as having gone "stork mad" for fathering eight children.[6]

If an athletic club or Elks Lodge in the Middle Atlantic States was honoring a baseball figure, chances are McGowan was at the head table with two or three of his hilarious stories to tell about his experiences in the minor and major leagues. Many of his stories were at his own expense. One that appeared in the *Herald* concerned an exhibition game between the Boston Braves and the Senators in 1925. "Most of my decisions were breaking against the Senators," McGowan wrote. "On one play I called Joe Judge [the Senators' first baseman] safe at first on a close play. Nick Altrock was coaching at first for the Senators. At this point there was some commotion behind first base in the stands. All of the players on the Braves and some of the Senators started in the direction of first base.

"'Go on back, fellows,' hollered Altrock, 'Everything's all right. A woman just fainted in the stands. McGowan called one right.'"[7]

His off-the-field ventures included being a pitchman for Longines watches during the '39 Series. Looking out from a quarter-page ad in *The Sporting News*, he's quoted as saying, "You can go to jail, lose a game, walk a base or garner a stiff fine if you are on the wrong side of time in the World's Series." To avoid such mistakes, McGowan let it be known that "the umpires I know in the American and National leagues wear Longines watches because time counts big in baseball."[8]

He played the horses with abandon and was a voracious writer. Though he had diabetes throughout most of his adult life, he indulged his fondness for chocolate. He would hide chocolate bars under stacks of papers on his desk and in between sofa cushions and dash into the corner pharmacy (Packett's in Silver Spring, Maryland) for a chocolate soda, telling his wife he was buying a newspaper to check the day's box scores. He would often consume a quart of ice cream at one sitting.[9]

He spent time in the garden of his Silver Spring home — a hobby known only to his close friends, according to a newspaper account of his death.

McGowan carried his umpire gestures over into his personal conversations by spreading out his hands, palms down, and jerking his thumb just as if he were calling players safe or out on the field.

"How are you feeling, Bill?" In answer he would spread his hands meaning, "swell."

"What do you say if we go to the movies?" He would give his right wrist a twist with the thumb protruding, meaning that suggestion is "out."[10]

On the Field

McGowan, like many umpires in his day, controlled the field of play as much with his personality as with the rulebook. Try and show him up, and he'd call a third strike on you regardless of where the ball was. As Lefty Gomez (who Billy Werber, third baseman and shortstop during the 1930s and '40s for five teams in the American and National leagues, said was known for "being goofy") found out, pranks weren't tolerated. Late in a game with Bob Feller on the mound and twilight approaching, Gomez brought a lit cigarette lighter with him to plate.

"Put out that lighter," McGowan ordered. "You're making a farce of the game. You can see the ball."

"I can see the ball fine, Mac," Gomez said. "I just want to be sure Feller can see me." On that note, Gomez quickly blew out the lighter.[11]

Until he got to know the rookies, he called all of them "Bush" or "Busher" to remind them of their place in the pecking order. Walt Masterson remembered this treatment from McGowan during Masterson's first major league game at the age of 18. After taking two strikes his first time at bat, he stepped out of the batter's box without calling time out to collect his thoughts, just as his high school coach had told him to do. "Hold it! Hold it!" yelled McGowan, who turned to brush off the plate but really to say to Masterson, "Bush, are you trying to show me up? Because if you are, you're outta here on the next pitch whatever it is."[12]

He was known to call a strike a ball for a player he thought to be deserving of a break; eject half a team for jockeying him; settle Ted Williams' nerves of the last day of the 1941 season when Williams went 6 for 8 to push his average over .400; advise Hank Greenberg on his home run swing; and umpire softball games for recovering amputees at Walter Reed Hospital near Washington, D.C., during World War II.

Through a combination of skill, hustle, and common sense he gained the respect of those who saw him work. He personified hustle long before Pete Rose became known as Mr. Hustle. McGowan rarely failed to be in position to see a play even if it meant a mad dash to first or third on a sweltering day. McGowan concluded his umpiring textbook with the following pitch for hustle to aspiring umpires:

> Always try to be a step ahead of the players. Hustle is the most valuable word in baseball. With the first pitch of the ball game, get in there and bear down. Be on top of your plays. Make your decisions with determination. Be alert. Take nothing for granted. The ball players make or break an umpire. If you are a hustler, they will love you for it, and hustling covers a multitude of sins. Among the American League umpires, three of the best hustlers I've seen in more than 10 years are Johnny Quinn, Bill Grieve, and Cal Hubbard. Their main forte is hustle. Here's hoping you fellows will always hustle.[13]

You have to be in shape to hustle, and McGowan was no stranger to preseason conditioning programs. During the spring of 1926, his second year as an American League umpire, he was seen putting on a uniform and rubber shirt for daily workouts at the YMCA in his hometown of Wilmington, Delaware. He said, "I like to be fast enough every season to get right on top of the plays I have to pass on, and the only way I can do it is to keep in shape so I can keep up with the players when they are heading for a play."[14]

Bobby Doerr (Hall of Fame second baseman for the Red Sox from 1937 to 1951) remembers asking McGowan, "Mac, what makes you such a great umpire?" He got his answer: "Always being in position to make the call."[15]

McGowan's 30-year umpiring career in the American League was among the longest in baseball history at the time of his death in 1954. His career rivaled in length those of Bill Klem, who was active from 1905 to 1940, and Tommy Connolly, who umpired in the majors from 1898 to 1931.

McGowan also personified endurance by umpiring almost as many consecutive games (2,532) as Cal Ripken, Jr., played (2,632). McGowan's streak began with the first game of the 1925 season — the same season that Lou Gehrig began his consecutive game streak of 2,130 games, which stood as the major league record for consecutive games until broken by Ripken on September 6, 1995.

McGowan didn't miss a game until a bout of neuritis forced him out on September 3, 1940. He returned to duty the night of September 5 for the night game at Comiskey Park. He didn't miss another game until May 1946, when he stayed out most of the season with another bout of neuritis. Al Cartwright reported, "The doctors said he wouldn't be back and so did President Will Harridge of the American League. But back he came ... and into a World Series, at that."[16]

Sportswriter Dick McCann noted that McGowan once worked 10 straight days on a broken toe. Several sportswriters explained that a foul ball had struck his toe at Shibe Park. In truth Bill had flung his hotel windows wide and was stripped for a nude nap when a mosquito began zooming around. McCann said at the time: "He folded up a magazine and started chasing the zinger zeppelin in his bare feet. But as he lunged at it savagely, he stubbed his toe on the iron leg of his bed — and down he went in a howling heap. I'm sure you understand why he let everyone believe it was a foul tip. He's a proud man, that McGowan — and like every umpire upon whose shoulders rest the entire structure of baseball, he has a right to be."

In the same article, written in 1941, McCann

A young Bill McGowan circa 1920 (from Bill Jr.'s photograph album).

noted that including McGowan's minor league career he umpired about 4,000 consecutive games, save one. That game occurred in his first year of umpiring, 1915, at age 19 in the Virginia League. He didn't get paid for eight weeks and went on strike for a game. His check arrived the next day.

It was during the 1915 season that he had his first and only serious doubt about the viability of his chosen profession. After being severely banged up at game's end by disappointed Portsmouth, Virginia, fans, he was debating whether to return to the fray. But he remembered that a sportswriter in his hometown had told him he'd be back home in two weeks because he'd find the work too hard.

He was behind the plate the next day. Thirteen years later, after umpiring his first World Series—the 1928 New York Yankees–St. Louis Cardinals affair—he wired the sportswriter: "It's been a helluva long two weeks."

McCann goes on to mention the two times the streak was almost broken. Once was when McGowan was en route from Washington to Philadelphia while his son Bill, Jr., was being operated on for appendicitis. McGowan went straight to the hospital, where he stayed until his son was out of danger. The next train wouldn't get him to Shibe Park in time so it cost him $15.50 to take a cab. "I made a mistake." McGowan said. "I shouldn't have told the cabbie I was an umpire. I think he hiked the rates."

The second time he almost missed a game was the famous Yankees–Philadelphia Athletics record-breaking doubleheader on May 24, 1928.

A sweep by the A's of the doubleheader that day at Shibe

Earliest known photograph of Bill McGowan in an umpire's uniform. Circa 1917–18 (from Bill Jr.'s photograph album).

Park in Philadelphia was the reverent hope of the thousands who came from as far as Maryland, Delaware, and Washington. The crowd overwhelmed the police, who were forced to open the gates an hour early. Though capacity at Shibe Park was about 27,500, paid attendance was 45,000, with another 15,000 waiting outside. The teams split the two games.[17]

The game was also notable because 17 future Hall of Famers took the field in the first game. The A's future inductees were Ty Cobb, Tris Speaker, Mickey Cochrane, Al Simmons, Eddie Collins, Jimmie Foxx, Lefty Grove and manager Connie Mack. Representing the defending World Champions were Earle Combs, Babe Ruth, Lou Gehrig, Tony Lazzeri, Waite Hoyt, Leo Durocher and manager Miller Huggins. Umpires Bill McGowan and Tommy Connolly rounded out the future enshrinees.[18]

Knowing the importance of the game, McGowan arrived at Shibe Park an hour earlier than usual to find thousands milling on the streets in search of tickets and the police admitting only those with tickets. McGowan, of course, had no ticket. He pleaded, "Honest, I'm one of the umpires," and was met with "Yeah, and I'm Judge Landis— now get moving, you bum." And, "Well, if I was you, I wouldn't be going around here boasting so loud about it." He managed to get in, and his streak was safe.[19]

He was prone to nervousness at times. Ed McAuley, a sportswriter for the *Cleveland News*, recounts the 1934 barnstorming tour of the Indians and Giants to which McGowan was assigned as the umpire. While most nights were spent on the train, when they spent the night in a city the club secretary would rent a block of hotel rooms for the press while McGowan and the players had their own block of rooms.

"Invariably," McAuley said, "we'd be in the room only a few minutes when McGowan came knocking. He just didn't want to be alone. He was tense and talkative and made no secret of his nervousness. When the tour ended in New York, he called my room to ride to the Polo Grounds with me.

"'What's the gag?' I inquired. 'You know how to get there, don't you?'

"'It's not that,' he answered. 'I just want company. I'm nervous as the devil.'"[20]

Whether out of nervousness or sociability, McGowan delighted in the off-duty company of players but never let social contacts color his judgment on the field. After one train trip from Philadelphia to Washington, Pete Runnels (all-star second baseman for the Senators, Red Sox, and Astros from 1951 to 1964) personally unloaded McGowan's huge equipment bags and arranged a taxi for him at Union Station. McGowan was recovering from an illness. The next night Runnels questioned a call and was immediately tossed by McGowan. "You're ungrateful," protested Runnels. "Did you forget what I did for you last night?"

"Now it's business hours," McGowan blandly replied.[21]

His most lasting contribution to the game is the school for umpires that he started in College Park, Maryland, in 1938. The school has undergone several changes in ownership since his death, and it continues as the Harry Wendelstedt Umpire School, one of only two accredited schools for umpires in professional baseball. The other is the Jim Evans Academy of Professional Umpiring.

1: Big Shot

Imagine walking on to the diamond in a distinctive blue uniform in front of thousands of people, knowing they are free to yell and boo at you, call you all sorts of names, and throw things at you with impunity. You also know that the players can express themselves freely to you, comment unfavorably on your ancestry anytime they disagree with a decision you make, and even take a punch at you. Your only recourse is to warn them and, if they don't take the hint, throw them out of the game, perhaps levy a fine, or punch 'em back. You have only one to three other people on the field to call on for help. You know you will be judged on how well you control the game, and the only school where you can learn how to do your job is the school of hard knocks. What kind of an umpire do you think you would have been in the 1920s and '30s when umpires faced these conditions?

What kind of an umpire was Bill McGowan? When asked, Mickey Vernon (Washington Senators first baseman in the 1940s and '50s, seven-time all star, and two-time American League batting champion) said, "He was a chesty kind of guy." To illustrate his point, Vernon recounted a time he disagreed with McGowan's call. "How could you call him safe?" said Vernon, referring to a runner McGowan had called safe on a close play at first base at Griffith Stadium in 1939.

"Because I'm the best umpire in the business. I'm number one," was McGowan's reply.[1]

Bill Werber agreed with Vernon's assessment. According to Werber, McGowan was, "arrogant, chesty, and sufficient unto himself... He wasn't well-liked, but he was well-respected."[2]

He knew he had an ego and often asked forgiveness for it. When asked to substitute for a week for sports columnist Bob Considine, he started his first column by asking readers to "please pardon the ego, but they tell me in the locker rooms that if a guy doesn't pat himself on the back no one else is going to do it. Therefore if I take a couple of bows, excuse it, please."[3]

Tommy Henrich (five-time all-star outfielder for the New York Yankees from 1937 to 1950) described McGowan as "autocratic." When asked by a fellow player in his rookie year of 1937 if he'd "had a run-in with Mac yet," Henrich answered, "No."

"Don't worry," the player said, "you will."

"On what grounds?" asked Henrich. "Don't worry," the player replied, "he'll find something."

And he did — more than once — according to sportswriter Bill Gilbert, who quoted Henrich as saying, "He's the best umpire I've ever seen, but he's an autocratic S.O.B."[4]

Gilbert also noted that McGowan could blow off enforcing the rules if he was in the mood to do so. During a game between the Athletics and the Yankees in the mid–1940s, A's Hall of Famer outfielder Al Simmons complained to McGowan that the Yankees Hall of Fame pitcher Lefty Gomez "was throwing the 'spitter'." The rule prohibiting the spitball was, and is, quite clear. "For ... delivering what is called the 'shine' ball, 'spit' ball, 'mud' ball or 'emery ball,' the umpire shall call the pitch a ball, warn the pitcher, and have announced on the public address system the reason for the action."[5]

When the rule went into effect in 1920, the names of pitchers who depended on it as their primary pitch were listed in the commissioner's office and allowed to continue throwing it until the end of their careers. Gomez, who made his first start in 1930, was not on the list. McGowan did warn Gomez but let stand Gomez's response to his warning, which was, "Tell Simmons to hit the dry side."[6]

Even though he might opt on occasion not to enforce the rule concerning spitballs, he brooked no queries from players who had an interest in the dampness of a particular ball. Such interest impinged on McGowan's realm of influence. Bill Gilbert recounted the time that Red Ruffing, Hall of Fame pitcher for the Red Sox and Yankees from 1924 to 1947, grounded out and asked McGowan to let Ruffing look at the ball to see if it had been doctored with a scratch or moisture. Most umpires considered this a fairly routine request. McGowan, however, waved his finger at Ruffing like a first-grade teacher dressing down a student. "You can't look at the ball. You can only ask. I'm the only one who can look at the ball."[7]

Nor was McGowan above using a threat to get his point across. Walt Masterson, known for his wicked fastball, was ordered by his Senators manager Bucky Harris to knock down the first three Yankees he'd face in a game in early 1939. Masterson obliged his manager. Down went Frank Crosetti, Red Rolfe, and Charlie Keller. Joe DiMaggio was the fourth batter up. McGowan called time and yelled out to Masterson for all to hear, "Knock down one more batter and I'll fine you $3,000." A rule allowing umpires to levy fines against players had been on the books since 1881 but was rarely used. A small smile broke across Masterson's face. Harris called time out and went to the mound to ask Masterson what was so funny. "Mr. Harris," Masterson said, "I only make $3,000."[8]

McGowan also used the threat of a fine against Ted Williams. It occurred in a 1942 game between the Red Sox and the Senators in Boston's Fenway Park. Fans in the left field bleachers were riding Williams particularly hard. Using his own peculiar logic, he decided to retaliate against the boisterous hometown fans by striking out. He gave a feeble wave at the first two offerings from pitcher Jack Wilson. Mac stepped in front of the plate to say to Williams, "If you take a deliberate third strike, you'll be thrown out of the game, fined, and probably suspended." Hearing that, Williams decided to swing for real, took dead aim at that section of the bleachers where the raspberries were coming from, and barely missed driving a line shot into that part of the crowd. He settled for a bloop single on the next pitch.[9]

McGowan was never bashful about ejecting players, particularly early in his career when he was establishing himself. At his first spring training in 1925 he was assigned to the Yankees. The first player he tossed from a game was Babe Ruth. Babe blinked in disbelief and then protested the heave-ho from this rookie umpire. "I know who you are and all about your reputation," McGowan said, "but when I'm wearing this blue suit you're just another ball player. Now, get out of here." The Babe got.[10]

McGowan may hold the record for ejecting the most major league players at one time with one mighty swoop of his thumb. Addressing a gathering at the annual banquet of the District of Columbia Baseball Umpires Association in 1938, McGowan told of the time he had joined the Senators in 1925 for a trial at umpiring during spring training. During the final exhibition game with the Boston Braves at Griffith Stadium the day before opening day, the Braves were calling him every vile name that popped into their heads until he could take it no more. Between innings he said to his fellow umpire James Y. "Shorty" Hughes, who was working the bases, "Shorty, that's a nasty bunch in the Braves dugout and they're giving me an awful shellacking. You try to pick out a couple of the worst ones, let me know who they are, and I'll throw 'em out of the game."

The next inning they conferred again.

"Did you spot 'em?" McGowan asked.

"Yeah, I got 'em," Shorty said.

"Who are they?"

"Good Lord. The whole team, Bill."

McGowan threw 18 Braves out of the game, and the following week received his appointment as an American League umpire.[11]

Fellow umpires were also fair game for McGowan's considered opinion. A rare instance of one umpire overruling another without being asked for help occurred when McGowan, as the third base umpire, disputed umpire-in-chief John Quinn's call during a 1940 game between the Senators and White Sox. Quinn ruled that White Sox catcher Jake Early, in reaching out to take a pitch from Rene Monteagudo to prevent a double steal, interfered with Senators batter Bob Kennedy. Quinn waved the White Sox runner Eric McNair home from third and motioned Mike Tresh to go from first to second. The Senators hotly disputed the interference call, but it stood. Then McGowan weighed in to say that if it was interference not only should the runners advance, but Kennedy should be given first base as well. Shirely Povich reported that "McGowan did everything but pull the rule book on the umpire-in-chief. Waving away the players who were grinning nearby at the spectacle of two umpires renting the air with shouts at each other, McGowan finally won his point with the aid of gestures."[12]

Umpire Jim Honochick, in his second year in the league, also found himself overruled by McGowan. "Bill McGowan was," Honochick pointed out in his account of the 1950 incident at Comiskey Park, "the oldest man in the league at the time." McGowan was going to be working the plate and asked Honochick and Ed Hurley to help him by calling balls hit down the line when it was close. Honochick, umpiring at first base, called one such ball hit by Chico Carrasquel "fair" and then immediately heard McGowan (who as umpire-in-chief was behind the plate and 90 feet farther from first base than Honochick was) call it "foul." McGowan told White Sox manager Johnny "Red" Corriden, who complained loudly about the double call, that Honochick had no business making the call because it was his (McGowan's) decision. Honochick was furious. He'd been asked for help, not humiliation. He explained what had happened to Corriden, saying, "It was a fair ball and it will be a fair ball until the day I die." "I know," Corriden said, "but what can you do. He's a sick man." Honochick got a call the next day from League president Harridge wanting to know why there was a double decision. Honochick explained things and Harridge just told him to go about his business.

Honochick told McGowan after the game: "If you were a younger man, I'd beat the daylights out of you right here and now. I respect you for your age. I respect you for the umpire you've been, but don't ever ask me again to help you out on a ball field again." McGowan told Honochick he hadn't seen him make the call. Honochick's one-word response was "Bullshit."[13]

McGowan prided himself on being tough, especially in his early years in the majors. For an umpire who'd just as soon throw a country ball player off the premises as look at him (according to St. Louis sportswriter Jack Herman), he made less use of the sweeping arm and thumb motion in the later years of his career. McGowan said in his interview with Herman in 1951, "I've thrown only one guy out of a game in the last 7 years and that was Aaron Robinson last September. When I came up," McGowan said, "I averaged about 30 players a season in the toss-out column. Yes, I used to be a tough baby on the field."[14]

McGowan expected players to be tough as well and expressed little sympathy to players who thought they had been mistreated. Tiger submarine pitcher Elden "Big Six" Auker, who pitched for the Tigers, Red Sox and Browns from 1933 to 1942, recounted the time he broke Lou Gehrig's big toe and that Gehrig complained about it to McGowan, to no avail:

> Gehrig was a low ball hitter and he would step in there with that big left foot of his and screw it into the ground, and then bring his right foot in. He just stood flat-footed and hit. And of course he was a low-ball hitter, and I was a sinker pitcher, a low-ball pitcher, and I was always pitting my strength against his strength, which wasn't a very good deal to do. So I used to throw at his feet and loosen up his feet. He kept saying to me, "Damn you, you're throwing at my feet." And I said, "Why would I throw at your feet? If I'm gonna hit you, I'll hit you in the head where it won't hurt you." One day in New York, he didn't get his foot out of the way and I hit him in the big toe, and he was rolling around on the ground. Bill McGowan was the umpire and he said, "Goddamnit, Bill, I told him he was throwin' at me. I think he broke my toe." McGowan said, "Oh, get up and go on to first base, there's nothin' wrong with you." But he wore some kind of an aluminum cast on his foot for about a week or so.[15]

Players got on McGowan for his assured attitude. Jimmy Dykes (who broke into the majors on McGowan's recommendation and played as an infielder for the Athletics and White Sox from 1918 to 1939) referred to McGowan as "Joe Chest Number One." Dykes reveled in trying to get McGowan's goat as he told a reporter, "All we have to do to get him wild now is hum a little rhyme the boys made up. You know they let the fans vote on umpires and McGowan was elected the best in the league. So the boys made up words like this: 'The American League fans voted me the best, but the players call me Little Joe Chest!'"[16]

McGowan was a tough baby with the players and managers, but he did show a considerate side to nervous ball boys. Sportswriter Robert Obojski, who was the Indians' ball boy in 1945, tells of the time during the second game of a Sunday doubleheader between the Indians and Senators at Municipal Stadium in 1945 when McGowan said to him, "Son, go over to the visitors' clubhouse and get me another dozen baseballs." Obojski knew the supply of balls was running low, and he encountered numerous difficulties in locating a box of new balls. It took him 15 minutes and all the time, "I was saying to myself, 'Geez, 33,000 fans out there and almost no baseballs left.' When I finally got to McGowan with the box of stuff he said, 'Good work, kid … we were down to our last couple of baseballs.'"[17]

McGowan also had a generous side. Shirley Povich recounted that "the pugnacious McGowan, who would raise himself to tiptoes and look down the throat of a six-foot player and challenge him to get tough, was a softie in other respects. Four of the neighborhood kids in his native Wilmington, Delaware, got their schooling from his largesse."[18]

The History of the Nickname

Early in his career he was tagged with the nickname "Big Shot." Some think it was conferred on him because of his fondness for landing a big shot in the gym or on the field. Others think it was the result of a letter he received from umpire Billy Evans, to whom he had written for advice.

McGowan, like many umpires, played several sports in his youth — baseball, basketball, and boxing in McGowan's case. He aspired to a major league career as a second baseman, could play a solid game of basketball, and was well known around the boxing gyms in his hometown. While he is not known to have struck a player in the majors, such was not the case in his 10-year minor league career. In one instance, the Orioles and Syracuse were playing a Sunday International League contest in Baltimore in 1922. McGowan called Otis Lawry, Baltimore second baseman, safe on a close play at first. Harry McCurdy (later to play catcher for the Cardinals but at that time Syracuse's first baseman) said to McGowan, "For that I ought to punch you in the nose." McGowan sat him down. McCurdy, egged on by his teammates in the dugout who were saying, "Why didn't you sock him?" came back to first base to ask if he was out of both games. It was a doubleheader. McGowan nodded in the affirmative. McCurdy swung a right to Bill's jaw. "I saw pink elephants," Bill said. McCurdy, thinking the matter settled, didn't realize that Mac could throw a punch with the best of them. McGowan regained his feet. He flattened both McCurdy and a policeman who had stepped between them. The benches cleared. The game was halted. McGowan paid a fine and was released by the police. John Conway Toole, president of the International League, suspended McGowan for 10 days and then fired him.[19]

It is testimony to the relative status of player and umpire in those days that the player, who was the one who threw the first punch in plain view for all to see, was not fired, suspended, or even fined.

McGowan was able to continue his umpiring career thanks to Judge John D. Martin, president of the Southern Association, who was sitting next to Toole at dinner during the minor league winter meetings. Toole explained to Martin that McGowan was the best young umpire he had ever seen but had to be fired because of the Baltimore fracas and, "we were trying to make Sunday ball stick there." Martin called McGowan and hired him for 1923 and 1924.[20]

In another dispute during his tenure at Baltimore, McGowan wisely shunned using his dukes in favor of a bit of acting. In a game with Louisville, McGowan made a call that displeased the spectators to the point where they swarmed onto the field demanding his scalp. To avoid the crowd's wrath McGowan snatched off his cap and mingled with the mob yelling like the rest of them.[21]

At the end of the 1923 season McGowan received a letter containing some friendly advice from J.V. Jamison, Jr., president of the Blue Ridge League, who had employed McGowan in previous years and thought highly of his work, and knew of his temper.

"I'm glad to hear you had such a good season and I hope you get back into the Majors," Jamison wrote. "If you do get back into the National League and are assigned to one of the old umpires, as you will be, don't try to indicate that you know it all. As a matter of fact, indicate that you don't know anything except how to call safe and out, and take all the other information these old heads choose to give you. It won't do you any harm, but to the contrary will put you in good with them and they can do more to boost you than anybody else, or on the other hand they can do more to break you."[22]

To what extent Jamison's advice had an impact on McGowan we don't know, but deference was never one of his stronger suits.

McGowan engaged in several other punching matches in his minor league days and, according to one account, acquired the nickname "Big Shot" because of his fondness for fisticuffs.

By another account he got his nickname from Hall of Fame umpire Billy Evans, to whom McGowan had written in 1912 at the age of 16 asking for advice about becoming an umpire. In answering the letter, Evans said, "Any man with enough courage to work in a powder factory ought to become a big shot as an umpire."[23]

McGowan acquired other nicknames that complemented his "chesty" image. John Kieran, a sportswriter for *The New York Times* in the 1930s, was known to refer to McGowan as "Wild Willie of Wilmington."[24]

Coping with Violence

McGowan was not the only minor league umpire to be the target of violence from players as well as fans. Many umpires in the Hagerstown, Maryland–based Blue Ridge League in 1920, for instance, resigned in mid-season or refused to officiate the second game of a doubleheader because of a safety concern, or failed to show up in a town, because of a lack of police protection. In one instance an umpire was slugged unconscious by a pitcher as he knelt down to scoop a cup of water from a bucket between innings. The pitcher was initially suspended for the season and fined but only served two months of his suspension.[25]

McGowan tells how Tom Walker, who was umpiring an important end-of-season game in the International League between Jersey City and Newark, avoided the fans' wrath with some clever subterfuge. Walker called a Newark player out on a close play at the plate in the ninth inning, resulting in a win for Jersey City. Walker needed the company of several officers to get to the dressing room, where he showered while Newark fans, "bent on having the umpire's gore," gathered at the dressing room's entrance, yelling curses and threats at Walker. Convinced the fans weren't leaving soon, Walker called the local hospital for an ambulance, saying he had pains in his leg and couldn't walk. The stretcher-bearers made their way through the boisterous crowd to see Walker lying on the training table without his coat. Several players loaded him on the stretcher, covered his face with a sheet, bade the attendants to hurry, and watched the stretcher-bearers make the return trip through the crowd to the ambulance. Once fully aware of the situation, the attendants drove Walker to the train station where he thanked them profusely and boarded his train.[26]

In addition to police escorts and ambulances, some umpires swam their way out of trouble. McGowan describes the nautical adventures of one Jack Vitter, an umpire in the Cotton States League, who McGowan quoted as saying, "I swam the Sunflower River at Clarksdale, the Pearl River at Jackson, and waded the Yazoo several times to spare the rope. The umpire racket is a cinch today. Why, we used to have to fight fans every day, swim the rivers, and battle the ball players for less than 200 iron men."

Looking for a less stressful league, Vitter threw his lot in with the Texas-Oklahoma League the following year only to be greeted by the league president with: "I'm glad to have a big strong fellow like you on my staff. You ought to be able to lick most of the players in this league."

"There it was again," Vitter lamented. "An umpire hiring himself out to fight the fans and players. Those were tough days. Yes, sir," he said.[27]

McGowan recounted an instance of how players turned the tables on an umpire by throwing him out of a game, literally. The incident occurred during a Blue Ridge League exhibition game in the coal region of Pennsylvania. The players of one of the teams picked up the umpire, "who was a little fellow," in their arms, marched to the outfield fence, and threw him over the fence and out of the park. The players, while debating among themselves who should umpire, heard a firm voice calling, "Play ball." The voice came from the recently deported umpire who was again attending to his duties by sweeping off the plate, showing the mettle it took to be the sole umpire for a game in those days.[28]

Even in the big leagues, umpires were targets for fans. McGowan tells of two such incidents. Billy Evans, working a game in St. Louis, was struck on the head by a bottle thrown by a fan. Evans was at the point of death for three weeks and didn't return to work for two months. The second episode involved "Red" Ormsby, who had the misfortune to also be hit by a bottle during a game in Cleveland in 1930. Ormsby was taken to a hospital, where he remained for several weeks.[29]

In a similar incident on July 26, 1936, umpire Bill Summers was forced out the game after he was hit in the groin by a pop bottle thrown from one of an unruly crowd of 50,000 at Comiskey Park. The crowd was upset with Summers' "out" call at first base on Ray "Rip" Radcliff, a White Sox outfielder. Judge Landis, commissioner of Major League Baseball and on hand to watch the game, offered a $5,000 reward over the PA system for the culprit, but only drew more boos. The deluge of pop bottles finally abated when Jimmy Dykes made a plea through the PA system.[30]

Life behind the plate was not always a struggle for survival. Occasionally umpires were accorded red-carpet treatment. St. Louis millionaire Arthur Donnelly, who made his fortune as an undertaker, offered such an example. He had become friends with the American League umpire Silk O'Loughlin and made it a point from the day he met Silk to drive him to and from the ballpark and often had dinner with him. He enjoyed Silk's stories so much that before long all the umpires in both major leagues made his acquaintance. His chauffeur-driven car picked the umps up at their hotel for the ride to the ballpark and waited for them after the game for the return trip. Donnelly would try to have dinner with the umpires in town three nights a week. He'd take them to the best nightclubs, exclusive country clubs and hotels, while tipping bus boys, waiters, head waiters, chefs, and check room girls or boys $10 each. Donnelly did this for 30 years. Umpires looked forward to the games in St. Louis.[31]

Learning the Business

While realizing he had to be tough to control the game, McGowan also appreciated the need to perfect his craft with help from his elders. Little formal instruction on umpiring would be available until 1935, when George Barr founded the first school for umpires, though there is a mention in *The Sporting News* of major league umpires being required to attend classes for the first time in the spring of 1936.[32]

Until then, umpires relied on their seniors for instruction. "Whatever I've accomplished," McGowan was quoted as saying, "I owe to Billy Evans, the former general manager of the Cleveland Indians, and Tommy Connolly, longtime American League umpire. Ban Johnson teamed me with Evans, then an American League umpire, and both Billy and Tommy coached me."[33]

Being teamed with Evans was, McGowan said, "the greatest break of my life. From the time I started umpiring I'd heard about Evans. What impressed me about Billy was his dignified approach to his work. I had heard how Billy, through his meticulous dress, put new dignity into umpiring. Billy used to pay $100.00 for his uniforms in the days before the League paid for them. They were custom-made. His caps cost seven dollars apiece. When he stepped onto the field, you could say he was the best-dressed man in the ballpark and not to be challenged. Anyway, under that influence, I got a new slant on umpiring. I decided to model myself after Evans. As I became a veteran, I passed along all the knowledge of umpiring and umpires' conduct to the young fellows who came under my guidance."[34]

McGowan expanded on his debt to Evans in a letter he wrote to Bob Evans, Billy's son, in 1953.

> He was my first tutor. He made me a good umpire. He was the highest-class guy I ever met or worked with. When I was a rookie working in the minor leagues I used to write letters to your Dad asking him advice and also asking for hundreds of answers to my hundreds of questions. He must have written me a dozen times over a four-year period. I had never seen your Dad nor had he ever seen me.
>
> Four or five years after I started corresponding with him I went south to spring training camp with the Yankees. I believe this was in the spring of 1924. I was standing on the corner of Canal and Corondelet St. in New Orleans, talking to the old Yankee scout, Bob Gilks. During our conversation, a dapper young man strolled by, and said with a haughty salute, "Hello, Bob." Bob returned the greeting with a very cordial "Hello, Billy."

I just noticed the warmth in the greeting of both men. We returned to our conversation. Finally, I said, "Bob, who was that dapper fellow who just spoke to you?" He said — "Mac, you don't mean to say you have been an umpire in the minors for ten years and don't know that fellow?" I said, "I cannot place him but he looks familiar to me." "Well that's the umpire Billy Evans." "Oh, no," I said, as I galloped up the street running at full speed after the most famous umpire of those days. Grabbing him by the arm I said, "Mr. Evans, I'm that rookie or bush league umpire who has been torturing you with all those letters for the past four or five years. I'm Bill McGowan." Well, he was more excited over meeting me that I was to meet my idol. A great friendship was carried on through the years from that point on.[35]

The coaching from Evans and others contributed to his proudest day to date in big league umpiring, which he said was "when I was named as one of the umpires for the 1928 World Series."

He also acknowledged a debt to Bill Klem (a Hall of Fame member, as are Connolly and Evans) incurred in the locker room just before Game One of that 1928 series. McGowan got to Yankee Stadium two hours early and, by his account, "walked nearly five miles around the dressing room because calling 'em in the World Series is as much the goal of every umpire in the bush leagues as playing in them is the ambition of every Class D rookie."

Klem, then the dean of umpires, saw McGowan pacing and said to McGowan, "Young man, how long have you been umpiring?"

"Thirteen years," McGowan answered. "Ten in the minors and three in the American League."

"Don't be nervous," Klem said trying to be reassuring, but McGowan kept pacing.

After the series, which the Cardinals lost to the Yankees in four games, Klem said to McGowan, "I'm glad you didn't believe me, McGowan. They're not just more ball games. They're the biggest show on earth, and if you ever get to the point in life where umpiring in the World Series is another routine assignment, do yourself a favor and quit. You won't be worth a quarter."[36]

McGowan had another reason to be appreciative of Klem's efforts; in this instance, it was the 1931 World Series in which the Cardinals defeated the A's in seven games. McGowan wrote that he had called Bing Miller of the Athletics safe on a close play at first with two out in the top of the ninth inning of the seventh game. Had he called Miller out, the series would be over with the Cardinals the winner. "The Cards," McGowan wrote, "surrounded me saying I was an American League umpire, and that I was a blind bum robber, etc. It looked for a moment like I would have to throw a couple of Cardinals out of the game. How the Cardinal fans would have loved that. Klem, a National League umpire, broke through the crowd looking at no one and while shaking my hand said, 'You made a great decision, Bill. That was great.' Frisch and his boys turned on their heels. That was the greatest thing one umpire could do for another."[37]

McGowan reported one lesson learned from Connolly was how to handle disputes with grace and respect. In a game in Boston, a Red Sox rookie disputed a strike one call by Connolly by saying, "All right old guy, get some oil in those lamps. That was six inches outside." Following Connolly's strike two call, the rookie dropped his bat, stepped out of the box, scooped up a handful of dirt, tossed it in the air and roared, "You blind bat, that was a foot outside." Still no response from Connolly who called the following pitch "strike three." "Geez," the rookie yelled, "what a league this must be, if they're all as blind as you. I couldn't 'a hit that from a ladder."

Connolly merely said, "Listen, Lad. In this league they may be high, they may be low, they may be inside or outside. But bear this in mind — they're all OFFICIAL."[38]

On one occasion during his rookie year McGowan took a piece of advice from Connolly that didn't turn out as he had hoped it would. As a new major league umpire he admired the natty attire of his fellow arbiters, particularly Tommy Connolly, and asked Tommy how he could afford to dress so well given his modest salary.

"It always pays to be friendly with all the salesmen you meet," Connolly said. "Strike up a conversation with them in the hotel lobbies, give them tickets to the ball games and the first thing you know they're making you presents of ties, socks, shirts, and occasionally, maybe something for your wife."

McGowan thanked Connolly and hastened down to the hotel lobby. He spied a likely prospect on a bar stool and struck up a conversation. The stranger admitted that he was indeed a salesman. This got McGowan's attention. He introduced himself as an umpire and discovered that his newfound friend was tremendously interested in baseball. The rush was on. McGowan sprang for dinner and wine and a couple of drinks in the bar, not allowing the salesman to pay for a thing while talking baseball all the while. The salesman loved it. They talked all evening, McGowan grabbing every check, all the while wondering what line the stranger was in. Finally, he could contain himself no longer and asked, "Say, I didn't catch what business you're in."

"Oh," said the stranger, "I'm a salesman for the Baldwin Locomotive Company."[39]

McGowan graduated from being the student to becoming the teacher.

One umpire, Ernie Stewart, credited McGowan with his success. In his rookie season of 1941, Stewart selected McGowan as the umpire he wanted to be paired with, to the puzzlement of American League president Will Harridge. Initially paired with Bill Summers, Stewart requested a change to McGowan. Harridge, who thought McGowan a bit on the wild side, thought that Summers would give a new umpire more reliable instruction.

"Why, Ernest," Harridge said, "there isn't an umpire in the league who likes Bill McGowan. He can't get along with anybody, he'll ruin you."

Stewart said, "I want a shot at him. I'd met him. He was like Jocko [Conlon]—a cocky, feisty Irishman [and eventual Hall of Famer as an umpire]. And he told me himself, 'You get a change and come with me, and I'll make an umpire out of you. Summers is going to ruin you.'"

Harridge reluctantly approved the change and throughout 1941 would say, "I just can't believe it," when Stewart would give glowing reports about McGowan. "I loved the way he called out his decisions," Stewart said. "Some umpires would just say, 'Strike,' McGowan: 'STRIKE!' Same way on the bases: a great big: 'YOU'RE OUT.' So I adopted his style and I say humbly, not cockily, he made me a good umpire."[40]

First Assignment

"Little Joe Chest" got into umpiring on a fluke.

When he was 16 he was an office boy for R.M. Carpenter of the Du Pont Company in Wilmington, Delaware. "I wanted to be a big-league ball player," McGowan said. "My heart was set on it. I was a second baseman. I could field and throw but when they started throwing curves and fast ones at me, I had a better bucket foot than Al Simmons."[41]

Not quite good enough to be a professional baseball player, he decided to take up umpiring, though he was also considering a career as a sportswriter and worked briefly as a newspaper reporter in Wilmington.[42]

Here's what McGowan told Don E. Basenfelder, reporter for *The Sporting News*, in 1936 about his entry into umpiring.

> My brother, Jack McGowan, now chief clerk of the fire department in Wilmington, Delaware, attended Villanova College and played in several sports. Eventually he umpired for semi-professional and college baseball teams. Jack was scheduled one day to umpire a game at Newark, Del., but couldn't go. He suggested that I take the job but I told him I did not know the rules. Nevertheless, he talked me into going.[43]
>
> It was quite an experience for me. In the first few innings I closed my eyes every time the pitcher threw the ball. I just guessed at balls and strikes but got away with it. In the fourth inning, with a great deal of

effort, I contrived to keep my eyes open with the pitch and had no trouble for the rest of the game.

That was back in 1912 and I was 16 years old. I had been playing on the infield of a semi-pro team then but after my experience in Newark, I decided to quit playing for umpiring. In 1913 I applied to George M. Graham, president of the Tri-State League, for an umpire's job. I misrepresented my age and succeeded in getting an opportunity of umpiring a few games in that circuit. At Graham's suggestion I umpired in the Delaware County (Pa.) League in 1914 and also called decisions for the University of Pennsylvania team that season.

Then, on the recommendation of Graham, I received a call from the Virginia League in 1915 where I umpired the two longest games ever played. On August 14, Norfolk and Suffolk went 23 innings in Norfolk. On September 4, the same two teams met again and battled to a 3-3 tie in 22 innings. And let me tell you this—the long ones are hard on umpires.

In 1916, I became a substitute umpire in the International League. Ed Barrow, then president of the league and later to become General Manager for the Yankees, brought me into Double A company to replace Bill Carpenter who was ill. Later that year I also umpired in the New York State League.

I had a job in the Blue Ridge League in 1917 but did not work at umpiring in 1918 on account of the war. But in 1919 I returned to the International League where I stayed until the end of the 1922 season. I umpired in the Southern Association in 1923 and 1924 and in 1925 succeeded in having the late Ban Johnson grant me a trial in the American League.[44]

Throughout McGowan's minor league career he established a reputation for taking control of games despite his young age. Everyone expected a speedy resolution to a McGowan game. He was known as "the fastest working umpire in the bushes," once handling a 26-inning game in 70 minutes.[45]

His major league debut began with a letter from Johnson that he received in New Orleans, where he'd finished the 1924 season, asking, "How much salary do you want to join my staff?" McGowan "let out a whoop that must have shaken Canal Street" and telegrammed Johnson to say he'd come up for two months for free to see what he could do. By return telegram Johnson said his salary would start at $4,700 with $750 for expenses.[46]

His first game in the majors was opening day 1925 in Griffith Stadium, where the Senators hosted the Athletics. Looking back on it, McGowan wrote: "Facing my first big crowd, something like 35,000 people, awed me at the very start. I will never forget the feelings that were mine after my first game in the majors. You can rest assured I was the last man to leave the ball park."

In the same article he described his worries about how he'd be treated by the "bench jockeys": "I suppose they'll yelp, 'Hey Dinneen [the umpire-in-chief], who is that new burglar with you? Where is he paroled from, Sing Sing or the Eastern Pen? Well he ought to cover a lot of ground with those dogs. What's he so nervous about? Hey, where'd you get that uniform, kid? Must have been Dinneen's. You look like his pup.'"

He caught a break for his first game. It wasn't until the second game that he heard these barbs. Many of the players knew him from his minor league days, including Sam Rice, Al Schacht, and

Bill, Madge, and Bill Jr. in New Orleans, 1924, when he was with the Southern Association (from Bill Jr.'s album).

Bucky Harris of the Senators and Eddie Rommel, Jimmy Dykes, Joe Boley and Chick Galloway from the A's. They helped ease his mind. Eddie Collins shook hands with him and wished him luck, adding, "We better shake hands now, for we won't have many chances to do it from now on."[47]

The Early Years

William Aloysius McGowan was born January 6, 1894, and baptized on February 2 in Wilmington, Delaware. He came from a long line of Irish Catholic ancestors. His father, John Aloysius McGowan, was born November 21, 1848, in Armagh, Ireland. John had three brothers—Alexander, Joseph, and William, and one sister, Bessie, all of whom were born in Ireland and eventually immigrated to Wilmington.

John married Catharine Agnes McCarthy on May 29, 1877, in St. Mary's Church, in Liverpool, England, where Catharine was living. Her mother was born in Ireland; her occupation in Liverpool was listed in the census records as "poultry dealer." John and Catharine lived for about six years in Liverpool, where he worked as a master porter at a hotel. They arrived in Wilmington, Delaware, about 1883 on a ship of the J&J Cooke Line with their daughter Elizabeth and eventually settled at 100 E. Front Street, the house where Bill McGowan was born.

John had three beer and whiskey stores in Wilmington. His first store was on First Street across the road from the railroad station. It proved to be a good location for the business because workers used the station to commute to jobs at Du Pont and other places.

Spirits had no appeal to Bill McGowan. He was a teetotaler his entire life, never partaking of beer, wine, tea, or even coffee. When he invited you for a drink, it was for a milkshake, as one player discovered with some disappointment. As a peace offering during spring training with the White Sox in San Antonio, Texas, in 1932, he said to White Sox pitcher Bob Fothergill (a heavy beer drinker whom McGowan had thrown out of several games), "Come on Bob, I'll take you for a drink." He steered Bob into a drugstore, where both had milkshakes. When they got outside, Fothergill said: "How come you steered me into the pill factory? I thought you wanted to buy me a drink." After McGowan explained that that *was* his idea of a drink, Fothergill said, "Well this may have been a gag but what I called you in Rochester and Detroit when you tossed me out goes double." This time, though, Fothergill was laughing.[48]

John signed a Declaration of Intention for Citizenship on July 21, 1888, at which time his brother Alexander, already a citizen, testified that John had been in this country for "five years and upward."

John and Catharine had six children who, with one exception, lived into the 1950s and beyond. In addition to Elizabeth, the family consisted of Catharine M., Jane Frances, John A., Alexander (who died February 7, 1894, of convulsions) and, lastly, William A. McGowan.

John later gave up the liquor stores to become a hotel manager and died of pneumonia in 1909, at age 58. His wife, Catharine, died in 1922 at age 68. Neither lived to see son Bill become an American League umpire in 1925. His sister Jane did, however, and according to family records "wouldn't let you in her door until she showed you her picture of Uncle Bill and told you that he was a major league umpire."[49]

Bill McGowan grew up in Wilmington, where he learned to box and managed several fighters before turning to umpiring for a livelihood. It is said that his boxing career ended with his being knocked out in the first round of his first professional fight, leading some players like Johnny Rigney to call him "K.O." or "canvas back."[50]

McGowan family circa 1900. Bill McGowan at age 4 with, from left, sister Jane, brother John, mother Catharine, Aleck (cousin of John), father John, and sisters Elizabeth and Catharine (from Mary Martelli, grandniece of McGowan, Sr.).

Players would remind him of his boxing days by calling out from the dugout, "Hey one-punch, you missed that one." Or, "Open up your eyes, one-punch."

"That would make him furious," said Charlie Metro, an outfielder with the Tigers and Athletics from 1943 to 1945. "You could see him cutting his eyes through his mask trying to figure out who the culprit was. If the phrase got repeated he'd walk over to the dugout and yell, 'You want me to clear this bench right now, because I will!' The guys would sit there all stone-faced till he walked away and then they'd break into smiles."[51]

Other references to his pugilistic past were more appreciated. The Boston press knew he had managed a fair fighter named K.O. Baker and during a quiet moments at a games in Fenway someone in the press box would shout down to McGowan when he was working home plate, "K.O.

Baker!" Usually aloof on the field, McGowan never failed to acknowledge the cheer with a deep bow.[52]

Here's McGowan on McGowan the pugilist:

> The gang I was raised with belonged to an athletic club known as the Du Pont A.C. named after the people who own the town....
>
> The Du Pont club went in big for boxing. Gee, I loved working out with the state featherweight champion. His name was "Kid Baltimore." And how he could sock. I had fooled around with 20 or 30 lads at the regular shows. (I say this blushingly.) After blinding 'em with science until it became tiresome, I had a serious talk with our champ.
>
> "Listen, Kid. I'm in good shape. I'm sure we're warm pals. Let's put on the gloves and go to it. As a test for me, I'd like you to fight your best. Don't pull 'em. And if you send me to dreamland, everything will be jake, and we will still be the same old friends."
>
> The bell sent us on our way. In the eleventh round, while in a clinch, the thought occurred to me that I was jabbin' and hookin' this bird into a pulp. If I lose this decision, it will be a case of "we wuz robbed." Then out of the clear blue sky, "locomotive 999," going a full speed, halted abruptly. Yes, it was my jaw and the kid's right. The floor came up and kissed me. The lights went out. What a queer feeling.
>
> The kid helped me to my corner and finally I asked, "Shall I continue? Shall I keep going? Let me have your advice!"
>
> The kid laughed and said, "My advice to you is TAKE THEM OFF."
>
> Did I take his advice? Well, I'm still in the American League.[53]

He maintained an active interest in boxing for the rest of his life. In 1952, two years before his death, he was photographed at the Touchdown Club in Washington, D.C., at a sports banquet telling Glen Flanagan "to watch out for that fast one" from his opponent for the lightweight title, Gene Smith. Flanagan didn't "look out" well enough. Smith, known as a knockout puncher with his right hand, got the best of Flanagan in ten rounds.[54]

Family Life

McGowan also played amateur baseball and basketball, and it was after a basketball game in which he had the winning shot in overtime, that he met his wife, Magdaline (Madge) P. Ferry. They married in a ceremony officiated by the Reverend Arnold in 1918 at the Church of the Immaculate Conception in Elkton, Maryland, and had one son, William Jr., who was born the following year. They also reared two children of Madge's brother, Bradford Ferry, who burned to death. He was at a gas station in Elkton when another man dropped a lighted match in a can of gasoline. The flames caught Bradford full in the face. The Ferrys had three with a fourth, a boy, on the way. The Ferrys were struggling to raise three children and a fourth would have made things even more difficult. Madge and Bill took in the newborn when he was five months old and named him Bill. The McGowan household now had three males, all named Bill. The newest arrival was soon given the nickname Bibbs. Bibbs lived with the family until he joined the Air Force. They also took in the Ferrys' youngest girl, Carol. She lived with the family until she was 13. The McGowans wanted to adopt both children but their mother wouldn't allow it.[55]

McGowan maintained an active interest in basketball until at least 1930,

"Madge" McGowan (from Bill Jr.'s album)

Bill, Bill Jr. and Madge at home circa 1942 (from Bill Jr.'s album).

The McGowan family at home circa 1939. From right: Bill, Bill Jr.'s friend Nancy, Bill Jr., Madge, and "Bibbs" (from Bill Jr.'s album).

when he was elected president of the newly organized Tri-State Basketball League. To help with publicizing the league, he managed to get mention of his election included in John Kieran's "Sports of the Times" column, along with the fact that the first game was to be played in Reading, Pennsylvania, on November 5, and that George Earnshaw (who had just won 22 games that year for Connie Mack's A's) would toss up the first ball.[56]

He also fancied himself a golfer, playing when he was in St. Petersburg, Florida, at the Jungle and Shore Acres Golf Course owned by Jimmie Foxx — Hall of Fame infielder for the A's and Red Sox from 1925 to 1941. The course was the links of choice for "the late Miller Huggins, Umpire Bill McGowan, and other baseballers. Ford Frick, National League President, is another who used to chop up its sandy fairways with his irons in the embryonic stage of his game."[57]

The McGowans' marriage would last 36 years, until his death in 1954. Madge, as her friends called her, was known as McGowan's number one rooter to the press. She died in 1981. She said in a 1952 interview at the time of his suspension in St. Louis: "We've been married for 33 years and I guess that's time enough to know anyone's faults. Sure, Bill has some. He is a bit quick-tempered for one thing. Don't forget he has a tough job. A lot of tension and a lot of abuse go with it. And no thanks."

Then, picking up his defense, she continued: "Bill has a million fine qualities, too. Nobody knows how charitable Bill is. For instance, he raised four children besides our own. Bill McGowan is a wonderful man, not the rowdy that some try to make him out to be."

She admitted that she may be a bit biased and that it's even all right with her if you want to boo the umpire. "That doesn't bother my Bill," she said.[58]

During their marriage Madge developed quite a reputation for her cooking, a skill Bill did not share. One night in 1918, a year in which he did not umpire, he came home after working late at Puessy and Sons, a steamfitters outfit, to his brother Jack's house on South Broom Street in Wilmington where he and Madge were staying. Tired and looking for something to eat, he spied a frying pan on the stove with something white in it and used it to scramble some eggs. He thought the eggs tasted a bit funny, but they hit the spot. Next morning he discovered he had scrambled the eggs in soap. Another time he offered to cook some sausage for Madge who was not feeling well. After about 30 minutes he came up to the bedroom "mad as a wet hen," saying, "I've been stirring that sausage and it never did get it into balls so I threw out the pan and everything."[59]

He did, however, get high marks as a father. Son Bill Jr. said: "He pretty much let me go my own way with my friends and would play baseball or football with me most anytime. He also said to me one day, 'You don't know how to box. I'll teach you.' He did, and that allowed me to challenge kids in the neighborhood I didn't particularly care for. One I really didn't care for was a guy named Riley. I popped him three good ones and his nose started bleeding."[60]

At the time of his father's induction into Cooperstown, Bill Jr. said: "My dad and I were pretty close. We were good friends. But I never looked at him as superhuman or anything like that. He was just my dad and went to work every day just like anyone else's dad. He went on the road for long stretches of time. We'd go see him at Shibe Park when he worked games there."[61]

Off the Field

McGowan had a full schedule during the off-season in addition to his umpire school responsibilities, as did a number of his umpiring colleagues. J.G. Taylor Spink, editor of *The Sporting News*, noted in 1938 that "the more social types of major league umpires, fellows like Red Ormsby, Beans Reardon, Bill McGowan, Cal Hubbard, Babe Pinelli, Bill Summers and a few others during the past few years, have been doing much to dissipate the long standing impression that umpires are hermits, autocrats, solitary brooders, misanthropes—aloof and morose souls who can have no off-the-field contacts."[62] In McGowan's case that meant writing and speaking.

He only had one hobby, according to Bill Jr. and that was writing. "He'd sit there from sunup to sundown and bang away at that Smith-Corona."[63]

Sportswriter Tom Meany recalled traveling with McGowan on his first major league assignment, which would have been in 1925. They were coming north from Florida on a barnstorming trip with the Yankees and Dodgers. "McGowan," Meany said, "was the only umpire I ever saw who carried a portable typewriter. His ambition was to be a sports columnist and an umpire.[64] He got an early start on both. A notice in the "Right Off the Bat" column of *The Washington Post* for February 3, 1920, stated, "Bill McGowan, International League umpire, is a newspaperman in the off-season."

He must have been using the typewriter, for a column under McGowan's byline appeared in the January 29, 1925, edition of *The Sporting News*. The column was titled "Through the Eyes of an Umpire" and the byline read By Bill McGowan, New American League Umpire. It was his first column in *The Sporting News* and the first of many more columns and articles that would appear in other newspapers and in several magazines.

His first *Sporting News* column set the tone and format for those that followed over the next 25 years. He included newsy items about individuals such as the off-season jobs held by several notable minor league players as well as a commentary on upcoming changes in player assignments to teams. He noted that players held such jobs as car salesman, insurance salesman, and one player working as a landscaper. Then he wrote three profiles, or "mini-stories," with a decidedly human-interest angle. He recounted the time Babe Ruth was late for a game because he was visiting a sick boy in a hospital; the time that his umpiring partner Harry (Steamboat) Johnson, a very well-liked umpire in the Southern Association, received more applause upon taking the field from the fans at a Rochester Internationals–Detroit Tigers exhibition game than did Ty Cobb during his first appearance at the plate (the game was even played in Augusta, Georgia, the Georgia Peach's hometown); and a story about a minor league umpire, Tommy Keenan.

Keenan in his off-season role as a fight referee officiated at a match between Jack Johnson, the heavyweight champion, and another fighter who was past his prime. Keenan let it be known to the press that "all is not on the up and up." Johnson had agreed to carry the other fighter for their six-round bout to give the fans their money's worth. Johnson was infuriated. The punch line (and nearly every McGowan story had a punch line) was that the next year during a barnstorming game, Keenan was brought on at the last minute to umpire. Unbeknownst to Keenan, Johnson was playing. Keenan, seeing Johnson advancing on him from the dugout while rolling up his sleeves, turned quickly to the stands and said, "Ladies and gentleman, it gives me great pleasure to present to you the strongest physical specimen to grace a ring and the cleverest man that ever donned a mitt — Jack Johnson." Johnson beamed.[65]

For a time McGowan wrote a syndicated column three days a week that appeared in 30 newspapers, including *The Washington Times-Herald* in Washington, D.C. Titled "It's Three and Tuh!" (since you'd never say the count was three and two), McGowan's column was sprinkled with personal anecdotes of players, managers, coaches, and umpires. If you wanted the straight story on Ruth, Cobb, Johnson, Speaker, Klem, Gehrig, Cochrane, Grove, Shawkey, Cronin, Mack, Schalk, Hornsby, and others, you read "It's Three and Tuh!" He also published articles in such magazines as *Liberty* and *Esquire*.[66]

He was a much-sought-after speaker because of his humorous tales of umpiring in the minors and majors. He started speaking at dinners and testimonials early in his career. The first reference I could find was a 1928 banquet held in West Chester, Pennsylvania, at the Elks Lodge to honor Yankee Hall of Fame pitcher Herb Pennock, who sat out the 1928 World Series — the first Series McGowan umpired — due to injuries. Others at the dais included Lou Gehrig and several other major league players and managers.[67]

Testimony to his speaking prowess can be seen in an article describing the audience's reaction to his speech after receiving an award from the Washington, D.C., Touchdown Club for outstanding service to baseball in 1944.

"As the Touchdowners presented a plaque to McQuinn [George McQuinn, first baseman for the American League Champion St. Louis Browns], they bestowed identical honors on Bill 'Old No. 1' McGowan and Bill countered with one of the most entertaining after-luncheon talks ever heard. Time and again the capacity crowd interrupted McGowan with prolonged laughter and applause."[68]

He might have told the story that he put in one of his columns about young Howard Burns, a pitcher trying to make the Cards roster. Burns got the ear of Cardinal scout Charley Barrett and told Barrett how he was going to burn up the big leagues as soon as he rounded into form. Barrett left the Cardinal camp for a few days to look at some college players in New

Orleans. He received a telegram one night at his hotel from Burns, whom the Cards had released outright. The telegram read, "Am loose." Barrett wired back, "Tighten up."[69]

Or perhaps he told the story of one of his umpire school graduates who was a carnival sleight-of-hand artist during the off-season. This umpire presented a deck of cards to a hitter who was roaring mad over a called third strike and asked the batter to select a card. The hitter did. "You just drew the seven of spades," the umpire said.

"That's right," the batter admitted, "but how did you know?"

"The same way I knew that last pitch was a strike," the ump yelled. "Now step away from the box — you're out."[70]

Another of his favorite stories was the one published in *Esquire*'s column titled "Comedy from the Field of Sport." His fellow umpire in a game in 1917 in the Blue Ridge League, a Class D League, had a particularly bad day behind the plate and decided to take his troubles to the bar that evening.

"Apparently," McGowan wrote, "he did a pretty good job of breaking training because when he reported for the game the next afternoon, there still remained a bit of the hangover. The heat of the day, plus the exercise necessary as the base umpire, stirred things up. Late in the game the umpire had a close call at second base — ball, runner and baseman all arriving at the same time — making quite a mix-up. Incidentally, by this time the umpire became quite dizzy as he raced down to second to get the play. Instead of rendering a decision, he just stood there, staring blankly at the situation. The manager of the home team, coaching at first, rushed down to second base yelling, 'Well … what is he?' He believed that the runner had beaten the play and was trying to influence the decision by rushing out on the field. '*That* isn't what's bothering me,' said the umpire. *Where is he? That's* the question.'"[71]

He was a frequent speaker at the annual banquet of the D.C. Baseball Umpires Association. He traveled to towns in Pennsylvania and Maryland to speak at various baseball events such as the one honoring Yankee slugger Charlie Keller, in Frederick, Maryland. Keller's bat helped the Yankees win the 1939 World Series. He also spoke at gatherings of local baseball players such as the 1937 annual meeting of the Union Printers International Baseball League[72] and the Eastern Branch Boys Club banquet honoring its three city championship baseball teams.[73]

McGowan often spoke at the weekly luncheons of the Washington, D.C., Touchdown Club, founded by Arthur "Dutch" Bergman in 1934. The club was founded to "cover every conceivable facet of football and had as its symbol, Timmie, the eternal little boy, happy, carefree whistling away in his make-shift uniform."[74] Baseball functions were also held at the club, where the likes of Lou Gehrig, Walter Johnson, Clark Griffith, J. Edgar Hoover, and a cast of other local and national notables would gather to honor selected sports figures. McGowan was occasionally among those honored, as happened when the club awarded him a plaque in 1944 for his outstanding work during his sixth World Series in 1944.[75]

Not limiting his appearances to baseball functions, he was the principal speaker at a luncheon sponsored by the Night Shift Athletic Club of the Engineering and Research Corporation in Riverdale, Maryland, to honor its bowling league championship performers in February of 1945.[76]

He officiated a special baseball games such as the first Washington Intercity Boys Club All-Star baseball game played on August 17, 1946, at Griffith Stadium, where Lefty Grove and Jimmie Foxx managed the two teams.[77]

McGowan took an active role in supporting the war effort. He offered his umpiring services at events held to sell war bonds such as the exhibition game played between the Senators and the New Cumberland, Pennsylvania, Army Reception Center Nine on September 9, 1943, where box seats sold for $1,000.00.[78]

He umpired softball games played by World War II vets who were recuperating from amputations at Walter Reed Medical Hospital. They played the games on the grounds of the army hospital for amputee convalescents at Forest Glen, Maryland, that had once been a fashionable girls school — National Park Seminary. McGowan distributed baseballs signed by the likes of Joe DiMaggio and Connie Mack. McGowan was also a frequent visitor to all the wards at Walter Reed, entertaining the men with inside stories of big league baseball.[79]

After his first game with the vets, he said he'd come out expecting it would take a couple of hours to retire one side. "Why hell," he said, "they played just like anybody else. They're marvelous."[80]

Before the start of the games, he'd often have an amputee pitch to an imaginary batter with himself calling balls and strikes. Once he called a high ball a strike and a kid from Detroit wanted to know if Hank Greenberg, a 6' 3" player for the Tigers, was at bat. He reportedly took no offense at the resulting chorus of "Three Blind Mice."

A few days earlier McGowan spent one of his off days at an army camp in Winthrop, Massachusetts, where "he spoke to the boys for 45 minutes and had them in stitches with his droll stories of incidents in games that he'd umpired. He conducted quiz programs, and don't think for a minute that the boys didn't fire questions that only a man as deeply versed in baseball lore as McGowan is could answer."[81]

Commenting on baseball's contribution to the war effort, McGowan was quoted as saying, "Such baseball men as Al Schacht, Emil [Dutch] Leonard, Mel Ott, and Frankie Frisch, who have entertained our American boys in direct line of enemy fire, have delivered up to baseball's finest traditions. Those performances topped any no-hit game ever pitched and any World Series game ever won in survival value."[82]

On a personal note, he was proud the fact that his son Bill Jr. had been promoted to staff sergeant in the Army while serving in North Africa.[83]

McGowan was also active in local radio and TV. He was a frequent guest of Arch McDonald, who did the play-by-play for the Senators and had his own radio show, and appeared on the local CBS television affiliate as a guest of sportswriter Morrie Siegel on his weekly TV show. A film on the training of umpires that featured McGowan and other umpires from his school was aired on WMAL-TV in Washington, D.C., in July of 1951.[84]

He was such a good friend of McDonald's that one day he asked Arch to say something on his radio show about losing his faithful dog. McDonald said, in a mock tone of gravity: "Like all other umpires, Bill is blind. He needs that old dog to lead him around the streets. That pooch had the heart of a gentleman. Poor old Bill. Why, he won't be able to find his way to the ballpark next summer. Pals, if you see this noble friend of man roaming around your neighborhood, give poor blind old Bill a ring at his home."

Ten minutes later McGowan received a call from a woman saying she wanted to give him her English bulldog. McGowan thanked her and suggested they wait a day or two to see if Jiggs would show up, which he did, much to McGowan's relief. He was able to thank the woman without having to tell her it was a joke about him being blind.[85]

Bill and Madge McGowan with their dog Jiggs at their home in Chevy Chase, Maryland (from Bill Jr.'s album).

Honors

McGowan saw well enough to receive many honors during his career. Perhaps his first was "The Sport Round-Up in honor of 'Bill' McGowan's 20 Years in Baseball" sponsored by Edward Abrahams, Jr., general chairman of the Sport Round-Up in Wilmington, Delaware. The invitation letter, dated January 16, 1934, read in part, "The home town friends of your friend 'Bill'

McGowan, will hold a Sport Round-Up in his honor on Friday Evening, January 26, at St. Elizabeth's Auditorium, Cedar and Rodney Streets this city at 7:45 o'clock. The Committee would very much like for you to attend, and pay honor to 'Bill.'"

One of his most notable honors was being voted by the American League players as Best American League Umpire of 1935 through a poll conducted by *The Sporting News*. He was presented with a handsome time-piece, suitably inscribed, at a ceremony held at Navin Field in Detroit on June 28, 1936. Councilman George Engleman, pinch hitting for Mayor Frank Cousens, made the presentation while members of the Tigers and Athletics looked on.[86]

An article at the time in *Sporting News* paid tribute to him by saying, "William A. McGowan, who topped the American League balloting, long has been recognized as one of the most capable veterans of the blue in the game. His ability is indicated not only by the fact that he led all other arbitrators of his league in the votes of players but also by his selection as one of the umpires officiating in the 1935 World Series between the Tigers and the Cubs. In that series, his keen judgment, cool-headedness in tense situations and general efficiency won high praise, from officials, players, and fans.[87]

He received a trophy for the award from the Philadelphia Sporting Writers' Association at its annual banquet at the Bellevue-Stratford Hotel. The banquet was a red-letter event for McGowan's hometown of Wilmington, Delaware. For the first time in the history of the event, three of the guests of honor were from Wilmington — McGowan, Jimmy Caras, world's pocket billiards champion, and Eddie Michaels, football captain at Villanova for 1935.[88]

2: When a Ball Was a Ball and a Strike Was a Strike

Behind the Plate

Known as "the best, the toughest, and the quickest-tempered umpire in the majors," he wasn't liked by all the players and fellow umpires, but no umpire's authority was more respected than his—as could be seen by the players voting him the best umpire in 1935. His election as the best didn't endear him to his fellow umpires, some of whom would mutter "Number One" and "Big Shot" when he was out of hearing range.[1]

Both Ted Williams, perhaps the game's finest hitter, and Yankee manager Joe McCarthy, the winner of seven World Series, admired his work behind the plate. "He was one of the sharpest guys with balls and strikes I ever saw," Williams said of McGowan. "I'd say he was probably 99.9 percent right." McCarthy regularly reminded his players not to ride McGowan "because he's the best balls and strikes man there is."[2]

Sportswriter Shirley Povich said of McGowan, "In 30 years in the league, Bill McGowan threw fewer ballplayers out of ballgames than any contemporary umpire. That's because disputes start with questionable decisions and McGowan's decisions commanded respect, even from the hostile players."[3]

Bob Feller, Hall of Fame pitcher for the Cleveland Indians from 1936 to 1956, except for the war years, recalled that questionable decisions were few and far between with McGowan behind the plate. "He was good on the bases," Feller said, "but he was an excellent ball and strike man. When you made a pitch you knew how he was going to call it before he called it; so did the hitter. Consistency, that's the name of the game — not what time the train leaves, not whether you got a dinner date, or what the weather is — he called 'em what they were."[4]

Sportswriter Jimmy Isaminger of the *Philadelphia Inquirer* wrote in 1933 that he'd been hanging around baseball since days when Jesse Burkett hit over .400 (1895 and 1896), yet never had heard an umpire subjected to the treatment that McGowan received from Connie Mack at an auditorium in Old St. Joseph's Church. "Mack paid the highest compliment to an umpire ever recorded since Abner Doubleday discovered baseball."[5] In Mack's words, "We have on this stage Bill McGowan, an American League umpire, who is a positive inspiration to the players through his spirit and hustling. His mistakes are very few and we always feel that he is on top of the play anyway and giving his decision as he thinks it should be and not loafing 30 feet away."[6]

Tommy Henrich recounted a remarkable instance in which the losing pitcher in a close World Series game went out of his way to compliment McGowan's acuity behind the plate. It happened after the first game of the 1939 World Series between the Yankees and the Cincinnati Reds. It was the ninth inning of the first game of the Series with the score tied 1–1 and Paul Derringer pitching. Charlie Keller of the Yankees hit a long fly ball to the Reds' Ival Goodman in right field who bobbled it, putting Keller on third. DiMaggio was intentionally walked. The Reds brought the infield in with Bill Dickey at bat, who foiled that strategy with a game-winning single over second base. "It was," Henrich said, "a heartbreaking loss for Derringer after one of the best pitching battles in World Series history."

Derringer, according to teammate Billy Werber, was so mad at Goodman after the game that once in the locker room he called Goodman "a gutless S.O.B." for failing to call off charging centerfielder Wally Berger, who caused him to misplay Keller's fly ball. Goodman "bopped him one on his nose." Reds manager Bill McKechnie yelled, "Lock the doors" and warned his players that anyone who talked about the fisticuffs would be fined $500.

After a few minutes the doors were unlocked and Derringer knocked on the door of the umpire's dressing room, asking for McGowan.[7]

McGowan was less than enthusiastic about talking to players after a game, particularly a losing pitcher, as experience had taught him that he was probably in for a complaint, long argument, or worse. He told the locker room boy to "keep that damn door shut." Derringer didn't give up. After hearing several pleadings that "this will only take a minute," McGowan relented. "Mac," Derringer said when he finally got his audience, "that's the best job of umpiring I've ever seen."[8]

McGowan received similar kudos from opposing catchers Mickey Cochrane and Gabby Hartnett. They both said McGowan didn't miss a play or call one ball or strike wrong in the entire 1935 World Series in which the Tigers beat the Cubs in six games.[9]

George Pipgras, American League umpire from 1938 to 1946 (and former right-handed pitcher for the Yankees from 1923 to 1933), said of McGowan, "If I was still pitching, I'd want Bill McGowan to work my game. I never saw him miss one."[10]

Some players respected McGowan's work to the point they would chide a sportswriter for printing a disagreement with a McGowan decision. Hugh Trade reports the time he publicly disagreed with a McGowan call in his column, Sports a la Carte, only to have the Baltimore players involved in the decision "belabor me for printing the story." The players, Ray Murray and Dick Kryhoski, said, "You just don't go around second-guessing or disagreeing openly with McGowan. He's one umpire you leave alone."[11]

In 1987, 33 years after his death, McGowan placed fourth among umpires in a survey given to all active and retired major league players, coaches, and managers who were asked to identify the best-ever players, managers, and umpires. Eugene and Roger McCaffrey sent 5,000 surveys to all the players, coaches and managers "whose addresses we could find." When the results of the 645 returned surveys were tallied, only Bill Klem, Al Barlick, and Jocko Conlan — Hall of Famers all — finished with more votes than McGowan.[12]

One might wonder why McGowan was singled out for such high praise in making the right calls on balls and strikes. After all, the official strike zone is the same for every hitter and, with minor changes, has remained the same for the last 100 years.

Calling Balls and Strikes

In 1907, the strike zone was defined in terms of a "fairly delivered ball," which was defined as "a ball pitched or thrown to the bat by the pitcher while standing in his position and facing the batsman that passes over any portion of the home base, before touching the ground, not lower than the batsman's knee, nor higher than his shoulder."

By 1950, the strike was "that space over home plate that is between the batter's armpits and the top of his knees when he assumes his natural stance." The upper level was raised to the top of the shoulders in 1963, lowered to be a horizontal line at the midpoint between the top of the shoulders and the top of the uniform pants in 1988, and in 1996 the lower level was expanded from the top of the knees to the bottom of the knees.[13]

The rub is that while the definition of the strike zone may be straightforward, not all umpires see the same zone.

Sportswriter Tom Meany made the case in 1955, a year after McGowan's death, that the strike zone, as seen by umpires, was shrinking. For instance he noted that many National League pitchers considered it a disadvantage to work when an American League ump is behind the plate because "They don't give you the low strikes because they can't see 'em." National League umpires worked from a crouch to the right or left of the batter and had a better view of low pitches than did American League umpires, who looked at pitches from directly over the catcher's head.[14]

Matt Batts, a catcher with the Red Sox, Browns, Tigers, White Sox, and Reds from 1947 to 1956, was of a similar opinion. "McGowan," Batts said, "used the American League stance — standing directly behind and leaning slightly over the catcher while facing the pitcher 'head on.'" Umpires who worked to the right or left of the catcher, the predominant National League style, Batts maintained, didn't have as good a view of the outside corner of the plate and would tend to call strikes on balls that were actually several inches off the plate.[15]

McGowan advised his students: "It's wise to bring that low ball up. This has been a war cry from the benches or dugouts for years. When you call a ball that has crossed the plate an inch or two below the batter's knee a strike, it appears to the players on the benches and the spectators on the right and left sides of the playing field, as a ball in the dirt."[16]

According to Meany, Paul Richards, longtime AL manager, also thought most umpires used the top of the letters rather than the armpits as the top of the strike zone. This coincided with McGowan's advice to his students. McGowan's comments on calling balls around a batter's shoulder were that "any ball that passes over the plate between the shoulder and the knee is a strike." He advised, "If you make it a point to guide yourself using the top of the player's shirt front letters as a line of demarcation, you will become more proficient behind the plate in the calling of balls and strikes."[17]

Another variation among umpires was the location of the ball over the plate, be it high or low. Meany reports that Bill Dickey, Hall of Fame Yankees catcher, said, "When I was catching, and it's still true today, some umpires would give you a strike if an edge of a ball was over the corner of the plate. Others wouldn't give you a strike unless the entire surface of the ball was over the corner. Since a baseball is almost three inches wide, you can see what a difference this made with corner pitches."[18]

McGowan's system for calling balls and strikes was to establish a strike zone that extended from the batter's shoulder to his knees and was 17 inches wide, the width of the plate, on which he fixed his attention. McGowan said it is impossible for an arbiter, or anyone else for that matter, to see both the ball and the plate at the same time.

McGowan sized up each batter as he stepped to the plate and immediately got this strike zone firmly fixed in relation to that particular batter. He then followed the flight of the ball until it passed through or outside the strike zone. If the ball entered the strike zone while passing the plate it was a strike, but if the ball went outside the zone, it was a ball. McGowan maintained an umpire couldn't possibly make the correct call if he tried to watch both the ball and the plate.[19]

Not everyone used the same strike zone to judge whether a pitch is a strike or a ball and this, as you might expect, led to disagreements. McGowan recalled a game during spring training in 1925 in which he was behind the plate. Walter Johnson was on the mound for the Senators, and Muddy Ruel was catching. Ruel signaled Johnson to throw a curve to Dave Bancroft, a switch-hitter batting left-handed, for the Boston Braves. Johnson did. Bancroft took it and Ruel caught it directly behind the outside corner of the plate. Ruel held it for an instant to show everyone it was a strike. McGowan called it a ball. The ball, McGowan said, had curved around the strike zone rather than passing through it. Walter Johnson ended the ensuing argument by saying to his teammates, "Just a minute fellows…. I think I have something to say. That ball was three inches outside — it curved around the plate!"

Before Johnson made his admission, McGowan said Ruel and the other Senators thought they were right due to the fact they see only the plate *after* the ball has passed it, because it's impossible for them to see both at the same time.[20]

The umpire also sees things differently on the bases than do players and fans which accounts, McGowan said, for why all umpires hate to make two types of decisions. In each case they make the umpire look bad to the crowd when in reality the umpire made the correct decision. The first occurs at first base when the first baseman, seeking to save a fraction of a second, reaches into the infield for the throw and inadvertently, or otherwise, lifts his heel from the bag. The crowd, not seeing heel lift, can't believe that the umpire could have called a runner safe whose foot touched the bag after the ball entered the first baseman's mitt.

The second situation occurs when the throw to second or third arrives before the runner but the man covering the bag fails to make the tag because the runner has executed a hook or fadeaway slide thereby barely avoiding the tag attempt. All the fans see is the ball arriving first and they assume the tag attempt was successful. How could the umpire not see it, they ask.[21]

It was just this type of call that McGowan rated as the "toughest call I ever had to make. It was the last of the tenth inning of a scoreless game between the Browns and the Indians. Bibb Falk, Indians outfielder, was on third with two out and the squeeze play was on. The batter missed an attempted bunt and Browns catcher Rick Ferrell's throw caught Bibb off third by several feet. He executed a hook slide and avoided the tag. I had to call him safe though it looked to all the world like he was out. Well, the same thing happened again and Falk hooked around the fielder and again the fans yelled. Finally, Falk scored the winning run and believe me, I didn't waste any time getting to the club house after the final out."[22]

Consistency

It was his consistency in calling balls and strikes correctly that set McGowan apart from his peers in the eyes of players and managers.

Mel Parnell (left-handed pitcher for the Boston Red Sox from 1947 to 1956) maintains that "many umpires differed in their strikes then just as you see today. You had to know your umpire and how he was calling 'em that day." Not so with McGowan, who Parnell says was "a great umpire because he had a consistent strike zone — high and low and in and out. You always knew where you stood with McGowan."[23]

Walt Masterson said that if a pitcher today is "working on one corner and goes astray by six inches, he'll likely get a strike call by a 'corner' ump." "McGowan," who Masterson said was not a high ball, not a low ball, nor a corner ump, "would never have called it a strike."[24]

He "always called a ball a ball and a strike a strike," said Sid Hudson (right-handed pitcher for the Senators and Red Sox from 1940 to 1954) except for 1943–45. "Pitches six inches off the plate were always called balls by McGowan," Hudson added.[25]

"A good umpire," said Joe Sewell (Hall of Fame shortstop and third baseman for the Indians and Yankees from 1920 to 1933), "will call a pitch a quarter of an inch outside the strike zone a ball. You've got to find out who they are and go accordingly. Bill McGowan, Tommy Connolly, they were good umpires."[26]

Not Always Right

Admired as he was for calling balls and strikes, he didn't get them all right and was not afraid to say so.

Joe Sewell recounts the time that he was in St. Louis with two strikes on him: "When the ball passed the bill of my cap and Bill McGowan — who was one of the good umpires— said, 'Strike three, you're out, oh my God I missed that.' All in the same sentence. He sure had missed it but I didn't say anything. I just turned and walked away. The next day he came up to me before the game and apologized. 'I did my best, Joe,' he said. 'Good enough, Bill,' I told him."[27]

Eddie Robinson, first baseman for seven American League teams (1942, 1946–1957), recalls a bases loaded, 3–2 count situation. "I took a ball that got the corner and thought I'd struck out. Mac calls it ball four and in comes the run while I go to first. The next day he asks me, 'Eddie, where was that pitch that I called a ball yesterday?' 'Outside corner,' I said. If I'd said it was a ball, he'd know I was lying."[28]

Gordon Cobbledick, a sportswriter for the *Cleveland Plain Dealer*, wrote: "Bill McGowan was the only umpire who ever admitted, in my hearing, that he had called one wrong. It was at Old League Park. He had called a White Sox runner out at first base to complete a double play that pulled the Indians out of a bad jam. From the press box it looked like an atrociously bad ruling. After the game he stopped at the office to pay his respects to his friend Billy Evans, who was then general manager of the Indians. Alva Bradley, the club president, was there, and asked McGowan if the White Sox runner had missed the base with his foot. 'Hell, no,' the umpire replied. 'I just blew that baby.'"[29]

He once confessed a wrong call to a player whom he had called out at first when the runner came back to the bag and said, "Listen, Bill. I know I was safe." McGowan said, "That's right. You know you were safe. And I know you were safe. But my hand went up when you crossed the bag, and 35,000 people in the stands know you are out."[30]

In another instance of admitting a mistake, McGowan recounted how he consulted with another umpire and reversed his initial call. During a game in Cleveland, he called a Red Sox batter, Dusty Cooke, out swinging on strikes but admitted that the third strike was a bit low and the catcher blocked his view for a moment. "The Red Sox's manager, Bucky Harris, said, 'Just a minute, Bill. You called Dusty out. But you thought he swung at the ball, didn't you? Would you care to ask Brick about that?'

'Sure Bucky,' I said. 'I'll ask Brick.' I motioned for Brick Owens to come in. 'Did Cooke swing at that ball?' I asked him.

'No Bill, his bat didn't go all the way around.' Owens replied. 'You win, Bucky,' I said."[31]

While willing to admit it when he blew a call, he could also deliver a sharp retort to a player who mistakenly thought he'd missed a call. To a runner who complained that McGowan called him out before the play was over, he retorted: "That's right. Any umpire can call the play after it happens. Only the great ones like myself can call 'em before they happen."[32]

By his own account, McGowan estimated that the umpire behind the plate, calling balls, strikes, foul balls, and plays at the plate will make 350 decisions during an average game and will average three mistakes a game, which is "not a bad average at all."[33]

He didn't take making a mistake lightly, particularly at World Series time when, he said, "I always said an extra prayer and hoped I wouldn't blow one. A bad call can change the whole complexion of the Series and take $2,500 to $3,000 out of a player's pocket — the difference between the winning and losing share. And it can make the guy in blue as notorious as Jesse James."[34]

To guard against making mistakes, he'd ask for help when need be. In a game at Yankee Stadium on August 16, 1944, he waved Johnny Lindell, Yankees outfielder, across the plate from second after Rusty Peters threw wild on Yankees first baseman Nick Etten's infield hit. The rules called for advancement of only one base. After conferring with fellow arbiters George Pipgras and Ernie Stewart, McGowan waved Lindell back to third.[35]

During a particularly tense game between the Yankees and the Red Sox in Fenway Park in 1952, Yankees manager Casey Stengel claimed Indians catcher Birdie Tebbetts deliberately stuck his foot in front of an Ed Lopat pitch in order to gain first base. McGowan's view was blocked by the catcher. He said to Stengel, "I don't claim to have seen the ball because the catcher blocked me. But I'll leave it to the other umpires. If they say it was deliberate, then you win and Tebbetts [can] come back to the plate. But if they say Tebbetts tried to get away then I want you to go back to the bench without a word."

The other umpires agreed there was no way to determine if Tebbetts had been deliberate, so he stayed at first, and Casey silently returned to the Yankee bench.[36]

Signaling the Call

Once the call has been made, be it ball or strike, the players, fans, and managers need to know what it is. An umpire is not required to call out his decision — a hand signal is all that's required.

Time was when an umpire was required only to call out decisions. There are several stories that purport to explain when hand signals for calling balls and strikes were used by umpires for the first time. One of the better known involves William Ellsworth Hoy, a deaf-mute insensitively nicknamed "Dummy" who came to the Bigs as an outfielder with the Washington Senators in 1888. Since Hoy could not hear the umpires' calls, he persuaded them to use hand signals — the right arm for a strike and the left for a ball.[37]

Some baseball historians put this story in with other myths of the game right alongside that of Abner Doubleday inventing the game, but there is one other reference in support of the Hoy story. Sportswriter Art Kruger says the same story was told to him by Paul Helms, founder and sponsor of the Helms Athletic Foundation and Helms Hall in Los Angeles. Kruger adds, "Helms ought to know. His middle name was Hoy and he was raised by his deaf uncle, one William E. Hoy, after his mother died and his father became ill."[38]

In another account provided by Paul Dickson, Brig. Gen. Reynolds J. Burt's father, Civil War hero Brig. Gen. Andrew Sheridan Burt, is credited with convincing American League president Ban Johnson to ask umpires to use hand signs to signal strikes. In a letter written by the younger Burt on file at the Hall of Fame, he recalls his father's habit of establishing baseball games at all of his posts as a morale builder after the Spanish-American War broke out. The letter says that the umpire would pick up a pebble in the right hand for a strike and one in the left hand for a ball, to ensure an accurate count, while calling out "ball" or "strike." The younger Burt umpired many of the games. In one game the crowd was so noisy that he was forced to raise his arms and use fingers to signify balls and strikes. This innovative tactic reportedly pleased his father, who some years later had difficulty hearing the umpire's calls on balls and strikes in Washington, D.C., "in Mr. Griffith's grandstand." Recalling his son's innovation, he sent a polite letter to Ban Johnson suggesting that right and left hand signals be used. In his letter, Burt states that Johnson directed his umpires to put the suggestion into effect with one difference. Hand signals would be used only for strikes, since if fans saw no signal, they'd know the call was a ball.[39]

Dickson reports two more accounts of the origin of umpires using signals. He points out that Bill Klem is recognized on his bronze plaque at Cooperstown as "introducing arm signals indicating strikes and fair or foul balls." Klem, Dickson says, credited an attorney with suggesting a signal to indicate fair or foul to avoid trouble with fans during a game in 1904. Dickson also reports that "noiseless" umpiring was used during a game in 1901 in Chicago's South Side in which the home plate umpire wore a red sleeve on the right arm and a white one on the left and raised the appropriate arm to make his calls—right for strikes and left for balls.

In yet a fifth account, Charles "Cy" Rigler, a National League umpire from 1906 to 1922 and 1924 to 1935, is credited with "introducing the gesture of raising his right hand to indicate a strike in 1905 while an umpire in the Central League."[40]

It would appear that using hand signals to augment the verbal calls was an idea whose time had come, albeit from several sources.

Umpires initially considered the use of signals to be an affront to the dignity of the game but, regardless of who first introduced the practice, by 1907 major league umpires were using signals to complement their verbal calls.[41]

In his minor league days McGowan worked on developing his own style of signaling if a pitch was a strike and practiced regularly. Along with fellow umpire Roy Van Graflan in the International League, each would jerk his arm over his shoulder and then freeze to see how it looked in the hotel room mirror. For the third strike they'd practice calling the batter out by bellowing "OW-i-i-t-t." They would practice and critique each other's style for hours. One night, so the story goes, a man in the next room called to say, "I don't mind the screaming but, tell me: do you guys ever call anybody SAFE?"[42]

McGowan finally adopted the motion of a clenched fist held about four inches above his head to indicate a strike.[43]

In the Stands

Respect for his ability was not limited to his work behind the plate or on the bases. Whitey Ford (Hall of Fame pitcher for the Yankees from 1950 to 1967) tells the story of McGowan's presence in the stands before a game deterring opposing pitchers from talking with each other. Players were barred from fraternizing on the field with players from opposing teams. An umpire was assigned to sit in the stands to see that it didn't happen.

One opening day, Red Sox pitcher Mel Parnell wanted to talk to Senators pitcher Chuck Stobbs about two Yankees, Bill (Moose) Skowron and Bob Cerv, that Stobbs had faced in the Yankees-Senators opener two days earlier.

Parnell knew the rule, but his manager, Lou Boudreau said, "Go ahead, things get confused on opening day. Nobody will be looking." Upon learning that McGowan was officiating, Parnell said, "Oh gee. He doesn't miss a thing. It will cost me $25 sure."

Boudreau kept needling saying, "Go ahead. We'll pass the hat for you. I'll put in $10 myself."

But with McGowan in the stands, Parnell wouldn't take the chance.[44]

Fraternizing with fans was also a no-no. "When we see a ballplayer talking to a fan," McGowan wrote, "we send a wire to league headquarters and it costs the player five bucks. Of course, it's ok if a fan hollers out to Sid Hudson and says 'Hello, Sid,' and Sid might answer, 'OK, how are you, Joe?' We're not going to be that petty, but if Hudson stops and holds a long conversation with a fan, he gets slapped with that fine."[45]

3: Not Born to Blush Unseen

If all McGowan had done was call balls and strikes with more accuracy and consistency than his peers, his performance as an umpire would not have been as memorable as it was. It was his *style* of umpiring that made memories. Deron Snyder said, "It would be fair to say the late Bill McGowan revolutionized the way umpires call ball games. Before McGowan, umpires were heard and not seen. He changed that with his colorful style, bordering on the pugnacious, which incorporated a host of vigorous and aggressive gestures. Generations of successors have been influenced ever since."[1]

Bob Addie, former sportswriter for *The Washington Post,* agreed. "Bill McGowan," Addie wrote, "was not born to blush unseen. In the first place, he's Irish. An Irishman is bred for combat. William Aloysius McGowan has had his share. In arguments, Bill McGowan was as great a Shakespearian actor who missed his calling. Bill would give it the grand gesture. He tossed players with a magnificent sweep of the thumb while the thunder of the crowd's wrath would bounce, wave upon wave, on his bald dome."[2]

In another article Addie described McGowan as "having more bounce to the ounce than you know what.[3] Willie is a colorful Irishman whose every story must be embroidered with magnificent gestures that would do credit to a movie star of the silent films, whose idea of making love was to get a headlock on a dame and wrestle her two falls out of two."[4]

In a similar vein, McGowan was noted for "calling a man out with such vehemence that even a dozing fan would take notice."[5]

Controlling the Game

Above all, McGowan accepted the time-honored dictum that the umpire's primary job is to control the game. From the fisticuffs of his early days to outright verbal abuse of players to the use of humor and tact, McGowan had a number of ways to control a game, the importance of which he learned early.

Max Kase tells of McGowan's initiation to the majors in 1925 during a spring training game with the Yankees in St. Petersburg, Florida. "Ruth, Meusel et al. rode Bill unmercifully and I recall how discouraged my new friend was as he poured out his troubles to me in the cool of the evening after each sizzling matinee at the old St. Pete park. It was the best introduction that Bill could have had to the majors because it convinced him at the outset that if he didn't take charge of the game on the field, he'd be taken charge of."[6]

It was a lesson he put to good use, but he left his fisticuffs behind him even when physically assaulted by a player, as happened on August 28, 1926, in front of 30,000 people. In a game between the Tigers and the Yankees at Yankee Stadium, Babe Ruth hit a towering drive to right that was very near the foul pole. McGowan called it a fair ball, making it Ruth's fortieth homer of the season. Tiger catcher John Bassler saw it otherwise and pushed McGowan roughly against the neck and chest. While McGowan may have been tempted to flatten Bassler with a right jab, he merely "asked Bassler to 'take the air' or words to that effect."[7]

What can happen if an umpire loses control of a game was amply demonstrated in a minor league game between Boise, Idaho, and Ogden, Utah, in which Augie Donatelli, later a major league umpire, was umpiring

The umps in spring training, St. Petersburg, Florida, circa 1926. From left, Bill McGowan, Emmett "Red" Ormsby, Clarence "Pants" Rowland, and Frank Wilson (from collection of Steve Steinberg).

in 1946. His partner, whose name he mercifully didn't mention, called a runner out at third on a close play.

"Maybe he was out —from where I was I couldn't tell — but while my partner is in his spin, giving the big 'out' wave, the third baseman dropped the ball. But he didn't see it. The Ogden players charged him but I got him out of the pack. He wanted to know what all the row was about, and when I told him the third baseman dropped the ball, he called the runner safe. Now the Boise players surrounded him and he was so upset he reversed himself again and called the runner out. That was when the fans came down out of the stands, and it was all the cops could do to get them back in. The cops took us off the field and put us in a patrol wagon and rode us down to the hotel."[8]

McGowan taught rookie umpires the importance of controlling the game. Ernie Stewart recalls how impressed he was that Bill McGowan could not stand to be yelled at. "He'd go to pieces," Stewart said, "but you'd know you were not allowed to holler one word at him. He was so sensitive when he worked the plate, he'd whip off that mask right away if that bench hollered at him. Why? No one can concentrate back of that plate with a bunch of guys hollering from the bench, calling you names, calling you impotent. You just knock them off real quick and they'll guard their words."[9]

Bill Summers, an American League umpire who broke in under McGowan, said, "He had a simple philosophy about umpiring and it guided me through my career. It was this— keep control of the players or they'll control you."[10]

While McGowan did let everyone, especially rookies, know who was in charge of the game, those rookies who showed McGowan due deference did not have problems with him.

In the second game of the 1949 season, Red Sox rookie Walt Dropo, who was known for having a tall strike zone, complained to McGowan about a called strike. "Get back up there, busher," McGowan barked. "We haven't even been formally introduced." In between at-bats, Joe McCarthy, Red Sox manager, warned Dropo that McGowan might make his life miserable for the rest of his career. Hearing that, Dropo decided to apologize to McGowan at his next at-bat. "That's all right kid, now we know each other," McGowan said.[11]

Sportswriter Shirley Povich tells of the time that Tommy Umphlett (outfielder for the Red Sox and Senators from 1953 to 1955) first encountered McGowan. Just breaking in with the Red Sox and fresh from North Carolina, Umphlett took one right down the middle. McGowan snarled, "Strike three," and for emphasis stepped out of position and pumped his fist in Umphlett's face as a warning he was willing to throw his official weight around if this was a fresh busher who wanted to make something of it. Umphlett, Povich reports, spoke up and "never did McGowan come so close to swooning. 'Yes, sir' he heard Umphlett saying."[12]

Those who attempted to influence his calls or disrupt the game by jeering opposing players were not as kindly dealt with. He had little patience with catchers who tried to umpire the ball game by attempting to make a pitch look good by swooping their mitt up into the strike zone. "I'd tell 'em all," McGowan said, "you move your mitt on me and you're dead. If it's a strike, you don't need to try to fool me."[13]

In 1943 when Tommy Byrne (left-handed pitcher for the Yankees and several other teams from 1943 to 1957) was needling some opposing players, McGowan told him to "Shut up, Bush." Joe McCarthy, his manager, went over to him and said, "Tommy, that's Bill McGowan, he can make your life absolutely miserable if he wants. If I were you I'd go to the far end of the bench and I'd shut my mouth." Byrne did, but it was too late. When Byrne was batting later in the game, a ball came in far wide of the plate. McGowan looked at it and called it strike three, adding, "How do you like that, you left-handed son of a bitch?"[14]

Sid Hudson, right-handed pitcher for the Senators from 1940 to 1952 and for the Red Sox from 1952 to 1954, relates the tale of Jack Wallaesa, a shortstop who, in his first or second major league game with the Athletics in 1940, looked back at McGowan twice after called strikes. McGowan called time and called out to Hudson, "Sid, throw it up here to me and I'll get rid of him for you." "I did," Hudson said, and "Mac" called strike three and threw Wallaesa out of the game.[15]

He also ordered batters to swing at the next pitch when he thought the batter was delaying the game. Charlie Metro recalled an exhibition game when he was with the Tigers and Mickey Cochrane was the manager. They were playing a service team, and Bob Feller, then in the Navy, was firing fastballs at him. "I fouled about five off," Metro said, "and three or four of them bounced off McGowan's chest protector. The last one caught him on his mask. He was mad because he knew I was just waving my bat at Feller's offerings trying to stay alive. 'Busher, you better swing at the next one 'cause it's going to be a strike,' he told me. And swing I did even though the next one was several inches above my shoulder because I knew he was going to call it a strike regardless of where it was. He called it a strike and added, 'Nice swing, kid. Nice swing.'"[16]

McGowan's "pugnaciouness" wasn't limited to rookies. Jimmy Dykes, who broke into the majors on McGowan's recommendation, ended up being tormented by McGowan throughout his career. For the slightest cause, McGowan would send Dykes to the showers early. Once, when McGowan ejected a teammate for using foul language, Dykes demanded to know what his teammate had said. McGowan shouted at him, "And you're out of the game, too, Dykes!"

"What for?"

"For expostulation!" answered McGowan.

"Nuts!" barked Dykes. "You're just showing off. You don't even know what the word means."

"I don't, eh," sneered McGowan. "Well I do, Mr. Dykes. It means holding up the game."[17]

Dykes relates another toss by McGowan:

> McGowan walked away. I followed. "Cut it out or I'll run you," says McGowan. Then he drew a line in the dirt. "Don't come any closer," he snorts, but I just stepped over the line.
>
> "You're outta the game," McGowan yells, giving me the heave-'ho with elaborate gestures.
>
> "What for?" I demanded.
>
> "Intimidation," snaps Mac.
>
> "Spell it," I said. "What's it mean?" He was still sputtering for a comeback as I strolled to the clubhouse.[18]

Perhaps McGowan was especially strict with Dykes because of Dykes' well-known penchant for disruptive antics on the field. American League president Will Harridge fined and suspended Dykes more often — 37 times — than he did any other player.[19]

McGowan could also be subtle with Dykes. Shortly after Dykes had assumed the reins of the Chicago White Sox as manager in 1934, Dykes, according to McGowan's lively and dramatic account, "rushed up to the plate in a wild rage to enter his objections to one of my decisions. I saw him coming. I knew he was red hot. I figured, 'If I can make him all the more sore he won't be able to say anything when he gets here.' Roaring, snorting, and howling at the top of his voice, there at the plate, trying to win a point, Dykes had the Chicago fans going mad. They urged Jimmy on. Jimmy kept coming too. His teammates were surrounding me. 'That's the old fight, Jim boy,' they said. Before he could collect himself, I brushed a few of the lads aside, and pleasantly addressed him: 'Now, Mister Manager, what can I do for you?' 'Mister Manager!' he barked. 'He calls me Mister Manager!' he gurgled. It burned him so much that Jimmy couldn't say a word. He didn't know whether to argue about the decision or to take me over the coals for the sarcastic remark — 'Mister Manager.' Jimmy gave me one dirty look and then started for the bench. 'Aw, to hell with it, let's get in there and win this ball game.'"[20]

The tension between Dykes and McGowan continued for all of Dykes' 21 years as a major league skipper. It got to the point in 1951, when Dykes was managing the Athletics and thought that McGowan had unfairly chased Ferris Fain from a game, that Dykes forbade his players to so much as say hello to McGowan on the field. Any player caught saying a word to McGowan was subject to a $50 fine.[21] Dykes let it be known that "I'm not speaking with Mr. McGowan at the moment," and, in games where McGowan was officiating behind the plate, would send coach Bing Miller up to the plate to discuss the day's lineups with the umpires."[22]

While he occasionally would slip a zinger to a troublesome player, McGowan generally counseled civility in dealing with abusive players. "The best way to get along is to give the arguing player a civil reply. You could tell them something sarcastic, but wisdom dictates a courteous answer. You're in the game to call decisions, not to have someone knock a chip off your shoulder. On the other hand, be firm with players and don't ever let any of 'em push you around. Once they find they can push you around, they lose their respect for you."[23]

While counseling civility, McGowan was not one to be trifled with. He tells of the time a Spanish-speaking White Sox pitcher, not understanding English, did not respond to McGowan's repeated summons to him to leave the bullpen and come to the mound.

"Each time I yelled at him I moved nearer the bullpen. Soon I saw Paul Richards, White Sox manager, on my heels. He said, 'You're losing your marbles.' I asked him, 'What was that you said?' Richards repeats it, 'You're losing your marbles.' I was burning inside as Paul turned away and I said, 'You can go in the clubhouse right now and start counting those marbles.' He did too, I saw to that."[24]

McGowan could also eject a player without being provoked. During a game between the Yankees and the Senators in Griffith Stadium on April 26, 1931, McGowan called a pitch a ball on Yankee outfielder Ben Chapman in the ninth inning. Senators catcher Roy Spencer turned as if to disagree and McGowan threw him out there and then.

"You can't do that," Spencer yelped. "I ain't done nothing yet."

"You're outta the game," McGowan said, "for what you were intending to say."[25]

McGowan once threw a player out of a game for his tone of voice. The player was Birdie Tebbetts (a catcher from 1936 to 1952 with the Tigers, Red Sox and Indians). Tebbetts had a talent for getting under anyone's skin. He knew the magic tricks that get a batter thinking about anything but the next pitch and he "chirped" his words in a high screechy voice. He was chirping from the bench one day when McGowan thumbed him out.

"What did I do?" Tebbetts asked.

"Nothing," McGowan said, "but your voice gives me a headache."[26]

Players and managers were not the only recipients of McGowan's "pugnaciousness."

Umpire Joe Rue recounts this story of his first game as a major league umpire with McGowan as a crewmate.

"I got off on the wrong foot with Bill McGowan. After the first game I worked with him in Detroit he said, 'You haven't asked me for any advice, Joe. I guess you're one of those kind who knows it all. You call your balls and strikes like some punk from the Eastern League.' I said, 'Bill, I want to tell you something. You're supposed to be the ace of umpires; but to me you're a pain in the ass, and if I ever ask you for anything, it will be over my dead body.' But I have to say this: McGowan was the best umpire in the league."[27]

Rue was not the only one to run afoul of McGowan and still compliment him on his skills. As manager of the White Sox, Jimmy Dykes, the longtime McGowan nemesis, resolved during the 1943 season to cease his arguing with umpires. His resolution lasted until August, when McGowan chased him. After that game, Dykes, in his own way, complimented McGowan by saying, "I haven't been bothering to fight with the umpires this season. I wouldn't dignify those bums by even going out there to argue with any of 'em except McGowan and Bill Summers."[28]

His control of games was legendary. There aren't many recorded examples of anyone putting one over on McGowan during a game, but it was known to happen. Joe McCarthy tells of the time he approached McGowan after the umpire had given the boot to Yankee catcher Arndt Jorgens, who challenged McGowan's call at the plate and pushed him during the argument.

"Mac," McCarthy says, "what the hell did you put him out for?"

"You saw what he did, didn't you?" McGowan said.

"Why he just gave you a little push like that," and McCarthy demonstrated what he meant by giving McGowan a little push.

"Isn't that enough?" McGowan asked.

"You mean to tell me," McCarthy said, "if a fellow gives you a little push like that"— demonstrating it again —"you're going to run him out of the game?"

The crowd was going wild watching McCarthy push umpire McGowan around with no consequences. McGowan got on to what McCarthy was doing and said, "Goddamnit, don't do that again."

"OK, Bill," McCarthy said with a wink and went back to the dugout.

McGowan never forgot it. Years later, McCarthy reported, he'd say to me, "You put one over on me that time, didn't you?"[29]

Tris Speaker (Hall of Fame centerfielder for the Red Sox, Indians, Senators and A's from 1907 to 1928), a player-manager for the Indians from 1919 to 1926, regularly put McGowan and other umps at a disadvantage with the crowd. At the close of an inning in which the visitors got the edge on a close call, the "Grey Eagle," as Speaker was called, would stop to chat on his way in from center field. "He would say, 'Nice crowd out today.' Then he would add, 'You bet it is a swell crowd. Yes sir, much better than yesterday.' By this time the crowd knew Speaker was bawling out the umpire and would immediately go to work with their howling and riding of the umpire. The umpires would walk away after telling the manager not to say another word. Sometimes the warning went unheeded and invariably, Speaker got the gate."[30]

More often McGowan got the upper hand in these tussles, as was the case with the Yankees' Jake Powell, who McGowan ordered out of a game

McGowan explaining how to tell if a pitcher has committed a balk to members of the Cleveland Indians during spring training, circa 1950. Tris Speaker, spring training coach for the Indians, is standing at left (from Bill Jr.'s album).

with a wave of his imperial thumb in Yankee Stadium in 1940. Yankees manager Joe McCarthy, not wanting to lose Powell, turned to reliever Marius Russo and said, "You go. Maybe he'll be satisfied." Russo walked from the Yankees dugout behind first base to the visitors' dugout behind third and got as far as home plate when McGowan said, "Where are you going? I want Powell, not you." McGowan turned Russo around and led him by the arm back to the Yankee dugout, saying to McCarthy and Powell, "When I want Powell, don't give me Russo. Get outta here, Powell."[31]

McGowan also enjoyed the occasional repartee. Sportswriter Bob Addie, noting that Casey Stengel and Willie (a common nickname for McGowan) were both actors, tells of a time in Comiskey Park in late September 1952 when McGowan called a play against the Yankees, and Stengel put on a tragic show. He thrust his hands high in the air and swooned into the waiting arms of two of his players.

McGowan walked to the Yankee bench and said, "What are you? Bernhardt? What's the fainting act for? Trying to show me up?"

"Why Bill," said the injured Stengel, "We're fighting for a pennant and I just fainted because we missed a splendid opportunity which you, in your infallible judgment, divined correctly."

"Harrumph, you ancient descendant of an improbable ancestor," replied McGowan (though perhaps not precisely in those words). The game continued without further conversation between the two men.[32]

Many of McGowan's actions can be explained as his ways of avoiding being shown up. Billy Evans had this to say about showing up an umpire.

"The umpire does not care to be shown up. It doesn't take much on the part of a player to arouse the wrath of the crowd. A shake of the head, a stepping out of the batter's box, or any one of a score of things, can call the attention of the crowd to the fact that the player doesn't look on the ruling with favor. Such actions are seriously objected to by any umpire."[33]

Humor

McGowan could also show a humorous side. If a pitcher today flipped the bird to an umpire to dispute a call, that would most likely be his last pitch of the day — and perhaps for a few days to come. Sid Hudson, recalling a game in Cleveland, said, "It was a tie game, bottom of the seventh, bases loaded, two out, a 3–2 count on Joe Gordon. I throw a side-arm curve over the middle of the plate and he calls it a ball. I'm so mad I give Mac the finger. With a nod of his head and a smile, he gives me the finger right back and says, 'OK, Sid, now let's play ball.'"[34]

Once, after disagreeing with a McGowan call, Moe Berg (noted American League journeyman player from 1926 to 1939 turned spy who was fluent in 12 languages but, of whom it was said, couldn't hit in any of them) turned toward McGowan from his catcher's position and said in his soft bass voice, "Bill, I want you to know that you can umpire better with one eye closed than most can umpire with two eyes. And I'll challenge any man who argues to the contrary." McGowan responded by closing one eye and blinking the other through his mask.

Thereafter, whenever Berg thought McGowan might have missed a pitch he would turn slowly and close one eye. McGowan would respond by bending toward the catcher and blinking one eye, reminding Berg of the umpire's supremacy. They winked at each for 14 years.[35]

Perhaps they had such an easy relationship because McGowan helped Berg get to the majors. McGowan was umpiring a Harvard-Princeton game in 1921 in which the Ivy Leaguers were calling him Mr. McGowan. He noticed a promising player for Princeton and asked him how he'd like to play in the majors, receiving an answer in the affirmative. McGowan got on his Smith-Corona and two years later Moe Berg was playing for the Brooklyn Dodgers.[36]

And there's the day Yogi Berra, who got back to second base too late in McGowan's opinion on a pickoff attempt, complained, "Damn it, Bill. I got back."

"You sure did," McGowan replied, "what took you so long?"[37]

He used the same line with Jimmy Dykes. Dykes was standing off second base with the bases loaded and one down when Tiger catcher Rudy York fired the ball to Tiger second baseman Charlie Gehringer, who put the tag on the diving Dykes, and up went McGowan's thumb.

"Out?" cried Dykes. "I made it, I got back."

McGowan looked benignly at Dykes and said, "Yes, you did, James, you made it. But what detained you?"[38]

McGowan used a story about Earle Combs, Yankees Hall of Fame outfielder, with his students to illustrate how to use humor to defuse a potentially explosive situation: "Earl [*sic*] Combs is as fine a gentleman as you'll ever meet. Once in awhile he becomes excited, and with palms downward will signal a runner (naturally a Yankee) is safe. I always manage to get a laugh, and at the same time an apology from the former great ball player by saying something to this effect: You'll be on our staff next year, Earl, if you keep improving on those close decisions." [39]

An umpire making himself the butt of a joke could also defuse a tense situation, as McGowan recounted in the case of National League umpire Bill Byron. He was known as "the singing umpire" as song was often his

response to players' complaints. In one case Byron had called a strike on
Phillies player Gavvy Cravath. Cravath thought it was a ball, as did two
of his teammates in the on-deck circle who had thrown up their bats in
disgust. The three of them crowded around Byron, who suddenly stepped
away, pulled out his whiskbroom and started to brush off the plate singing,
"Oh, he's growing old and feeble, and his eyes are dim with age." The two
players started to laugh, as did Cravath, who took his place in the batter's
box without another word.[40]

He could also assume a professorial air when responding to complaints. John Carmichael recalls the day in Yankee Stadium when Manager Casey Stengel approached the plate to ask Yogi Berra if the pitch
McGowan had just called a strike "was a good strike."

"I dunno, Casey. I never really got a good look at it," Berra replied.

Then McGowan broke in with, "Gentlemen, I had a full view of the
pitch. It was a thing of beauty. It took about two inches off the outside
corner and I will further say that it was a very fast ball, very fast. That is
my considered opinion, gentlemen, and I will not change it."[41]

Not Always a Stickler

While McGowan would bend the rules when he wanted to make a
point with a player, he also prided himself on knowing when to bend the
rules in the interest of common sense, at least as he saw it.

In a game in the Southern League, he gained nationwide publicity for
calling a catcher's balk in a game between Little Rock and New Orleans in
the Crescent City. With the bases full, a New Orleans runner started to
steal home on the Little Rock pitcher's windup. The catcher stepped past
the hitter to the front of the plate to get the pitch. McGowan sent the batter to first and advanced every other runner one base, not on the grounds
on interference, but because the catcher in preventing the pitch from reaching the plate had caused an offense similar to the one when the pitcher starts
his delivery, but fails to throw the ball.[42]

He recalled the time during his first year in the majors, 1925, when
Al "Bucketfoot" Simmons, Hall of Fame outfielder for several major league
teams from 1924 to 1944, threw a handful of dirt at him after being called
out at second. McGowan would have been within his rights (according to
the rules) to have reported the dirt-throwing to the League president and
Simmons would be suspended.

However, it was September and Simmons was in a tight race with
Harry Heilmann, Hall of Fame outfielder for the Tigers from 1914 to 1929,
for the batting title. Simmons rushed up to McGowan, talking rapidly.

The fans thought Simmons was arguing the call and were yelling things that fans yell at such a time, like "Take a punch at him, Al. Kill the big stiff."

Simmons was apologizing profusely for throwing the dirt and making his case for not being suspended. He prevailed.

"It would," McGowan wrote, "have been unjust to rob Simmons of his chance to lead the league in batting because of a momentary fit of temper, especially when he apologized."[43]

As it turned out, Heilmann won the batting title with a .393 average to Simmons' .387.

McGowan recounted a game in 1926 in which he chose a tactful way to deal with George Sisler, Hall of Fame first baseman for the St. Louis Browns from 1915 to 1927. The game occurred toward the end of Sisler's 41-game hitting streak — the major league record until Joe DiMaggio took it to 56 in 1941. McGowan called a third strike on Sisler who slammed his bat on the plate and called McGowan a vile name. This was more than enough provocation to toss Sisler from the game. He didn't, and Sisler apologized at his next time at bat.

McGowan explained his reasoning for not tossing Sisler. "I wouldn't have taken that abuse from an old hand who was in the habit of saying sharp things to umpires.... But, sometimes in the stress of a game, as when Sisler was working on that record, something is likely to slip out for which the player is likely to feel sorry. Often one just doesn't need to hear such things."[44]

In other situations McGowan would dispense with tact. During a 1945 game in Cleveland, Indian pitcher Jim Bagby, Jr., snarled, "Good day for you today, Bill. You only missed two on the last hitter."

"Miss that junk you throw?" McGowan exploded. "Any time I can't count the stitches on your fastball, I'll give up. Why, when you pitch I shut one eye to rest it and just work the other eye."[45]

At times he would go beyond using common sense and flat-out break the rules, as he did with Buddy Lewis.

In August 1945, Buddy Lewis (third baseman and outfielder for the Washington Senators from 1935 to 1949) was just back from World War II after flying 350 missions in a C-47 over the "Hump" in the Chinese-Burma theater of operations. Lewis had been an All-Star for the Senators in 1938 and would be again in 1947. He re-joined the Senators at Comiskey Park and faced White Sox pitcher Earl Caldwell in Lewis' first time at bat since Pearl Harbor. After the first two pitches, which were over the plate, but which McGowan called balls, Caldwell came halfway to plate and yelled to McGowan. "What's going on?" Caldwell wanted to know. "Those first two were right down Broadway."

McGowan said, "Don't you know who this is? This is Buddy Lewis. It's his first day back. Ain't no way I'm calling a strike on him during his first at bat." Caldwell motioned the catcher out of box and issued an intentional walk.[46]

Ed Joost, slick-fielding shortstop for the Reds, Braves, and Athletics from 1936 to 1955, gives another example of how McGowan took liberties with the umpires' creed of objectivity. This time it was in the form of a reward to Joost for looking out for another American League umpire, Ed Jones. During a game with the Senators in Washington, Jones was standing in front of the Senators' catcher, Al Evans, and unintentionally blocked a throw to the plate from first baseman Mickey Vernon attempting to force the runner from third on a bases-loaded bunt from A's pitcher Bobby Shantz.

Several fans expressed their displeasure by throwing cans of beer from the upper deck in Jones' direction. They ceased only after the public address announcer warned that any fan throwing beer on the field would be ejected.

After the game, as both teams and umpires were passing through the Senators' dugout on the way to their dressing rooms, Joost found himself behind Jones. Joost happened to look up to see a fan about ready to hit Jones with a bottle of beer from above. Joost reached out and pushed the fan away, knocking him over.

Before his next game in Philadelphia, the clubhouse boy told Joost that McGowan wanted to see him.

Joost said, "What's he want?"

"I don't know," the clubhouse boy said, "just go over and see him."

So Joost went over and McGowan let him in the door, and Joost said, "Number one — what do you want?"

"Sit down," McGowan said. "I heard what you did in Washington last week."

"Oh, hell, anybody would have done that," Joost said.

"Yeah, but you did it, didn't you," McGowan said. "Let me tell you something. I'll never call you out on a close third strike EVER!"[47]

Even though he would break the rules at times, he did know the rules and how to apply them to game situations. Two of the most widely reported incidents about McGowan's umpiring involve his correct application of rules. One cost Lou Gehrig sole possession of the 1931 home run title. That April 26, Gehrig hit the ball into the center field bleachers in Washington. The ball popped back out of the stands and into the hands of center fielder Harry Rice. Yankee base runner Lyn Lary was confused and slowed down. Gehrig kept running and accidentally passed Lary. McGowan called Gehrig out to end the inning. Gehrig and Ruth ended the season tied for the American League home run title with 46.[48]

In a more colorful incident that made front-page headlines in the *Cleveland Plain Dealer*, McGowan ejected Cleveland pitcher Johnny Allen for refusing to cut off part of his right shirtsleeve, which dangled as he pitched, distracting the batters.

Many considered Allen as among the most talented pitchers in baseball. Jimmie Foxx said he was by far the toughest pitcher he ever faced. He was also one of the most volatile. Allen littered the 1930s with famous tantrums, smashing up barrooms and hotel lobbies, and once attacked the other team's third-base coach in mid-inning.[49]

Early in the 1938 season Allen was feuding with McGowan. James Isaminger reported that "the incorrigible Johnny Allen fumed and threatened Bill McGowan when the Chevy Chase man [a reference to McGowan's hometown in Maryland at the time] was calling balls and strikes perfectly. The Indians won 4–1, but Allen acted as if McGowan was stealing victory from him."[50]

It came to a head between Allen and McGowan on June 7, 1938, when Red Sox manager Joe Cronin complained to McGowan that Allen was wearing a sweatshirt in which holes had been cut at the right elbow for ventilation — but distracted batters by flapping.

As McGowan tells it: "The right sleeve of Allen's undershirt was torn and every time he tossed the ball up there it emerged from the fluttering shirtsleeve right at the batter making the ball difficult to see. I told him he would have to remove the torn shirt.

"'I've been pitching with this shirt for five years and nobody said anything was wrong with it before,' Allen growled.

"I told him either to change shirts or get out of the game. Allen strode to the dugout, grabbed his jacket, and headed for the dressing room."[51]

Sportswriter Gordon Cobbledick reported that the "unstable right-hander indulged in a violent quarrel with McGowan," walked off the field to the clubhouse and refused the urgings of his manager Ossie Vitt to return, arguing that he'd worn the shirt several times before.

Allen says a little more about the violent quarrel.

"I had a few arguments with McGowan over called balls in the first inning and in the second inning he comes out to the mound and says, 'You gotta take that shirt off.'

"'For why,' I demanded.

"'Because it's ragged,' he stormed.

"'It isn't ragged,' I insisted. 'It has some holes in it but it's perfectly legal.'

"'Well, it's not legal for me,' Bill shot back. 'It's got to come off, or you're out of the game.'

"By that time I was hot and shouted back, 'That's OK by me!'"[52]

Cleveland manager Oscar Vitt told Allen that while no one had complained before, McGowan was right in asking him to trim the sleeve. Allen wouldn't budge, and Vitt fined Allen $250 on the spot. Allen later asked to appeal his case to American League president Harridge. Harridge refused to see him and fined him another $25.

The rule in question stated, "Pitchers are not permitted to work with ragged or slit sleeves which have the effect of confusing the batter."[53]

Allen's shirt is currently in the Hall of Fame due to the intervention of Indians owner Alva Bradley. Bradley hurried to Boston and bought the shirt from Allen for "right close to $500," according to Allen, and then displayed it in his brother Bradley's Higbee's Department Store in Cleveland. From Higbee's the shirt went to Cooperstown.[54]

The McGowan-Allen brouhahas continued to make for media stories that year. An article in *The Sporting News* in the winter of 1938 reported that "noting the 'Umpire School' advertisement of Bill McGowan ... Ed McAuley of the *Cleveland News* expresses the belief that McGowan's sticking his chin out for Johnny Allen who had a couple of run-ins with Bill last season."

"You can imagine with what rich variations on the 'Physician, cure thyself' theme this off-season enterprise will suggest to Allen," chuckles McAuley. "For in McGowan's ad he promises to teach students 'Stance Behind the Plate and Positions to Take on Various Plays.'

"Unless you have seen Allen's side-splitting imitation of Bob Feller jumping off the bench to take a bow before a Southern exhibition game, you have no appreciation of the fellow's flair for pantomime."[55]

Coaching

Though as an umpire he was tacitly forbidden to advise players on the field, McGowan would often offer advice or encouragement to rookies and stars alike, most famously involving Ted Williams.

On the last day of the 1941 season, 10,000 people turned out at Shibe Park on a rainy Saturday afternoon for a doubleheader to see if Williams could end the season hitting .400. He was leading the league with a .39955 batting average going into the game. Joe Cronin, Red Sox manager, offered to bench him so his average would be rounded off to .400, making him the first American League batter to hit .400 since Harry Heilmann of Detroit had hit .403 in 1923.

"No thanks," Williams said. "If I couldn't hit .400 all the way," he said later, "I didn't deserve it."[56]

At Williams' first at-bat, the A's catcher Frankie Hayes said to Williams, "Ted, Mr. Mack told us if we let up on you he'll run us out of baseball. I wish you all the luck in the world today, but we're not giving you a damn thing." Hearing that, McGowan called time and slowly walked around the plate, bent over and began dusting it off. Without looking up, he said, "To hit .400 a batter has got to be loose. He has got to be loose."[57]

The advice took. Williams was loose. He singled his first time up off Dick Fowler, homered his next at-bat, and got two more singles off relief pitchers in the first game. In the second game he combined a single with a ball hit off the outfield loudspeaker horn for a double to go 6 for 8, ending the season with a .406 average.[58]

Later in Williams' career McGowan's advice helped Williams break out of a slump. McGowan told him: "The reason you're in a slump is you're trying to break the ball. You can't do that. Just hit it."

Hank Greenberg (another home run slugger and eventual Hall of Famer) credited McGowan's advice with helping him get a $70,000 salary. He begged McGowan to tell him what was wrong with his swing. After several entreaties, McGowan agreed and said, "There's nothing wrong with your swing. There's just too much of it. Just shorten up a little bit. You don't have to knock those homers into the twentieth row, the first row is far enough. A homer by this much counts just as much," and McGowan held up two fingers an inch apart to demonstrate a sufficient margin.[59]

Showing the confidence he put in his advice, McGowan was quoted as saying in January 1938: "Hank was about ready to go to town and barring accidents, he should set some records this coming season."[60] And set some records Greenberg did. He hit 58 homers, missing Ruth's record single-season mark of 60 by only two, and led the American League in runs scored with 144.

Even "bushers" were occasional beneficiaries of his advice. Irv Noren, recently called up from the Hollywood Stars of the Pacific Coast League, had McGowan behind the plate for his first major league game, with the Senators in 1950. "I swung and missed at a borderline high pitch. Mac says, 'That's a Coast League strike, kid. In the majors, it's a ball.' I appreciated him saying that," Noren said.[61]

Gil Coan recalls McGowan telling him what to look for from the opposing pitcher during his rookie year with the Senators in 1946. "He always encouraged the young ball players," Coan said.

He may not have always encouraged the veterans. Billy Werber, a noted base stealer, made a point of saying that while it wasn't unusual for other umpires to "to give me some encouragement by saying 'Go ahead,

Billy, you can take a little longer lead,' you never heard anything like that from McGowan."[62]

Ira Smith points out that such kindness is not always expected of umpires. Extensive research, he says, has proven that umpires *can* be kind and sympathetic. Even so, some folks just can't picture one of them helping an old woman across the street, caring for a crippled pigeon or holding up a ball game to soothe the nerves of a jittery young pitcher.

Yet that's just what he did for Tommy Bridges, who had been called up from the Three-I League to the Tigers in late August 1930. Bridges had just watched the Yankees blast two Tiger pitchers for 13 hits in five innings when manager Bucky Harris summoned him to the mound. His warm-up pitches were "outlandishly wild." McGowan called time to speak to the young pitcher.

"Listen, son, you threw the ball past bats in the Three-I League that are just like the ones these fellers up here have in their hands. You're bound to do better than those last two guys who were in before you. So just figure it's another ball game and do your best. Good luck to you."

The advice took. Ruth popped up on an easy fly to right, Lazzeri got a fluky hit through the infield, Gehrig fanned, and Harry Rice grounded out.[63]

McGowan was also known to advise players on their dress. In a 1944 game against the Tigers, he told rookie Yankee pitcher Mel Queen that next time he should wear a cleaner pair of pants. Misunderstanding McGowan's meaning, Queen delayed the game while he changed pants.[64]

Yogi Berra, in a story told by columnist Maury Allen, describes how an encounter with McGowan led him to officially adopt Yogi, a nickname he'd had since childhood, as his professional name.

"'Umpire Bill McGowan arranged for me to autograph a couple of baseballs,' Berra writes of a 1947 event allowing the underpaid umps to hustle a few bucks at dinners with signed baseballs. Berra signed the balls as Larry Berra and McGowan asked, 'Who the hell put Larry Berra on here?' Berra protested that his name was Larry Berra and McGowan said, 'The hell it is. Sign them Yogi. That's your name, ain't it?'"[65]

Scouting

Early in his career, when McGowan saw a minor leaguer with major league potential he made sure the right people knew, as he did in the case of Moe Berg.

In 1916, McGowan, then 20 years old, wired Connie Mack about the talents of three ball players in a league of two teams from Maryland and two from Delaware. Mack sent his chief scout, Mike Drennan, to see a game. Drennan took a liking to the third baseman, Jimmy Dykes. Shortly thereafter Mack also signed knuckleballer Eddie Rommel and shortstop Joe Boley on McGowan's recommendations. [66]

Dykes played in the majors for 22 years and Joe Boley played for six years. Eddie Rommel played for 13 years, became known as the father of the knuckleball for Connie Mack's A's, and went on to a long career as a major league umpire.

McGowan's most prominent find was Leon "Goose" Goslin, whom he first spotted in 1919 while working a game between the employees of the du Pont plant, where Goslin repaired elevators, at Carney's Point, New Jersey. They became friends, and Goslin traveled from his home in Salem, New Jersey, to McGowan's in Wilmington, Delaware, every day for weeks to talk baseball. McGowan thought so highly of Goslin that he recommended him to Connie Mack, who at that time was loaded with prospects and couldn't use another. [67]

McGowan, who by now was umpiring in the Sally League, got Goslin a tryout with the Columbia, South Carolina, team in the South Atlantic League by sending a message to manager Zinn Beck: "Guarantee this boy will win games for you and that big league clubs will want him inside of two years." [68]

In his first year with the South Carolina team, Goslin did win six games but he also lost five, which prompted Beck, who was also the third base coach, to give Goslin a little advice.

"Listen, young man," Beck said to Goose. "I've been in baseball a long time, but the fact is I'm not thirty-one yet. Won't be till the season ends. If you keep this up I'll never make it, 'cause the way they're hitting you I'll get killed out here for sure."

Goslin became an outfielder even though Beck told him he needed a clothes basket to catch flies in the outfield. Two years later McGowan sent word to Clark Griffith that Goslin, now called "Goose," was ready for the big time. [69] Griffith agreed, was most appreciative, and was able to return the favor.

"McGowan," Griffith said, "did me one of the greatest favors of my life back in 1921 when he was umpiring in the Sally League. I was coming north on a train from Charlotte when I first met him. He introduced himself to me and immediately told me about a great-hitting outfielder playing for Columbia named Goose Goslin. He told me Goslin was a real slugger and that I ought to look him over.

"I made a personal trip to Columbia to see Goslin and signed him immediately. I'll never forget Bill McGowan for that alone. Later, it was my pleasure to recommend him to Ban Johnson, president of the American League, when Bill applied for work in our circuit."[70]

Goslin was the key slugger in Washington's pennant victories of 1924, '25, and '33. He won the American League batting championship in 1928 with a .379 average and became one of the greatest money players in all of baseball. He hit seven homers in World Series competition and held the World Series mark for consecutive hits. The high point of his career came in the ninth inning of the sixth game of the 1935 Series against the Cubs. He stepped to the plate with Mickey Cochrane on second, the Tigers ahead in the series 3–2 and the score tied 3–3. Goslin called to his teammates, "Get for those showers, boys, it's all over." He promptly singled sharply over second baseman Billy Herman's head, sending Cochrane dashing for the plate to score the run that gave the Tigers their first Series title.[71]

Goslin was not the only player of note that McGowan spotted for Griffith. In 1919 McGowan wrote Griffith, whom he'd not yet met, a note saying that there was a sweet-looking second baseman in the International League who had the facility of waiting out the pitchers and seemed ready for the majors. That was Stanley "Bucky" Harris, who, as a player-manager for the World Championship Senators in 1924, became known as the "Boy Wonder" and, along with Goslin, would end up in the Hall of Fame.[72]

McGowan and Griffith were to have a close association throughout McGowan's career. They often appeared at speaking engagements together, and McGowan was usually a guest at the "Old Fox's" birthday parties.

Several years later McGowan was again locating talent for the Senators, who were looking for an additional coach. McGowan recommended Ben Egan, a former catcher for the Athletics and Indians, whom McGowan had worked behind in the International League. McGowan was of the opinion that Egan was responsible for the development of all the players that Jack Dunn, Orioles owner, had sold to the majors from the Orioles. Leading that list of players was Babe Ruth.[73]

McGowan was a backer of Walter Johnson's youngest son, Eddie, who was a star baseball and basketball player as well as president of the student body at the University of Maryland. "A sure-fire major league shortstop," said McGowan. Eddie Johnson did play shortstop for Easton, Maryland, of the Eastern Shore League, after which he moved up to Norfolk, which had just lost Phil Rizzuto to the Yankees. Injuries to Johnson's legs were the only thing that prevented McGowan's prophecy from coming true.[74]

Later in his career McGowan was quoted as saying, "Nowadays we umpires can't recommend ball players to any club owner. It's in our contract that we can't. But back in my International League days they didn't care what we did and I was always placing young ball players. I got a kick out of it."[75]

The condition against recommending players was item four in McGowan's 1952 contract, which paid him a salary of $13,000 plus $2,500 for hotels, meals, and incidentals and reimbursement for travel expenses. The condition read in part, "The Umpire shall not in any manner, act as advisor or agent in recommending players to, or securing players for, any club member of the League, nor except with the written consent of the League's president, for any club member of any other league."

4: Why Don't You Umpire?

While his occasional one-on-one tutorial to a "busher" or a manager about who was running the game never caused McGowan any problems, he did get into trouble when he put his displeasure on public display. Many umpires have been asked to resign or were quietly fired. McGowan is the only major league umpire to be suspended twice for his conduct on the field.[1]

His first major league suspension came in 1948. Ray Scarborough, right-handed pitcher for the Washington Senators from 1942 to 1949, was a key figure in that suspension.

Scarborough, Mel Parnell said, "was one of the best bench jockeys I've ever seen. He'd run guys berserk. Scarborough was known as Pickle Nose because he was a pickle salesman during the winter in North Carolina."[2]

McGowan, no doubt, knew of Scarborough's reputation. On July 15, during the ninth inning of a close game at Griffith Stadium against the White Sox with McGowan behind the plate, Scarborough shook his head, which McGowan took as displeasure with his calls. McGowan took a few steps toward the mound and threw his ball-strike indicator at Scarborough, who ducked as it went by, and then picked it up and pocketed it. McGowan finished the game without his indicator.[3]

Senators manager Joe Kuhel, concerned that the incident could lead to trouble in the future, asked McGowan after the game why he threw his indicator. "Because," McGowan said, "he was trying to show me up."

When asked about the incident the next day by a reporter, Scarborough said he had told McGowan earlier in the game, "'Bill, I believe you missed a couple of pitches on me,' but I said nothing in the ninth inning when he threw the indicator to the mound. I merely shook my head in disgust when I pitched the fourth ball to Luke Appling. I knew it was a ball and I was mad because I didn't get the ball over the plate."[4]

While the incident may have been a case of McGowan misunderstanding Scarborough's reason for shaking his head, Kuhel was correct in seeing it as an omen of trouble to come. On the following Monday night at Griffith Stadium in a game between the Indians and the Senators, McGowan was at first base and Scarborough was on the nearby Senators bench. McGowan made several uncomplimentary remarks to Scarborough and, to hear Scarborough tell it, McGowan called him a "bush *****."[5]

Later in the same game, several Senators reported seeing McGowan intentionally throw a ball at Senator outfielder Ed Stewart. Stewart was arguing with umpire Joe Paparella, who had just called him out on a close play at home plate on what would have been the winning run in the ninth inning.

Stewart said he was so busy arguing that he didn't see the ball but said that McGowan did curse him on his way to his outfield position. "McGowan called me names which I don't want to repeat. He also threatened to chase me out of the ball game and told me never to speak to him again, either on the field or off the field. I felt so mad about the things he called me," Stewart said, "that I could have punched him in the nose."

In the locker room, Senators manager Joe Kuhel, left, pitcher Ray Scarborough and outfielder Ed Stewart discuss the 1948 McGowan ball-throwing incident that got him suspended.

On the following morning, July 20, Clark Griffith telephoned a complaint to the office of American League president Will Harridge demanding speedy punishment of McGowan and saying the charges would be backed by affidavits signed by Washington players. Harridge notified McGowan of his suspension and $500 fine that afternoon. Harridge said his office had received several complaints about McGowan during the year but the suspension was for the July 19 episodes only. Asked for his reaction, McGowan, in a rare instance of taciturnity, merely said: "I don't want to talk about that. Mr. Harridge is running the show."[6]

Harridge's decision, released to the press at noon on July 28, read as follows:

> After a thorough investigation, I find that the charges filed against Mr. McGowan for his conduct and use of bad language on the ball field at Washington have been substantiated. It is regrettable that an umpire should be involved in a situation of this kind because he is the League representative on the ball field, clothed with absolute authority and should at all times realize and appreciate his responsibility to baseball. I acted as I would have if the situation had been reversed and similar charges had been made by an umpire against a player. Mr. McGowan will remain under suspension for a period of ten days without salary. He will again be eligible to officiate in American League games on and after Friday, July 30.[7]

Harridge's decision sat well with the Nats, who released a statement saying, "If a ball player is fined and suspended for cursing and abusing an umpire, it's only fair that an umpire get the same punishment if he abuses a ball player."[8]

A day later McGowan regained his voice on the matter and said that he was astounded at the suspension and "that Scarborough kicked on at least 20 pitches during the game. He was trying to show me up and I didn't like it because he was trying to incite the crowd. I didn't throw my indicator at him, I just flipped it a few feet toward the mound suggesting that he umpire the game.

"As for cussing Stewart or other Washington players, I may have mumbled a couple of cuss words out there but they weren't directed at anybody. I was talking to myself about the heat and the tough time the umpires were having.

"And I didn't throw a ball at anybody. I picked a baseball up that was on the ground and rolled it toward Paparella so he could hustle the game along."[9]

Among the charges made by several of the older Nats was that McGowan had been abusive to many of the Nats rookies, particularly Al Kozar, the Senators' second baseman from 1948 to 1950.[10]

Kozar supported that charge. In his account we see an example of how McGowan could hound a player for no apparent reason. Several months before the suspension incident, in a game with the Browns, Kozar thought the Browns' Pete Layden took off early for third after a fly ball to center so he stepped on second with the ball and looked at McGowan for his call expecting that it would be "out." The call was "safe."

Kozar said he threw the ball to the pitcher and returned to his position without saying a word.

"McGowan said if I didn't like his call he'd send me back to the minors. He kept screaming, calling me rookie and cursing. Then he looked up in the stands and said. 'Do you think you're gonna get those people on me? I'll rub your ass in your nose.' I'd walk away but he'd follow me until finally he quit. My manager Joe Kuhel said to me in between innings, 'Christ, you never say anything. Why don't you leave this guy alone? He's been in the big leagues for twenty years.' I said 'Joe, I'm not arguing. I didn't argue with anybody.' 'Sure didn't look that way to me,'" Kuhel replied.

"Then," Kozar continued, "a few days later in Chicago I'm talking to reliever Forrest Thompson, when all of a sudden I'm pushed in the back. It was Bill McGowan again, cursing me and demanding the ball. Then Kuhel comes out to say, 'If you say one more word to McGowan I'm taking you out of the game.' He wouldn't listen to me. McGowan kept it up. I thought he was sick and having a nervous breakdown.

"After the Cleveland game, Kuhel wanted me to write him up. I told Kuhel, 'You didn't want to listen to me before. I had no beef with the guy tonight.' I wouldn't write anything down and they got McGowan suspended without my help."[11]

Word of Kozar's refusal reached McGowan, who gave Kozar one of his special exemptions from the rules on opening day against the Yankees the next year, 1949.

"The first pitch," Kozar said, "from Allie Reynolds was waist-high — a perfect pitch. McGowan calls, 'Ball one.' Catcher Yogi Berra grumbled, 'Oh, come on.' Then Allie threw a low strike and I heard, 'Ball two.' Yogi said, 'Goddamn, Bill. Let's cut out that shit.' McGowan said, 'Berra, do you want me to shove the ball down your throat?' Then he called time, walked by Berra and was face to face with me. 'Kid,' he said, 'you were the only Washington Senator not to write me up last year. I gave you two; I'm not giving you any more. We're even. Take that goddamn bat off your shoulder and swing!' And he turned to Berra and said, 'You shut up.'"[12]

Shirley Povich, sportswriter for *The Washington Post*, ended his article on McGowan's suspension by saying it was rumored that McGowan was not in the best of health and was suffering from diabetes.[13]

New York Times columnist Daley added that while you'd expect most ball players to say something to the effect of "serves the ole buzzard right" upon hearing of an umpire's suspension, most said softly, "Too bad about Willie, isn't it?"[14]

If McGowan got some sympathy from some players, it was a different story with his fellow umpires. "The bald truth," wrote Shirley Povich, "is that McGowan is not too popular with a certain group of umpires who rated higher in league politics than did McGowan. They would have joyfully received any little thing that came to pass to deflate Mr. McGowan. The trouble with him, as other umpires saw it, was that he was out in front by a country mile as the best umpire in the league."[15]

McGowan returned to umpiring on July 30 at first base for a game between the Yankees and the White Sox at Comiskey Park. Contacted by a reporter on July 29, McGowan said: "I'm ready and eager to go back to work. I still love my league and have no hard feelings toward anyone."

He said he had received instructions to start umpiring the next day but could not disclose where.[16] Turned out it was Comiskey Park, home to the Chicago White Sox, who had been the Senators' opposition for the game in which he threw his indicator at Scarborough.

Later that same year Harridge selected McGowan to be the umpire-in-chief for the first-ever American League pennant playoff game on October 4, 1948, in which Cleveland defeated Boston 8–3. The selection was a clear signal that Harridge considered McGowan to be the best umpire in the American League. McGowan often cited his selection to be the highlight of his career, saying, "Never had a guy turn his head on me all day. It was the only time both clubs congratulated me after a game."[17]

On a more humorous note, McGowan's suspension did bring an offer of temporary employment. Lefty Craig, umpire supervisor for the Big State, Evangeline, Lone Star, Sooner State, and Mexico leagues, wired McGowan, "Have opening on Evangeline League umpiring staff if worse comes to worse." Craig had great respect for McGowan's work as a teacher, since he employed 16 umpires in his league who were graduates of McGowan's school. Craig was also a fan of McGowan's work on the field but was just ribbing McGowan by offering him a Class D position, though he did add, "If he should call my hand, I'd certainly place him in the Evangeline League."[18]

The incident also inspired a melodramatic account of the happenings by a writer who didn't know McGowan or his reputation. Nevertheless, after noting the anonymity under which the writer assumed McGowan had labored for 24 years, the editorial continued: "But then at last, the emotion blew out. Like Ajax, Bill shook his fist at the gods and dared the lightning.

He has given a lift to the meek everywhere. Husbands will talk back to their wives with renewed courage; perhaps some inspired drivers will get out of their cars in the stalled traffic and punch the horn honkers behind them on the nose. There ought to be a Bill McGowan Day."[19]

Friction with the League President

McGowan had good reason to be astounded at his suspension. Complaints about umpires were routinely made to the league office, as were formal protests with charges. If umpires were taken to task, the public didn't hear about it. Umpires had been called on the carpet before, but always in the private chambers of the president's office. Never had an umpire been publicly rebuked and stripped of his uniform pending an investigation.

The case can be made that the suspension and the way it was done was retribution for McGowan's style. He was seen as not only the best but also the most irritable of the umpires. Complaints against him came mostly from his irascible reactions to criticism, his fondness for showing scorn toward any disputant, and his chip-on-the-shoulder, swaggering approach to every argument. It's significant that this complaint was not about any call he made but that he'd abused Washington players.[20]

This was not the first time he'd thrown his indicator in a fit of pique. Two years earlier he'd thrown his indicator in the direction of the Senators bench because he was more than slightly irked at the catcalls coming from that direction.[21]

In addition to his occasional piques of temper on the field, his opinions—as expressed in his newspaper and magazine articles—received a chilly reception in the American League's executive offices. Some were of the opinion that his pen cost him more than one World Series check.[22]

Harridge had acted on the previous complaints privately, by denying McGowan appointment to the profitable World Series umpiring job for a stretch of several years. In 1940 he not only ordered McGowan to stop writing his articles, but also refused McGowan's wife permission to sell a magazine story about umpires.[23]

Titled "So You Hate My Husband" under Madge McGowan's byline, the piece was also partially written by sportswriter Dick McCann (who also suggested the catchy title). It was accepted for publication pending Harridge's OK. He failed to give it because he thought McGowan had a hand in its writing. Harridge was of the opinion that umpires should be seen and not heard, and especially not talk for publication. Jack Miley, sportswriter for the *New York Post*, pointed out the higher standard Harridge held umpires to as compared to players, saying,

Ball players are allowed to endorse cigarettes and breakfast foods, they can spiel on the radio and plug everything from candy bars to galoshes. Managers can write magazine articles on how they'll beat the Yankees or why they don't like night ball. But an umpire's wife can't say a few words in defense of her husband's profession without being told to pipe down or they'll send her old man to Siberia.[24]

Another indicator of friction between Harridge and McGowan was reported in 1945: "McGowan long ago gained disfavor with Harridge and his chief of umpires, Tom Connolly, because of his outspokenness. They'd like to fire him, but they scarcely dare because McGowan is so far the best of the league's umpires that they don't have the nerve."[25]

These episodes were not McGowan's first run-ins with the powers that be. Before Harridge became American League president, Judge Kenesaw Mountain Landis, the baseball czar from 1920 to 1944, had taken exception to McGowan writing articles for *The Wilmington Star* in Delaware in the early '30s because Landis thought the articles were too revealing.[26]

It appears that by 1948 Harridge was fed up with McGowan and wanted to let everyone know.[27]

Can You Write?

For the next three-plus years, McGowan conducted business as usual, complete with articles. Then in 1952 he had a series of disputes during St. Louis Browns games that culminated in his second suspension.

On June 12 (just two days after taking over as manager from Rogers Hornsby), shortstop Marty Marion pushed McGowan in a dispute over his overruling fellow umpire Hank Soar's call that Browns shortstop Joe DeMaestri was safe on a play at third.[28] McGowan ejected Marion.

Marion and Browns owner Bill Veeck claimed Marion did not push McGowan, though according to one account at the time, "the entire Fenway Park press box agreed that McGowan was pushed." Veeck took such exception to McGowan's ruling that he asked Harridge to give McGowan a lie detector test. Harridge declined.[29]

After conferring with Marion, Veeck, and McGowan, Harridge did issue a statement that read, "Marion's actions in jostling and bumping umpire McGowan not once but several times were entirely uncalled for and was the type of action which will not be condoned in the American League."[30] Marion was subsequently reinstated and fined $100.

At the start of the Red Sox–Browns game of July 27, Red Sox manager Lou Boudreau told Browns player-manager Marty Marion and McGowan that he had just signed a player contract and was eligible to play.

When asked by the press what the discussion was about, McGowan replied, "It's none of their business."

Then on August 6 at Sportsman's Park in St. Louis during a game between the Tigers and the Browns, his temper got the best of him again. McGowan let the St. Louis sportswriters know exactly what he thought of them in full view of the spectators.

As Oscar Ruhl, writing for *The Sporting News,* tells it, McGowan called Cliff Mapes, Detroit outfielder, out on a third strike in the seventh inning, bringing loud protests from the Tigers' bench. McGowan turned toward the Tigers' dugout and gave the motion of thumbing out a player.

A writer in the press box telephoned field information attendant Bernie Ebert to ask McGowan which player he had ejected. McGowan is said to have told Ebert, "Tell 'em it's none of their ****** business." As Ebert started back to the phone, McGowan added, "Tell 'em I'll write them a letter."

When informed of McGowan's response, one writer, Ellie Veech, sports editor of the *East St. Louis Journal,* called down to the field from the press box to say, "Hey, McGowan, can you write?"

McGowan, a widely published author, was no doubt galled by Veech's question. He "made an offensive gesture directed to the press box." He told Ebert to "tell those in the press box that if there were any good writers up there they'd be in New York," and he repeated his gesture.

Immediately after the game, Robert L. Burnes, sports editor of the *St. Louis Democrat,* wired a protest to Harridge on the grounds that McGowan had failed to supply information and had made obscene gestures.

The next morning, G. Thomas Duffy, managing editor of the *East St. Louis Journal,* sent a protest to Bill Veeck, president of the Browns, saying unless McGowan apologized, his paper would no longer cover the Browns' games.

Harridge wasted no time replying to Burnes by wire that afternoon saying, "Have your wire. Umpire McGowan was wrong when he refused to advise members of the St. Louis press box name of player he ejected from the bench. His personal conduct and remarks are most regrettable and as president of the American League I personally apologize to all writers who witnessed the affair. McGowan has been relieved of any further umpire assignments for an indefinite period."

Harridge called Duffy with a similar message. Harridge also stuck McGowan with a $650 fine — the biggest fine ever meted out to an umpire up to that time.[31]

An indefinite period turned out to be four games. Billy Hoeft was the player in question.[32]

McGowan's suspension drew fire from Knocky Thomas, the manager of the Touchdown Club in Washington, D.C., that hosted many functions for athletes and where McGowan was a frequent speaker and occasional recipient of an award.

"You sportswriters are a bunch of jerks," Thomas began.

> Here's the greatest umpire in the business and yet he's knocked off because a few prima donnas in the St. Louis press box didn't like it when he wouldn't tell him which Detroit player he ordered off the bench.
> I'm not saying McGowan was right but don't you writing guys ever make a mistake? When you do, you don't appreciate anyone running to your boss, do you?[33]

As in Povich's article on McGowan's 1948 suspension in *The Sporting News*, Ruhl noted in his article about the 1952 incident that McGowan was reported to be in poor health.

5: The School

McGowan's most lasting contribution to the game is the school he founded for umpires known then simply as Bill McGowan's School for Umpires. National League umpire George Barr opened the first school for umpires in 1935 in Hot Springs, Arkansas.

McGowan opened his first school in 1938. An article about it in *The Sporting News* read as follows:

"Bill McGowan will conduct a school for umpires this winter with classes due to start November 25. Enrollment will be confined chiefly to students living in the Washington and Baltimore and vicinity for amateur and semi-pro arbiters who aspire to the minor leagues. He will school the students on handling various situations that arise, positions to take on plays, interpretation of rules, and similar details."[1]

The school was headquartered at 6143 Thirteenth Street Northwest in Chevy Chase, Maryland, which also served as the McGowan residence. Students got their experience by officiating at University of Maryland games.[2]

At the same time McGowan had initiated a correspondence school for umpires. "This complete, low-cost mail course," as it was described in an ad in *The Sporting News*, "is designed especially for amateur and semi-pro umpires who cannot attend the schools now being conducted at Washington, D.C. and Baltimore, Md., by Bill McGowan, veteran American League umpire." McGowan described the lessons as "not one of those learn-to-be a big leaguer in ten easy lessons, but a rational attempt to improve men who have had some experience in umpiring college, American Legion, and independent games."[3]

Walter Stewart of the *Memphis Commercial Appeal*, upon learning of the correspondence school, observed that "this might be a happier world if the boys could do all their work through the postman. It's easier to dodge bottles by mail."[4]

In 1939, Bill McGowan joined forces with fellow umpire Red Ormsby to open for business in Jackson, Mississippi. The school moved to Florida several weeks later. That year the McGowan-Ormsby combine also had charge of the umpiring department of Babe Ruth's new baseball school in Palatka, Florida.[5]

John "Red" Flaherty (an early graduate of the McGowan-Ormsby combine who made the majors) recalled, "In the late 1930s I got a chance to go to Bill McGowan's umpire school. The first couple of weeks we were in Jackson, Mississippi and then we went over to Florida for about 2 weeks."[6]

"It's good work," McGowan explained, "and the pay is good. It has something for which we are all striving these days— security. If you behave yourself and your health holds out, umpiring is the greatest work in the world. It keeps you outdoors. The hours are short. The responsibility is terrific, but if you got the right start and learn the business from the ground up, you don't have to worry about shouldering the responsibility. It becomes automatic."[7]

McGowan always took great pride in his school. In 1948, he was quoted as saying, "I give my schools as much thought and work as I do umpiring in the regular season. I get a great kick out of taking these boys and turning them into good umps. I had to come up the hard way and learn by the trial and error method. If I can save these boys heartaches, then I'll be happy."[8]

You can see his pride in letters he wrote to applicants. In a letter dated April 3, 1946, to Roman Bentz, McGowan said, "We had 68 fellows in the school at Cocoa, Florida. We started on Feb. 1st and ran through Feb. 28th. Fifty-six veterans attended. I placed all but three of the G.I.s in the minor leagues for the coming season; these three did not care to make a start this year. Placed all but two of the civilians. One of my boys was a Purple Heart

Bill McGowan (left) with Navy Lt. Oliver F. Naquin, skipper of the ill-fated *Squalus* submarine that sank off the New Hampshire coast May 23, 1939. Naquin lived with the McGowan family for a time in 1941 (when this photograph was taken).

Instructor at Bill McGowan's School for Umpires demonstrating proper position and signal for calling a runner safe.

winner and I placed him in the Class A. South Atlantic league. I placed about 10 in Class B. leagues and 12 in Class C. The rest in Class D. leagues. None received less than $178 per mo."

Since the school operated between January and March, McGowan was excused from the requirement to work during spring training, as were other veteran umpires like Emmett "Red" Ormsby and George Moriarty. This arrangement didn't sit well with Clark Griffith, who favored spring training for all umpires, saying, "How can a fellow who hasn't seen a baseball for six months accurately call balls and strikes on opening day?"[9]

Others didn't share Griffith's concern. One was Jimmy Dykes (whom McGowan had ejected from any number of games), who proudly told a sportswriter that even though McGowan was voted the best umpire in the American League in 1935, "we like to call him 'Little Joe Chest.'"

Eighteen years later Dykes had high praise for McGowan. He noted that McGowan didn't take spring practice in 1953, since he was busy with his school. "On opening day," Dykes said, "he stepped into Yankee Stadium. Let the others have spring training. Let them loosen up their legs and sharpen their eyes and firm up their judgment after six months off. He didn't need it. The only spring training he needed was practice breathing hard so he could blow up his chest protector. Kellner is pitching against Reynolds and McGowan calls the greatest game I ever saw in my life."[10]

The school reached booming proportions in 1947, the year it came under the GI Bill of Rights, with 251 graduates, 95 percent of whom were veterans. The average age of the students was 23 or 24. Of those who graduated in 1947, about 100 found work umpiring.[11]

McGowan was tireless in seeking jobs for his graduates. In 1951 he talked to 48 minor league presidents trying to find positions for students who would be graduating from the January 1952 umpire school at Daytona Beach, Florida.[12]

Life at the School

One who made it to the majors in 1955 via McGowan's school and the GI Bill of Rights was John Rice. Rice used the GI Bill to enter Bill McGowan's umpiring school in West Palm Beach, Florida, in 1948.

"It lasted about a month," Rice recalled, "and you weren't guaranteed a job when it was over. You were completely on your own. Two of the teachers were Bill McKinley and Ed Hurley, two major league umpires.

"They'd teach you positioning and how to handle various plays and we even played some ball. The last week or ten days there were people

Instructor demonstrating how to put on the mask.

Students practicing their "out" signals.

there to evaluate you, and they recommended you to leagues looking for umpires."[13]

Rice attended the school in 1948 and 1949. "We'd stay in the barracks," Rice said, "while the faculty stayed in a hotel and McGowan had his own place. There was no drinking in the barracks—beer or otherwise. If McGowan found out about any drinking he'd raise hell. He wouldn't ask for names but in that shrill voice of his that he used when he was mad, he'd let us know that we were expected to be ready and alert every morning.

"Al Somers, an umpire in the Pacific Coast League, was in charge of the activities on the field during the day while McGowan would stand around in his blue shirt to be ready for pictures. Reporters were always around taking pictures for ads that were shown in movie theaters and occasional newsreels. But McGowan always let you know that he ran the ship; not in a pushy or loud way, but you knew he was the boss. After hours he'd always go to the dog races."[14]

While he was at the dog races, many of the students would gather around for a singing of the school song after the evening meal. Bill McGowan's School for Umpires was informally known as "The Institute for Objective Umpiring," or I.O.U., and voices raised in unison would belt out:

"We're loyal to thee, I.O.U.,
You taught us to be, I.O.U.
Defenders of Honesty,

Fair play and integrity,
We'll call every one as we see (Ball three!)
We want you to know, I.O.U.,
Wherever we go, I.O.U.,
We're faithful to you
'Cause we're your old Boys in Blue,
The alumni of I.O.U. (Strike two!)"

Graduates of at least one class received diplomas to mark their successful completion of the school. At the end of the 1949 sessions, McGowan and the faculty put on a full-blown graduation ceremony. Against a backdrop of swaying palm trees and "Dean" McGowan dressed in a white academic gown and a white mortar board, graduates, dressed in their umpire uniforms, lined up to receive M.A. (Master Arbitrator) degrees from a faculty member dressed in a black mortarboard and academic gown.[15]

In 1946, Bill McKinley was McGowan's first graduate to be promoted to the American League. McKinley was a graduate of McGowan's school as well as Barr's school. On comparing the two, McKinley said, "There wasn't too much difference between the two schools other than Barr

Instructor demonstrating proper position and signal for calling a runner out at home.

taught you to use the inside protector (used in the National League) and McGowan the outside protector (used in the American League)." McGowan got McKinley a job for the 1940 season in the North Carolina State League and the next year got him a job in the Michigan State League.[16]

A major league umpire-to-be, August Joseph Donatelli (better known as Augie), enrolled in McGowan's school in 1946. Just back from the war and a none-too-pleasant experience as a prisoner in German camps, Augie completed the school and McGowan placed him in the Pioneer League. "To show you how bad they needed umpires," Donatelli told sportswriter Frank Graham, "there were 60 candidates in school and Bill got jobs for 59 of us. Don't tell the ball players what I said, but the one that didn't get a job wasn't even bright enough to be an umpire."[17]

The faculty was usually made up of seven or eight graduates of the school who were umpiring. In 1946 the faculty included McGowan as umpire-in-chief, Al Somers of the Pacific Coast League as assistant chief, and instructors Lou Adragna, of Carolina; Vince Alcoser, Vernon Stephens, Jr., and Al Mutart of Ohio State; Augie Donatelli of Pioneer; Rocco Flammia of Georgia-Florida; John Gallin of Appalachian; Jim McClellan, of Pony; and Frank Prince of the South Atlantic League.[18]

McGowan would often use a combination of former and current players and umpires on his faculty. In 1951, for instance, members of the faculty at Daytona Beach, Florida, included McGowan, the dean, former players Buddy Lewis (former third baseman and outfielder for the Washington Nats), Hall of Famer Travis Jackson (former shortstop of the New York Giants), Andy Seminick (then a catcher with the Phillies), and umpires Art Passarella (then in his ninth year in the American League), new National League umpire Augie Donatelli, and Jake Early (a former catcher with the Nats and the Browns).[19]

By 1955 the full-time faculty consisted entirely of professional umpires. Al Somers was chief instructor and was assisted by Frank Cifrese, Jr., Bill Kinnamon, Eddie Sudol, and Francis Walsh. Each man was a graduate of McGowan's school.[20]

McGowan would bring in big-name ballplayers such as Babe Ruth and Joe DiMaggio when he could. Babe Ruth and Joltin' Joe DiMaggio appeared in 1948 when the school was held in West Palm Beach, Florida. While the ball players would share their experience and advice with the students, they also provided everyone with some light moments. During DiMaggio's appearance, for example, he agreed to don the umpire's mask and chest protector over his business suit and demonstrate the gestures he'd use if he were the umpire behind the plate calling a runner out. McGowan played the role of runner and thoroughly enjoyed himself, as evidenced by the huge smile on his face in a photo taken of the event.

John Rice recalled that "one day McGowan got a call saying Babe Ruth was on a train, a regular passenger train, near the school that that year was held at the West Palm Airport, en route to a fishing trip. Did McGowan want the train to stop so the Babe could say hello to the guys? Well of course he wanted the train to stop. It did. Babe got off for a few minutes and we all gathered around to say hi."[21]

Ruth came to the vestibule of the train door and looked down at the umps who asked him to come out. He went hesitatingly down the steps to pose with the boys. The exertion caused beads of perspiration to pop out on his forehead. "I'm not feelin' well," Ruth complained when he retired to his drawing room. He occasionally brushed his hand over the left side of his neck. "It pains me constantly," he said. "They don't seem to be able to do much for the nerve."[22] The Babe died of throat cancer six months later.

Other major league stars who made appearances over the years included Hank Greenberg, Al Rosen, Red Ruffing, Ed Lopat, and Al Lopez. By 1954 the school had been in operation for 15 years and had found a permanent home in Daytona Beach, Florida, where students stayed at the Riviera Hotel, two to a room. By this time over 1,200 of its graduates had been placed in organized baseball. Tuition in 1954 came to $85 for five weeks of instruction. In addition, students were responsible for their food and paid $7 a week in lodging.[23]

It was also in 1954 that McGowan operated the first professional umpire school outside of the United States. He conducted the Provincial Umpires School in Montreal, Canada.[24]

Requirements

McGowan required several things from his students. All students were required to have knowledge of the rules but "if they don't," he said, "we try to give it to them." McGowan also required good eyesight of his students and would take no applicant who wore glasses.[25]

Perhaps this requirement was due to the fact that an umpire's eyesight was a primary target of barbs and taunts from fans and players, and wearing glasses would be seen as a glaring vulnerability. It wasn't until 1956 that major league umpires first wore glasses when Ed Rommel and Frank Umont broke the long-standing taboo. Wearing glasses was officially condoned in 1974. Roland Hemond, White Sox general manager and chairman of the Umpire Development Committee, and Barney Deary, administrator of the Umpire Development Program, changed the wording of the eyesight requirement for umpires from "good vision-uncorrected" to read, "good vision-corrected is now accepted."[26]

Wearing or not wearing glasses is no longer an issue for umpires though good eyesight is, according to Jim Evans, major league umpire from 1972 to 1999. "Wearing glasses," he remarked, "is often a sign that an umpire is taking care of his eyes."[27]

McGowan's own eyesight was frequently questioned. One instance that was notable for its good-natured tone was during a game at an army hospital during World War II. Each time this catcher caught a fast one the jolt dislodged his temporary glass eye. "Look, son," McGowan said, "why don't you play the outfield? What would you do if you got socked in the other eye?"

"That's easy, Bill," replied the catcher, winking his good eye. "I'd become an umpire."[28]

Physical stature also mattered to McGowan. "The day," McGowan said in his textbook, "of the 5' 7" [Klem's stature] 147-pound umpire is over. Players do not respect little umpires."

As McGowan put it in a letter to an applicant, Roman Bentz, who attended the school in 1947 and would later be an instructor after a one-year career as a tackle with the San Francisco 49ers:

"Your age is very good — your height all in your favor — and your weight seems all to the good — Hope you are not on the fatty side... But if you are, we will have to cut down on some of it. Might also tell you that most minor league heads prefer big men. We have had too many letters from little fellows weighing 140 and 21 years old, five feet seven... Too small."[29]

Hall of Fame umpire Jocko Conlan learned firsthand about the importance of size at that time from Tommy Connolly. Connolly told Conlan he couldn't place Conlan in the American League because "we think you're a bit too short to be an umpire." Conlan, who stood 5' 7½", went on to a successful umpiring career with the National League.[30]

McGowan was a bit of an exception to the size requirement, standing 5' 9" and never weighing more than 160 pounds. Ed Barrow, who hired many an umpire when he was president of the International League, said, "Size is something I liked in umpires. A big fellow looked authoritative. But if a fellow had the ability to run and control a ballgame, and had the judgment to go along with it, size became secondary." Of McGowan, Barrow said, "Bill McGowan, whom I discovered and named to my staff when I was president of the International League, is a present-day example of outstanding umpires who are little men."[31]

Finally, McGowan required "heart" of each student but acknowledged this was one requirement that couldn't be taught: "We can give them everything but the heart after a class of 5 weeks."[32]

McGowan's Fact Sheet

He mailed each student a Fact Sheet before the school started. The Fact Sheet for 1950 classes consisted of the following.

School

The first of my two classes for the coming year will start January 6, 1950. The second begins February 11, 1950 and each runs for five weeks. Both classes will be held at Cocoa, one of the more beautiful spots in Florida.

The tuition is $85. The VA will pay same and allow subsistence while at the school; if single — $75, if married — $105. Married with one or more children — $120. All students will live at the Indian River Hotel, two students to a room, and arrangements have been made to accommodate married couples. Rooms will be $2 per person per day. Meals are extra and arrangements are being made to furnish meals at the Hotel at reasonable rates or you may eat out. Twin beds and semi-private bath.

Features

From time to time we will have well known visitors such as Mister A.B. Chandler, Commissioner of Baseball, Mr. Connie Mack, Manager of the Athletics, Bill Carpenter, representing the National Association of Professional Baseball Clubs, and minor league presidents and scouts, Joe DiMaggio, Billy Evans and others.

We have had considerable trouble with some of the students making their appearance in the lobby of the hotel objectionable. Some of the students would sit around with their short sleeve sport shirts open at the neck. We will have to ask each student to please wear a long sleeve sport shirt buttoned at the neck or better still to wear the coat or jacket of their business suits while spending time in the lobby where we have many refined ladies staying at the hotel. For the most part they are elderly ladies— please oblige.

Clothing

Many of the boys are concerned about the type of clothing to bring to the school. Usually Florida weather runs true to form and it is generally warm. The best way I can describe it is not to bring down the real heavy overcoats—a lightweight top coat, sweaters, business suits, etc., should answer the purpose. To be on the safe side I'd suggest taking your best business suit ... just in case! The bathing beach is quite an attraction, so be sure and bring along a bathing suit. (Swimming Pool at the Hotel.)

Pay of an Umpire

Perhaps you may interested in the average monthly pay of an umpire in organized baseball. Well here it is:

Class D Leagues— Minimum $250. Class C Leagues— Approximately $285; Class B Leagues— Approximately $325; Class AA Leagues—from $400 to $600; Class AAA — Around $500 to $700; and the major leagues start their men at $5,000 and all expenses [per year] and you can go as high as $12,000 per year.

Usually transportation around the circuit is furnished by the League.

Equipment

A lot of fellows ask what equipment is necessary for league baseball. Here 'tis.

Umpire Cap for plate work, with short peak.

Umpire Cap for work on bases, with long peak.

Blue Serge Uniform — with pockets large enough to hold three balls in each pocket, and with enough room to take out balls quickly. Coats are pleated down the back on both sides.

Chest Protector.

Umpire's Mask.

Shin Guards.

Spiked Shoes.

Jock and Cap.

Indicator, for balls and strikes.

Small Whisk Broom.

Watch — any kind.

Black or Dark Blue Bowtie, or four-in-hand tie.

White Shirt.

Official Rule Book.

The above is the equipment an umpire *MUST* have in league baseball although not necessary for the school; however it is to your advantage if you come to the school equipped with a dark suit, dark tie, umpire's cap, spiked shoes and whatever other umpire equipment you may have. Your appearance will go a long way in helping you impress the various officials and scouts who visit us, and sign students to contracts.

Remember, I do not guarantee anybody a job — it is up to the student to qualify.

This year equipment may be purchased at the school. A sporting goods man will be on hand the early part of each class to take orders for chest protectors, masks, shin guards, spike shoes and indicators.

For the past three years, three of the largest newsreels have taken movie shorts of the school. We hope to have this repeated for the coming session.

We will show movies of the 1949 World Series and other features.
Signed
Bill McGowan
American League Umpire

The Curriculum

McGowan described the school's 1955 curriculum in his brochure for interested applicants as follows:

> The course consists of six days of fieldwork per week. We start at 10:00 A.M. and continue until 3:00 P.M. The schedule of work on the field will begin with limbering up calisthenics. This is followed by a period of mass formation, where the students will be taught the proper stance behind the plate. We will then teach the proper timing on calling BALLS and STRIKES and the gestures for making them. We will also teach the gestures for calling Interference and Obstruction plays. All other types of plays will be covered during these hours. We will have blackboard classes two nights a week. Here we will learn and discuss the Rule Book of baseball and the instructors will give talks on handling situations, and we will have our examinations or tests on the evening class work.
>
> Some of the students will act as ball players one day and as umpires the next. After this preliminary period of learning the fundamentals, all the students will have the opportunity of umpiring games for the Cleveland farm teams— under the supervision of an instructor. Some of the students will then be chosen to umpire schools for the St. Louis Cardinals' farm teams at Deland, Florida, which is about 20 miles from our training quarters.
>
> The daily work on the training field will be graded daily by your unit instructor. In our night classes we will also cover the Infield Fly Rule, and when and when not to eject players or managers from ball games, and many other fine points of the job of being an umpire.[33]

McGowan also instructed his students in such details as how to wear the mask, adjust the protection pad, and dust off home plate. Students had to make gestures for the calls that were emphatic enough and in just the right form to get favorable marks. A point system was used to judge these activities.

Finding a Job

The most exciting times were the visits by six to ten minor league executives who were selecting umpires for their staffs. Notable among them was George Johnson, who had been an umpire with the American Association for 27 years, and was chief supervisor for the National Association of Professional Baseball Clubs. Johnson would spend three weeks at the school observing students and was instrumental in placing a large number of students in various leagues.

Jobs, as Rice had said, were not guaranteed, and graduates only got a card to show for their studies. However, McGowan and his faculty were proud of the fact that 85 percent of all minor league umpires had attended the school, and that every league in the United States under organized baseball rule had one or more of the school's graduates. As of 1955, seven graduates had made the majors: Bill McKinley, Grover Froese, John Flaherty, and Larry Napp in the American League and Augie Donatelli, Hal Dixon, and Augie Guglielmo in the National.[34]

While not promising anyone a job, McGowan was an effective agent for his students, as can be seen in the case of John Rice. Rice's route to the majors was typical of that followed by McGowan graduates. Rice's first assignment was with the Illinois State League on the recommendations of scouts from that league brought in by McGowan to look over the students. In the winter of 1947 Rice went to the baseball meetings held in Florida where, thanks to an introduction to the president of the Mid-Atlantic League by McGowan, Rice landed a position with the Mid-Atlantic League for the '48 season. "My objective," Rice said, "was to get to the Pacific Coast League, and McGowan helped with that by introducing me to the president of the California League where I worked for the '49 and '50 seasons. Then the Western League bought me in 1950, thanks to McGowan contacting a senator from Colorado who was the league president.[35] I worked there for two years and then was interviewed by the supervisor of umpires for the Pacific Coast League. He interviewed me in a bar in the South Side of Chicago where I lived. But before I heard from him I was offered a contract to umpire in Venezuela for two years, which I accepted. Then I was invited to try out with four or five other guys for McGowan's position."[36]

Umpires could expect to be reimbursed for mileage at the rate of 5 cents to 7 cents a mile, depending on the league they worked in, with the understanding that the umpire with the car would take his partner along without cost. In class D and C leagues, umpires usually took a room in a private home for the season in one of the centrally located towns in their league.[37]

On the Job

Once a graduate got a job, he needed to be "broken in," and McGowan had ideas on how best to do that. "It goes like this," he said. "A new man is nervous and jumpy. You can help him over the rough spots and keep up his confidence, or you can make him look bad and maybe ruin him for keeps. If a young umpire gets in a jam with the ball players on the field you can take him out of it. If you see he isn't moving around to get himself in the right position to see plays you can tip him off quietly."

McGowan goes on to give an example of how not to break in a rookie umpire: "We had a promising young umpire break in a few years ago and he was so nervous he forgot to move down to second base when a runner reached first. Instead of catching his eye and waving him down where he belonged the umpire-in-chief yelled 'Time' and strutted halfway down the line to bawl him out in front of all the ball players and all the customers. That's the wrong way to start a new umpire."[38]

6: No. 1

Bill McGowan died at his home on Thursday, December 9, 1954, of a heart attack brought on by complications from his long battle with diabetes and the intensity he brought to his work.[1] The day before he died, his wife, Madge, was quoted as saying, "He loves baseball, and baseball has ruined his health. I wanted him to retire five years ago but he wouldn't hear of it. I think night games sapped Bill's strength because he never ate properly and he couldn't sleep because he was so intense. Here he is now, lying on his back and fighting this heart attack, and yet I know he wouldn't have traded a single minute of his experiences."[2]

Madge knew her man. When Bob Addie of *The Washington Post* asked him in August of 1954 if he missed baseball since he was unable to work, McGowan replied, "Like my right arm. I look at every scrap of news. I listen to the radio, watch television, and it's still not enough when you've been in the arena for 30 years. I hope I come back."[3]

In January 1953, Addie wrote, "Like many others this past season, McGowan was worn out by the many twinight doubleheaders and long single games. He would love to work two more years to make it 30 in the American League, but he doubts if he can stand the pace even that much longer."

Addie goes on to quote McGowan as saying, "I think I'll wind it up after next season. I hate to give up the game but it's getting rougher on me all the time."

"When McGowan does retire," Addie concluded, "it will be the end of another fabulous career in baseball the like of which may not pass our way again."[4]

McGowan did work the 1953 season but was forced to leave the diamond midway through the second game at Detroit on July 26 because of the heat. He returned several days later.[5]

McGowan worked part of the 1954 season, one more than he thought he might in his interview with Addie, to finish his career with an even 30 seasons. He umpired his last game in July 1954.

Others, including fellow umpire Jim Honochick, also knew McGowan had health problems at the time. As Honochick tells the story:

> There were days in 1950 when he shouldn't have worked. He was a diabetic and had only so much energy in him, but if he wanted to give you a game, he'd say, "you want to see an exhibition? I'll give you one today." Then he'd go out and really bear down behind the plate. The man was uncanny on balls and strikes. When the game ended, he was completely exhausted. He couldn't do anything on his own. You had to help him take his coat off. The worst thing he could have was Coca-Cola, but he'd drink six bottles before he'd remove his clothes to take a shower. He was drained, physically and emotionally drained, but he had given you the best game of umpiring that you'd ever seen. After McGowan there were only good and bad umpires. He was the greatest umpire I have ever seen, a superstar.[6]

McGowan also had another disease, namely a gambling addiction. As Ernie Stewart tells the story, "Bill McGowan was a great horseplayer. It was frowned on, but it didn't make any difference. Mr. Landis called him in a couple of times but, of course, Bill denied it.[7] He had to bet horses every day…. Being around Bill as close as I was I came in contact with probably all the outstanding bookies in the United States…. If we had a rained-out game he'd say, 'Come on, Ernie. Let's go down to the bookie joint.' Sid Wyman rented a second story of a building just outside of St. Louis. He had ten or fifteen operators hooked up to every track in the United States. Bill was in his glory out there…. He let Bill bet every race in the United States and just called it even at the end of the day. I've seen Bill lose $2,500 in a day. Sid would say, 'Why Ernie, I wouldn't take a nickel from him. He's got a disease. He's sick, the man's sick.'" Stewart added that playing the horses never affected his umpiring a bit — when he walked out on the field, his mind was just on the game. The minute the game was over, he'd say, "Hurry, got to get downtown, see what my horses did."[8]

Not all bookies were as generous as Sid Wyman, and occasionally McGowan's trips to the track took a toll on his wallet. Bill Werber got a call at his house in University Park, Maryland, from McGowan in 1934 or 1935 asking $500 to tide him over for a few months, explaining that he'd "experienced some financial misfortune." He didn't tell Werber any details. Werber knew from talks with his Red Sox teammates that McGowan loved to play the horses. Werber sent the check, expecting to be repaid the next spring when umpires, unlike players, were paid for their preseason services. When the check hadn't arrived when the season started, Werber alerted McGowan that if the debt were not repaid soon, he'd bring it to the attention of Commissioner Landis. "His check," Werber said, "came by the next mail and it was good."[9]

This episode didn't dim Werber's respect for McGowan. "To give the guy his due," Werber wrote, "I can recall no ill will or any questionable decisions against me. He worked hard and took his responsibilities seriously."[10]

Werber was among those who respected McGowan's hustle, saying, "We only had two umpires in those days. One behind the plate and one at first who'd have to run to second and third when plays developed on the bases. McGowan could run to second as fast or faster than most players, even during games in St. Louis in August when it got to be 110 degrees."[11]

Even though his health had prevented him from umpiring since late July 1954, he maintained an active speaking schedule. There are conflicting accounts of his last public appearance. A United Press article puts it at the 85th birthday party for Clark Griffith on November 21,[12] while Washington sports columnist Bob Addie says it was on a television show urging people to get checkups to detect diabetes.[13] I tend to go with Addie's account, as he was close to the Washington sports scene and well known to McGowan.

McGowan suffered a heart attack just three days before the fatal attack as he and Madge were preparing to go to New York to attend the major league meetings. Messages and phone calls and a long telegram from Boston Red Sox owner Tom Yawkey arrived at their home as the news of the first attack spread quickly.

The doctors were initially optimistic, as was Madge, who said, "I want to correct the impression that Bill's condition is extremely serious. It's true that he will be in bed from four to six weeks. The doctors say he needs absolute rest right now, but they also add that within a couple of months he'll be able to carry on his baseball school." "Actually," she continued, "Bill learned of his heart condition last July when he became ill from diabetes. Then he suffered this heart attack on Saturday morning. While the cardiograph taken last night didn't show much improvement, Bill is doing well and the doctors assure us he'll be able to carry on his duties. Of course, he'll have to slow up."

She added that he wasn't giving any consideration to an offer he'd received to become president of the Piedmont League.

"We'll have to decide that later," she said. "Right now we're concerned with getting Bill back on his feet. He's been wonderfully cheerful and has been heartened by the many messages he's received from his baseball friends."[14]

Just two days before his death, the American League paid him a special tribute by voting to double his pension to $6,000 a year from the

McGowan (center) seated between Hall of Famers Nap Lajoie (left) and Tris
Speaker at a 1952 baseball meeting. (Bill, Jr.'s collection)

$3,000 that he was entitled to under the league's retirement plan. Yawkey
proposed it, and the motion carried unanimously — but not before Spike
Briggs (owner of the Tigers, with a penchant for deflating some of the
other AL owners' stuffiness) had his say, seconding Yawkey's motion with
"I wish we had 16 umpires like Bill McGowan." Another owner added his
tribute to McGowan, saying to Briggs, "That's the first time you've been
right all day."[15]

The Reverend William Buckley, a nephew of McGowan, conducted a
requiem on Monday, December 13, at St. Michael's Catholic Church in Silver Spring, Maryland. McGowan was buried the same day in the family
plot in Cathedral Cemetery in Wilmington, Delaware.

Many baseball notables attended the mass, including William Harridge, president of the American League, and his entire staff of umpires,
headed by Chief Umpire Cal Hubbard. Harridge, who had twice suspended

McGowan hustling into position to make call on Dodgers Dixie Walker, sliding into second base in the third game of the 1947 World Series.

McGowan, said, "I feel McGowan ranked as one of the all-time greats of his profession."

Clark Griffith, also in attendance, said that McGowan was "a fine fellow and the greatest umpire in the business." Noting that McGowan had the reputation of being a pretty tough customer behind the plate, Griffith said it never cost him a friend, stating, "Bill always wanted to be right and sometimes he had to be tough to make it stick."

Others attending the mass included Bucky Harris, manager of the Tigers; former Senators Joe Judge, Sam Rice, and Ossie Bluege; Jim Busby, with the Senators; and Al Somers, umpire-in-chief of the Pacific Coast League and lead instructor at McGowan's umpire school.[16]

J. Edgar Hoover, director of the FBI, sent a telegram of condolence to Mrs. McGowan on December 9, 1954. The telegram read, "It was with the greatest regret that I learned of your husband's passing, and I want to offer you my heartfelt condolences. During his many years of dedication to the highest principles and traditions of true sportsmanship, Bill won the affection and admiration of a host of friends. He will always live in their hearts, and I hope that you can derive some comfort from this thought. You have my deepest sympathy in your bereavement."[17]

A few days before his death he had been notified that he was to be the recipient of the Touchdown Club's Clark Griffith Trophy for being Baseball's Man of the Year. Griffith presented the trophy, a silver pitcher from

Commissioner Happy Chandler, to Bill McGowan, Jr., at the club's twentieth annual dinner, held at the Hotel Statler in Washington, D.C., on January 8, 1955. In presenting the trophy, Griffith said, "McGowan started his American League career by umpiring our spring games in Tampa and he's been No. 1 ever since. He was fearless, competent and fair."[18]

At the start of the 1955 season, I.O.U. graduate John Rice filled the vacancy created by McGowan's death and opened that season at third base at Griffith Stadium. "I was fully expecting an announcement over the loudspeaker saying something about McGowan but there was no such announcement. They just started the game as usual."[19]

The School Continues

After McGowan's death, his son, William A. McGowan, Jr., ran the school with Al Somers until 1957. The 1955 school opened in Daytona Beach, Florida, on March 1, 1955, with Al Somers as the chief instructor and Bill Jr. doing the paperwork at his Maryland home. Bill Jr. said that the school's opening "would be his wish, and the school will continue to operate as a monument to him."[20]

During this time Somers wanted to buy the school but the McGowan family refused. McGowan's wife, Madge, hired a lawyer to make sure Somers didn't change the school's name without the McGowan family's permission. To be doubly sure that her wishes on the matter were known, she sent a telegram to Somers on May 16, 1956, stating, "Permission to use any part of literature or name of McGowan school is hereby emphatically denied. I am still in possession of ownership." On the same day she sent a telegram to J.G. Taylor Spink, editor of *The Sporting News*, where ads for the school frequently appeared. The telegram read, "The name Bill McGowan is not to appear in any school advertisement under any circumstances. Thank you."

Spink, by return wire the same day, answered, "Re Tel. Your wishes will be respected."

Mrs. McGowan's last telegram of May 16 went to W.T. Mayburry of the regional office for the Veterans Administration in St. Petersburg, Florida, saying, "I am still owner of McGowan school which will not operate in '57. Permission for anyone to use this school is emphatically denied."[21]

Finally, Somers came to the McGowan residence to talk with Madge where arrangements were made to sell the school to Somers. He operated it under his name for the first time in 1957.[22]

Somers ran the school until 1977 when Harry Wendelstedt took over the then-named Al Somers Umpire School. Wendelstedt umpired in the National League from 1966 to 1999. He is a former Marine and University of Maryland graduate. Wendelstedt still runs the school as of this writing with his son, Hunter, a major league umpire, on the staff.[23]

Upon taking over the Somers School, Wendelstedt made clear during the final days of the 1977 school that the path to the majors for umpires had changed. Gone were the days when an old-time ball player of whatever league could get a chance as an umpire because he was introduced to a minor league president.

"We have," Wendelstedt said, "sixteen aspiring umpires here who have college degrees plus 28 others who have two or more years of college."

"First," Wendelstedt continued, "a man must go to our school or the one run by Bill Kinnamon over at St. Petersburg. The two schools then select the students we feel are best qualified to enter pro ball."[24]

In 1997, the school still lasted five weeks, and the tuition had risen to $2,100, not including meals. The curriculum remained much the same as it was in 1954. Classes met six days a week, beginning at 8:30 A.M. with 90 minutes of classroom instruction on the rules followed by instruction on ball fields emphasizing mechanics, positioning, and voice control for calling balls and strikes and safe and out calls. The school day ended at 3:30, after which high school and college games were umpired.

Hall of Fame Induction

Bill McGowan finally achieved the recognition he so justly deserved when he was elected into the Hall of Fame on the first ballot taken during a four-hour meeting of the Veterans Committee at a Tampa hotel on Tuesday, March 18, 1992 — 38 years after his death.[25]

McGowan had been on the Hall of Fame Ballot since at least 1976.[26] In 1981 the Veterans Committee reported that McGowan was among the men on its "list of those who figured prominently in the balloting."[27]

"This should have happened a long time ago," William A. McGowan, Jr., was quoted as saying at the time. "They waited all this time; it's sorta like a dishonor to him. It's like they're saying, 'You ain't so much.' I'm pleased, yes," McGowan Jr. continued, "but on the other hand I'm a little disturbed. If they're going to wait so long to induct him, you almost wonder what's the point. My dad was one of the greatest umpires who ever lived. One thing that's always bothered me is that the Hall of Fame inducted an umpire named Cal Hubbard [in 1976] and I've got to say that that guy never did anything that would have put him in front of my dad. My dad broke Cal Hubbard in as an umpire, trained him and put him in his back pocket for most of his career. And then he gets elected before my dad. I never understood it."[28]

Sportswriter Izzy Katzman was of the same opinion. "How," Katzman said, "Conlan and Hubbard could have been selected over the Wilmington native long has puzzled this observer."[29]

Why did it take 38 years for Bill McGowan to be inducted into the National Baseball Hall of Fame? As one Hall of Fame official said on the occasion of McGowan's enshrinement, "It's unusual for anyone to gain Hall of Fame election after having been deceased for so many years, but this only illustrates that Bill McGowan's reputation as a top caliber umpire lives on."[30]

Some have speculated that his relationships with some of the sportswriters who vote on candidates was not all it could have been, particularly in light of his treatment of the St. Louis sportswriters during the 1952 incident for which he was suspended.

Bob Broeg opined that the reason was more politics than McGowan's relationships with the press. Broeg, longtime sports editor for the *St. Louis Post Dispatch* and a member of the 1992 Veterans Committee that elected McGowan, said umpires generally had a hard time getting to Cooperstown. For years, beginning with the Hall of Fame's founding in 1939, many, including its founder Ford Frick, wanted only players in the Hall of Fame.

That sentiment can be found today. Brad Harris asks rhetorically, "What would an umpire have to do, as an umpire, to have contributed to the game on the same level as a Branch Rickey or Babe Ruth?" Harris notes there isn't a measurable way to say that one umpire is better than another; there isn't any "correct calls per opportunity" statistic for umpires so none, in Harris' view, should be elected to the Hall of Fame for his accomplishments as an umpire.[31]

The National Baseball Hall of Fame opened in 1939. It wasn't until 1953 that an umpire was inducted, when Bill Klem and Tommy Connolly were honored, each serving as a "representative for their league"—Klem for the National and Connolly for the American. Connolly did umpire in the National League, but only from 1898 to 1900. He was an American League umpire from 1901 to 1931. The next umpire, Billy Evans, wasn't elected until 1973. Jocko Conlan was elected in 1974 as a result of "Warren Giles leading the charge for him," Broeg said.

Cal Hubbard, Broeg continued, was inducted in 1976, becoming the first person ever inducted into three national sports halls of fame (the other two were the college and professional football halls of fame).

Broeg said that Al Barlick was elected in 1989 as a "consensus candidate."[32] Citing "reliable sources," an article in *The Sporting News* reported that Barlick was a trade-off by members of the committee who said they would vote for Barlick if McGowan were given similar support in 1990.[33]

Ted Williams, also a member of the 1992 Veterans Committee, "was strong for McGowan," Broeg said.[34]

That Williams thought highly of McGowan was evidenced by his telephone call to him shortly before his death in December 1954. Williams, who many thought was self-centered and hard to get along with, had a soft spot for McGowan.

"How are you feeling, No. 1?" Williams asked. "They tell me you'll be out for the rest of the year. Take it easy and don't rush it. Don't forget, you're still number 1."

The call gave McGowan a big lift. "Imagine that," he said, "the greatest player in the league calling up to see how I felt."[35]

John McGowan, a grandson of Bill, recalls another example of the esteem in which Williams held McGowan. John and three of his young nephews encountered Williams in the hallway of the hotel in Cooperstown where they were staying during the induction ceremonies in 1992. "He was in sweats and looked like he was coming back from exercising," John said. "I asked him, 'Mr. Williams, could these little guys get your autograph?' He said this wasn't a good time and that he was on his way to a meeting. But when I said, 'These guys are Bill McGowan's great-grandsons,' Williams said, 'There's one thing I don't sign and that's bats. See me at dinner tonight, and bring three bats with you.'"[36]

There is a published report of Williams pushing for McGowan's induction as early as 1980, but it wasn't until Williams became a member of the Veterans Committee in 1986 that the McGowan bandwagon began to roll in earnest.[37]

Baseball historian Larry Gerlach contributed by writing a several-page letter of support for McGowan that included lots of quotes from contemporary players and sportswriters as to his excellence. Rather than trying to make the case for McGowan, Gerlach's strategy was to let contemporary ballplayers and sportswriters make the case, as they knew his work better than people who never saw him in person. Ted Williams later told Gerlach that he liked what he'd written and that he had spoken strongly in favor of McGowan.[38]

By custom, many members of the Hall of Fame attend the induction ceremonies. Those in attendance at the 1992 induction ceremony were Luis Aparicio, Al Barlick, Johnny Bench, Yogi Berra, Ray Dandridge, Bobby Doerr, Bob Feller, Rick Ferrell, Rollie Fingers, Charlie Gehringer, Bob Gibson, Billy Herman, Ferguson Jenkins, Al Kaline, George Kell, Ralph Kiner, Bob Lemon, Buck Leonard, Al López, Juan Marichal, Johnny Mize, Joe

Morgan, Stan Musial, Hal Newhouser, Jim Palmer, Gaylord Perry, Pee Wee Reese, Robin Roberts, Brooks Robinson, Red Schoendienst, Tom Seaver, Enos Slaughter, Warren Spahn, Billy Williams, Ted Williams, and Early Wynn.[39] Many of those in attendance signed a copy of Norman Rockwell's famous *Saturday Evening Post* cover showing three umpires looking into the heavens as the rain falls on the diamond.

McGowan had been inducted into the Delaware Sports Hall of Fame on May 26, 1977, at the du Pont Country Club where Lee MacPhail, then president of the American League, was the main speaker. William A. McGowan, Jr., accepted the plaque for his father.

Delaware later honored McGowan with a monument to him at Frawley Field in Wilmington, which was unveiled on August 30, 2001. Another native baseball son of Delaware, Vic Willis (The Delaware Peach), was honored as well. Willis' 45 complete games in 1902 for the Boston Beaneaters were the most in the National League at the time. The keynote speaker at the dedication was Delaware State Senator Bob Marshall, who, in cooperation with the Delaware Stadium Corporation, had arranged for the funds for the two monuments. McGowan was described in the program as "an umpire who came close to being the exception to the old adage that fans don't pay to see the umpire. He introduced a colorful umpiring style with vigorous, aggressive gestures, which bordered on the pugnacious—yet he ejected very few players. His enthusiasm never waned over 30 American League seasons, while his hustling style and umpiring skills commanded the ball players' respect. He was an iron man among umpires, not missing an inning for 16 years (2,541 consecutive games)."[40] That description was taken from the wording on his Hall of Fame plaque in Cooperstown.

Greatest Players and Plays

McGowan saw many of the best players who ever played the game on a day-to-day basis over many years, including Ty Cobb, Babe Ruth, Walter Johnson, Ted Williams, and Joe DiMaggio. How did McGowan rate the players of his day? Unsurprisingly, not only by their talent on the field, but also on the extent to which they challenged calls, as we can see in his 1954 interview with Max Kase. A favorite, according to Kase, was Walter Johnson.

"Walter Johnson," McGowan said, "never kicked on a ball or strike in his years of pitching for Washington. He was the greatest pitcher of them all." [41]

Johnson was known for having definite ideas on when a new baseball was needed and when the one in play was OK. McGowan noted, "It has been the custom in the American League that when Johnson is pitching and the batter wished the umpire to look at the ball, the umpire usually yells to Walter, 'How's the ball, Barney?' If the ball is satisfactory to Johnson's way of thinking, it is all right with the umpire and the batter."[42]

Of Babe Ruth, McGowan said, "When he thought he had a kick coming he'd blow up his cheeks and say 'Good strike, two feet over my head.'"

Lou Gehrig did considerable kicking, particularly on half-swings. Gehrig and Lazzeri were particularly adept at starting a full swing and then stopping it by pulling the bat up. Since McGowan's attention was focused on the strike zone, he often couldn't tell if the bat had crossed the plate. In these instances McGowan would shoot a quick glance at one of the base umpires who'd shoot back an equally fast signal of swing or no swing allowing McGowan to make a call without any delay being noticed by players or fans. Gehrig didn't always agree with McGowan's call.[43]

As a rule, McGowan said, "It's the .248 hitter who throws his bat on the ground and jaws. Players like Williams and DiMaggio are gentlemen. If they have anything to say, they'll whisper, 'Bill, was that high enough to be a strike?'"[44]

McGowan noted that often the .248 hitter's opinion of the umpire often depends on which team the calls are favoring. The Browns' players dubbed McGowan "Broadminded" in a particular game as his calls were to their liking. They continued to refer to him as "Broadminded" until he ejected Browns third base coach Bill Killefer for arguing over a play at third. Killeffer's parting salutation was, "All right Broadminded, I'm on my way. But don't forget that's only the first part of your name. The other part is BLIND FATHEAD @#$%*!."[45]

As far back as 1920 Billy Evans had come to the same conclusion about who does and who does not gripe about calls. The reason that star players rarely make a scene is, Evans said, "simply that they never find it necessary to seek an alibi in order to cover up either lack of ability or failure to have properly completed a play or to compensate for an umpire's mistake. Umpires make mistakes. So do star players. The star player who has some brains, or he wouldn't be a star player, is broad-minded enough to take all things into consideration."[46]

The most unusual feat McGowan said he ever witnessed on a ball field was performed by Lu Blue (later to become a first baseman for the Tigers, Browns, and White Sox) while playing for Martinsburg in a game at Frederick, Maryland, in the Blue Ridge League. Blue, a switch hitter, connected while batting right-handed for a grand slam home run against a left-handed pitcher. The bases were again loaded for Blue's next appearance at the plate, and the Frederick manager changed pitchers and brought in a righty. Blue went to the other side of the plate and hit his second consecutive grand slam to win the game in the tenth inning, 12–8.[47]

His nomination for the best play he ever saw was executed by the Athletics in 1929 against the Yankees. It was, he thought, instrumental in breaking the Yankees' spirit and deciding the pennant race. "It was the ninth inning with Earle Combs on third, one out, Babe Ruth at bat, and the A's a run ahead. The Bambino rifled a line drive over second that looked like a sure hit. Mule Haas came tearing in from deep center, just managed to spear the ball and flipped it to Max Bishop at second base who relayed it to the plate and got Combs for the double play to end the game."[48]

The "most amazing performance" went to Babe Ruth calling three home runs in the fourth game of the 1928 World Series, which the Yankees won from the St. Louis Cardinals in four straight. The game was played at St. Louis, and the fans were razzing Ruth something fierce. He turned to the crowd from his position in left field, pointed to the right field seats (where, as a left-handed hitter, most of his home runs landed) and made a high arc with the sweep of his hand. Ruth hit a home run to right at his next at-bat. The crowd kept razzing Ruth, so he turned to them again from left field holding up two fingers and curving a bigger arc in the direction of the right field fence. Sure enough, Ruth hit homer number two his next at-bat. Now the fans applauded him, but the "Babe was no piker." He held up three fingers while making the gesture toward right field. Before the game was out, he had his third homer. "I've heard some doubts," McGowan wrote, "voiced about the famous home run which Ruth is supposed to have called against Charlie Root in the 1932 series with the Chicago Cubs. I didn't see that one, but take it from me, I did see Ruth call *three* in one game at St. Louis."[49]

Ty Cobb got the nod as the best player he saw. "Nobody was in his class," McGowan was quoted as saying. "He could win a game without a bat. He'd come up there, grab five bats, and smack his lips like a tiger. Could scare the life out of a pitcher. Then he'd walk, steal second, third, and home and beat you 1–0."

McGowan did say that the first time he worked a game in which Cobb played, "I thought he'd undress me at second base. Instead Cobb told him, 'I might get mad and be thrown out today, but tomorrow I'll start all over with a clean slate. Just keep hustling and you'll be alright.'"

Ruth was not far behind Cobb in McGowan's estimation. "Ruth was the greatest slugger who ever lived," McGowan said. "Take away all his home runs and call them singles and he's still one of the greatest players. Great arm, smart, and fast for a big man. But he couldn't beat Cobb."[50]

McGowan's nomination for the best all-round hitting and defensive outfielder that he ever saw was Al Simmons. "He was the best I ever saw for three seasons when he was helping the Athletics win pennants." After Simmons' era, McGowan said, "Ted Williams is the greatest hitter to come along."

Joe DiMaggio, McGowan thought, was the "best all-round modern ball player. He had a great arm, was a terrific base runner, a fine hitter and one of the all time great fielders. A lot of people don't realize it but Joe was a great base stealer.... Joe could steal that extra base. I never saw his equal for instinct on bases. He was rarely thrown out going from first to third."

McGowan rated Tris Speaker as the greatest defensive outfielder he'd seen. "He used to play only about 60 feet back of second base for Speaker could really go back." Of the "current" crop, he rated Jim Busby of the Senators and the Red Sox's Jimmy Piersall as the closest approaches to Speaker in the field.[51]

McGowan's nod for the nicest player went to Cecil Travis, Washington Senators infielder from 1933 to 1941 and from 1945 to 1947. "He wouldn't say a word if you called a strike on him on a ball that came up to the plate on three bounces."[52]

As for the most difficult game he ever worked behind the plate, it was the fifth game of the 1947 World Series between the Yankees and the Dodgers. "Shea [Spec Shea of the Yankees] when he was right — and he was right that day — is the kind of pitcher who threads the ball through the eye of a needle and then cuts the corners with it. He was either an inch from the outside or an inch from the inside corner, but no one had a kick."[53]

7: That's a Sure-Fire Way to Lose Your Job

What kind of an umpire would McGowan be today? Umpiring, like the rest of the game of baseball, has changed since McGowan's day, though the changes have more to do with style than substance. The basics remain the same. The umpire's job is still to control the game by enforcing the rules.

While McGowan left his impartiality in the locker room every so often, umpires are still well served by this advice offered by *Beadle's* in 1867: "It is almost unnecessary to remark that the first duty of an umpire is to enforce the rules of the game with the strictest impartiality; and in order to do so, it would be well for him, the moment he assumes his position on the ground, to close his eyes to the fact of there being any player among the contestants, that is not an entire stranger to him; by this means he will free his mind of any friendly bias."[1]

To help maintain that impartiality, *Beadle's* advised the umpire "to avoid any conversation with any party during a game, turn a deaf ear to all outside comments on his decisions, and constantly bear in mind that upon his manly, fearless, and impartial conduct in a match mainly depends the pleasure that all, more or less, will derive from it."[2]

Not only is the ideal umpire of any era expected to be a paragon of impartiality while talking to no one and not reacting to any negative comments, the umpire (as Billy Evans pointed out in 1920) is expected to perform the duties "in a capable manner" while knowing there will be no applause to a call well made, only boos, catcalls, and perhaps worse when a fan or player thinks the umpire has blown a call.[3]

Nevertheless, with all of its hazards and pressures, there were still those who aspired to the position, though many became disillusioned when the reality set in. Evans noted in 1920 that "the number of people willing to take a chance" is surprising, though he went on to say, "The minor leagues receive the most applications during the winter when the stove leagues are in session." By spring, many lose their "desire to satisfy fandom and decide to stick to their winter job. By July, the sun and the withering sarcasm of the fans usually has burned up the crop, and officials are eagerly sought."

Evans relates the story of a young man who approached him for a job in his dressing room in Chicago as he was talking to a well-known minor league president. "I could use a good umpire," the president said, "but I can't afford to pay much money, as my league is an easy one for umpires. All you have to do is satisfy the players, managers, club owners, public, and the press, and you won't have any trouble holding your job." That was all the applicant needed to hear. He left the dressing room without another word.[4]

The public image of umpiring has also remained about what it was in McGowan's day. Jim Evans (no relation to Billy), a major league umpire from 1972 to 1999, notes that parents don't always look upon umpiring as a profession they'd want for their children.[5]

"Umpiring," Jim Evans says, "was and is a special calling and is as an important part of the game as playing, managing, or coaching." While acknowledging that the game couldn't be played without umpires, he admits, "You don't look at your kid in a crib in the hospital and think, 'Someday I want him to be an ump.' You think more like Mickey Mantle." This was certainly true in his own father's case.

"My dad," Evans said,

> was a carpenter. When I was 14, I'd work with him for eight or nine hours a day on weekends and during the summer and make about ten bucks. It was hard work under a hot sun, and my hands would get sore and blistery. I would also umpire Little League games once in awhile, sometimes three a night, and make nine dollars in three or four hours. It wasn't nearly so hot, and I liked the work. So one day when my dad and I were taking a break, I said to him, "Dad, I've decided what I want to be when I grow up." My dad said, "What's that?" "A major league umpire," I said.
>
> My dad, who was a big tall man with massive hands said, "Come here!" I walked over to him. He grabbed me by both shoulders, pulled me right to him so we were nose to nose and said, "Have you been screwing around with drugs?"[6]

While the duties and the public perception of umpires haven't changed much since McGowan's era, the way in which umpires are selected and trained and how they perform their duties have changed.

Selecting and Training Umpires

Umpires in McGowan's era were selected, oftentimes handpicked, by the league president, perhaps at the suggestion of a club owner. Ban Johnson, who was president of the American League from 1901 to 1927, personally selected his umpires with an exacting eye for ability and character. Among his selections, in addition to McGowan, were some other well-respected umpires such as John F. "Jack" Sheridan, William G. "Billy" Evans, and Thomas H. "Tommy" Connolly.

Previously, umpires were selected by the home team in a number of ways. In 1871 the National Association of Professional Base Ball Players allowed the home team to choose the umpire from a list of five names submitted by the visiting team. National League president William A. Hulbert in 1879 appointed baseball's first umpire staff; a group of 20 men from which teams could choose an arbiter.[7]

The great majority of aspirants in McGowan's day were themselves former players of varying ability. Many, like McGowan, came from the sandlots or from the minors, while others came from the majors and, occasionally, other professional sports.

Jocko Conlan, a Hall of Fame umpire and outfielder for the Chicago White Sox in 1934 and 1935, is a notable example of a major league player who made a successful transition from playing to umpiring. He got his umpiring start one day at Comiskey Park when the heat overcame third base umpire Emmett Ormsby. Conlan, who was on the bench sitting out the game because of a broken finger, was drafted as Ormsby's replacement. He took his position on the field in his White Sox uniform and called teammate Luke Appling out on a close play at third. Evidently that sufficiently demonstrated his impartiality, for the following year American League President Will Harridge got him a job as an umpire in the minors.[8]

Other major league players who made the transition to umpiring were Ed Rommel and George Pipgras. Rommel, a knuckleballer for Connie Mack's Athletics from 1920 to 1932, was an American League umpire for 22 years. George Pipgras, right-hander for the Yankees and Red Sox from 1923 to 1935, was an American League umpire for 11 years.[9]

Former football players were another source, with Cal Hubbard being the best-known example. The only man to be elected to the baseball, college football, and pro football halls of fame, Hubbard was a huge man for his time at 6' 3" and 235 pounds. At little Centenary and Geneva colleges, he won nationwide fame as a bone-crushing tackle. In his professional football career, he played offensive end and linebacker in addition to tackle for the 1927 champion New York Giants and the 1929–31 Green Bay Packers championship teams. He was named at tackle on the first three official All-NFL teams, 1931–33. He began umpiring minor league games during the summers while he was playing pro football. He became an AL umpire in 1936, his last season with the New York Giants. In 1944, Hubbard gained notoriety as the first umpire to eject a pitcher (the Browns' Nels Potter) for throwing a spitball. Hubbard's imposing size and keen eyesight made him one of the best at his trade. He was once examined at the Boston Optical Lab and was found to have 20-10 vision, the strongest ever recorded — even better than Ted Williams.[10]

Hank Soar played professional football for the New York Giants before becoming an umpire and ended up under McGowan's tutelage. During his first two years in the majors Soar pointed with pride to the fact that "they've teamed me with the best umpire in the world. I've been trying to learn half of what Bill McGowan knows about umpiring."

McGowan was evidently not a gentle teacher. Soar took as much grief from McGowan as from the players when he made a bad call. "He glares at me like I let him down," Soar said. "In the clubhouse after the game he calls me down, and says I was a lousy football player, too. He said he used to see me play and that the Giants didn't use me except in the last three minutes and then they wouldn't let me carry the ball for fear I'd fumble."[11]

McGowan was far from accurate in his dismissive estimation of Soar as a player, as he starred for the Giants for nine years starting in 1937 and played offense and defense for most of the game. McGowan's teaching did work, though, as Soar, like Rommel, was one of the American League's top umpires for 22 years.

Bill Summers was a boxer before joining the men in blue. He fought for about eight years as a featherweight in his native New England, where he was known as Marty Summers. Like McGowan, he worked for 10 years in the minors before getting his appointment in the American League.[12]

Selecting former players wasn't an infallible means of recruiting umpires. Some players who put on the blue suit didn't last long. Fred "Firpo" Marberry was one. After 13 years as the first major league star relief pitcher for the Washington Senators and Detroit Tigers, from 1923 to 1935, he was offered a job as an American League umpire toward the end of the 1935 season. McGowan was "schooling the big Southern boy in the techniques of the job." He did fine on the bases, McGowan reported, but it was after his first game behind the plate that he decided to retire from umpiring. Marberry said of his first and only day behind the plate, "I learned something out there today. When I go back home to Texas and get on my farm, I know I won't load my mules down with so much harness.

Hell, I wasn't worried about the balls and strikes. I couldn't see through the mask; the chest protector didn't seem to fit right, and those shin guards under my pants had me crazy. Too much harness for me," Marberry snorted.[13]

The equipment bothered him because he was unable to find any equipment large enough to fit his 6' 2", 225-pound frame. Available shin guards, ankle guards, and breast protectors, as Shirley Povich referred to them, were all too small. Larger ones were ordered, but that was not sufficient inducement for Marberry to remain an umpire even though he had the basic skills. "Marberry," according to McGowan, "has a great start in this umpiring business. He breathes authority. When he makes a decision it ought to stick. Ordinarily it takes six or seven years to develop an umpire, but Fred looks like a natural."[14]

Other players who found umpiring not to be to their liking included Bobby Wallace, a Hall of Fame infielder for the Cleveland Indians and St. Louis Browns for 25 years before retiring in 1918. He gave up the idea of umpiring after trying it for only a year as did Big Ed Walsh, a Hall of Fame pitcher for the Chicago White Sox from 1904 to 1916. It was not unusual to find that the best umpires of the day had never played in the major leagues. Four of the best umpires during the 1920s— Tommy Connolly, Bill Klem, Billy Evans, and Ernie Quigley — were never known as ball players.[15]

A Call for Standards

By 1952 the quality of umpiring throughout the majors was becoming an increasingly frequent topic of conversation. Managers Al Lopez of the Indians and Jimmy Dykes of the Athletics complained loudly about the declining quality of umpiring as they saw it. An Associated Press photograph from the 1952 World Series between the Yankees and the Dodgers showing Johnny Sain of the Yankees stepping on first base and being called out by umpire Art Passarella while the ball had yet to reach Gil Hodges' glove added fuel to the debate.

In response to these concerns, an editorial appeared in *The Sporting News* suggesting to National League President Warren Giles and American League President Will Harridge that something be done to improve the quality of umpiring. The editorial suggested raising salaries and improving the conditions of umpires' rooms, but their strongest suggestions involved training and supervision. George Barr's and McGowan's schools were each given high marks, but it was noted they were seasonal operations conducted by private individuals. The editorial suggested year-round training and that senior umpires, many of whom were on the verge of retirement, be employed by the leagues as supervisors and mentors for rookie umpires both in the classroom and on the field. The editorial noted that the "mere mention of their names would do much to attract ambitious young arbiters and that their tutelage would cut years from the time consumed by novices who have to learn their trade by the trial and error method."[16]

Some of the suggestions in that editorial about year-round supervision have since been implemented. Today, there are no walk-ons and no former major league players in the ranks of major league umpires. Jim Evans was the last person to get a job as an umpire in professional baseball without attending a school for umpires. He was umpiring college games in Texas during the summer following his graduation from the University of Texas. Several scouts admired his work and helped him get a job umpiring in the Florida State A League for a year in 1968. Subsequently, he did attend an umpire's school in 1969 before ascending to the majors in 1972.

Major League Baseball requires that all umpires in professional baseball attend one of the two accredited schools for umpires, the Jim Evans Academy of Professional Umpiring in Kissimmee, Florida, or the Harry Wendelstedt Umpire School in Daytona Beach, Florida. Most applicants are younger than 30 and seeking a position in professional ball.

The top graduates from each school are invited to a tryout sponsored by the Professional Baseball Umpires Corporation (PBUC). Those who excel at the tryout are assigned to entry-level positions and work their way up the minor league ladder under the evaluative eye of PBUC. PBUC recommends selected Triple A umpires to Major League Baseball as permanent and temporary positions become available in the majors.

Style and Tactics

At the end of the nineteenth century umpires were afforded little in the way of support or protection. They were routinely spiked, kicked, and cursed by players, and fans hurled epithets and all manner of debris at them. Physical assaults on umpires were so frequent that police escorts were frequent and familiar sights to the arbiters. Umpires couldn't seek relief from club owners or league officials, for they recognized that umpire baiting was good for the gate receipts. Owners often refused to support the umpires' decisions, did little to curb rowdiness, and would pay a player's fine that an umpire had levied. Some umpires would retaliate by throwing objects back into the stands or (as McGowan did in Baltimore) punching players.

Given these conditions, umpires were forced to devise their own methods for keeping control of the game. They used whatever personal skills they felt most comfortable with. Some, such as Robert V. Ferguson, known as "Death to Flying Things," ruled as iron-fisted autocrats. Others, like John F. Gaffney, known as the "King of Umpires," relied on tact and diplomacy. Some umpires even started compiling a professional code for arbiters under the leadership of Benjamin F. Young, who drew up a professional code of ethics for umpires as well as a ten-point proposal in 1887 to improve their status.

But it wasn't until Ban Johnson assumed the presidency of the upstart American League in 1901 that umpires received strong support from league officials. Johnson insisted that umpires be respected and backed up his words by supporting their decisions and suspending players who were guilty of flagrant misconduct. The National League soon followed suit, perhaps because its presidents, Thomas J. Lynch and John A. Heydler, were former umpires. By the end of World War I, umpires enjoyed "unprecedented authority, dignity, and security." As umpire, manager, and baseball executive Clarence "Pants" Rowland put it: "All umps ought to tip their hats whenever Ban Johnson's name is mentioned."[17]

One result of Johnson's support for umpires was that umpires became prestigious figures in their own right. Notable among them were "Silk" O'Loughlin, who matched wits and words with the best of players; "Big Tommy" Connolly, who became the first league umpire-in-chief; Jack Sheridan, who was the first to crouch behind the plate; and Billy Evans, who set the standard for appearance and dress for all umpires who came after him.[18]

While umpires were gaining greater support and respect from their leagues, McGowan and his colleagues were learning their trade from more experienced umpires who, in turn, had learned from their elders. Umpiring was an apprenticeship process until 1969, when Major League Baseball mandated attendance at an umpire school. While the first school for umpires was established by George Barr in 1935, becoming a professional umpire before 1969 was largely a matter of chance opportunity or personal contacts. Systematic evaluation and supervision was lacking and advancement, even to the majors, was often determined as much by politics and personality as by ability.[19]

As a consequence of required attendance at one of the two schools and ongoing performance evaluations there is greater consistency, some would say professionalism, among umpires in the tactics they use to control the games.[20] Graduates are more knowledgeable about the rules and more skilled in techniques than were the apprentice umpires. Formal training has imposed uniformity of style as students were taught by the book and maverick characters were weeded out. As these changes were taking place and as umpires were gaining more support from league officials, they portrayed themselves not as omnipotent enforcers of the law who demanded respect, but as impartial judges who deserved it.[21]

Without the requirement to attend a school, and without unions, instant replay, and ESPN, umpires in McGowan's day had greater freedom than do umpires today to fashion their own style and tactics. McGowan took more advantage of his freedom than did many of his colleagues. Umpires had only the league president to contend with, and he was rarely in attendance at games.

"McGowan," Jim Evans said, "couldn't use today the tactics he used. Those tactics were his survival tools. He had to let people know who was in control. In order to control the game he had to say, in one way or another, 'Son, don't question me. It may be a strike but if I want to call it a ball I will. Just watch me.'" [22]

Making a wrong call intentionally today is grounds for dismissal, as Erik Stahlbusch, who called a player out at first when he was clearly safe just to get back at him, found out in a Class A game in Cedar Rapids, Iowa, in 2001. The player's manager, Tyrone Boykin of Cedar Rapids, was wearing a mike for a story by a local TV station and caught the following on his tape.

> Boykin: "So you call him out and he's safe?"
> Stahlbusch: "Yeah."
> Boykin: "And that makes it even."
> Stahlbusch: "Yeah, that does make it even."
> Boykin: "So you're saying right there that he was safe, but you called him out for the hell of it?"
> Stahlbusch: "Yeah, I did."

Stahlbusch resigned shortly thereafter.[23] Doing an occasional favor for a player by calling a ball a strike, as McGowan did for Buddy Lewis, would be today, according to Evans, " a sure-fire way to lose your job. In 28 years of umpiring, I never miscalled a pitch as a favor. That's unethical."[24] Evans did say that an umpire today might occasionally give the benefit of the doubt to a pitcher with a reputation for pinpoint control. A pitch just a hair off the corner of the plate might be called a strike if it was thrown by a pitcher such as Greg Maddux, who gets the corner most of the time.

Umpires were barred from recommending players to owners toward the end of McGowan's tenure, and the same holds true today. "It's against the rules to recommend players," Evans said. "It's in the code of conduct that is posted in the umpires' dressing room. You're not even supposed to think about it."

Similarly, umpires no longer dispense advice to players because as Jim Evans said, "You'd get one of two reactions, and neither one is good. First, the player could well tell you where to put it by saying, 'You've got enough trouble umpiring. You do your job and I'll do mine.' And secondly, as happened to one umpire whose advice to a hitter 'to stand further back in the box' resulted in a batter getting a hit to break out of a slump, the manager of the opposing team could loudly express his displeasure by saying, 'What's going on here? Are you a coach or an umpire?'"

By the same token, umpires today tend to be less expressive than they were in McGowan's day. Today, McGowan most likely would not return the flip of a bird to a pitcher, as he did with Sid Hudson. "If an umpire did that today," Evans said, "it would be the lead story on ESPN's *Sports Center*, and the umpire and the player would immediately be called on the carpet by the league president. You'd have a call waiting for you from the league president or commissioner."[25] Such actions received little notoriety in McGowan's day because the only media attention they might draw would be a mention in the local paper.

It's also unlikely that today's umpires would comment on a player's performance, as did McGowan and his colleagues. Charlie Metro recalled McGowan saying, "My, sonny, that was a dainty tag," when Metro reached back to tag home with the point of his index finger after safely sliding past the plate to avoid the catcher's mitt during a game against the White Sox in 1943.[26]

Billy Evans once asked Al Schacht (a pitcher for the Washington Senators from 1919 to 1921, but much better known as The Clown Prince of Baseball), "Have you thrown your fastball yet?" After Schacht had replied, "Yes, about ten times," Evans replied, "Good, I guess I won't need this," and let the air out of his chest protector.[27]

McGowan told another story of umpire-player relations: Mickey Cochrane (Hall of Fame catcher for the Philadelphia A's and Detroit Tigers from 1925 to 1937) was charging at umpire Dick Nallin after Nallin called Cochrane out for failing to touch third base. While Bill Klem might have drawn a line in the dirt and said to Cochrane, "Don't cross this line or you're out of the game," Nallin pulled his bag of chewing tobacco from his hip pocket, took a chew, then offered the bag to Cochrane. Cochrane stopped cold, accepted the offer, and went back grinning to the dugout.[28]

Players would occasionally kid the umps. McGowan recounts the time before a game in Yankee Stadium when "Lou Gehrig asked with a grin, 'Which of you three fat men are working behind the plate?' Vernon 'Lefty'

Gomez, popped off with 'Hey, Mac, they tell me that any one of you three guys could work behind the plate on a minute's notice.' Getting no response, Gomez continued, 'Yes, I never knew you wore your chest protectors [as did National League umpires] under your coats before.' Just to prove we didn't, all three of us opened our coats sorta unconsciously."[29]

Increased restraint on the part of umpires may have improved the quality of play in some instances. One day in Fenway Park, normally reliable Red Sox second baseman Johnny Pesky let a routine ground ball go through his legs. Joe Cronin, his manager, wanted to know, "How in the world could you let such an easy ball get through you?" "I was listening to Larry Napp [second base umpire] singing," Pesky replied with a bit of a red face.[30]

Another restraint on an umpire's behavior has been the player's union. There were no unions in McGowan's days. "You controlled the game in any way you could in those days. That's how you earned your respect," Evans said. "If someone gave McGowan a hard time, he'd more or less stick it to him to teach him a lesson." Today, umpires and players have unions to back them up.

Unions have, in Jim Evans' opinion, contributed to higher level of professionalism on the part of players, umpires, and everyone connected with professional baseball. And, as has been the case in other businesses, unions have improved the benefits of its members. The average major league player salary in 1972, Evans' first year as a major league umpire, was $17,000–$18,000; now it's more than $2 million a year. Umpires, "always the step-children," according to Evans, have seen their conditions improve, but not as dramatically. McGowan, as the top-paid umpire in 1954, earned $15,000. Now a major league umpire's starting salary is about $100,000, with the top of the scale being more than $300,000. An umpire's per diem in 1972 was about $40; now it's more than $300, and umpires rate first-class airfare.

Having a Feel for the Game

As the level of professionalism among umpires has increased, the opportunities for personal expression by umpires have diminished. No umpire today would call a rookie "busher" or throw a player out of a game for "expostulation," much less make two "indecorous" gestures to the press box, or throw their ball and strike indicator at a pitcher who's questioning the umpire's judgment. The day of the colorful umpire with his own style is behind us. Does that mean that the quality of umpiring is better today than it was in McGowan's day?

Not necessarily. John Lopez, writing for the *Houston Chronicle* in

August 2003, takes major league umpires to task for inconsistent strike zones, losing control of games, and having as-contentious-as-ever relationships with players and managers. Lopez is of the opinion that these conditions exist because Major League Baseball hasn't made the needed investment in umpire development. While Professional Baseball Umpires Corporation staff members constantly evaluate minor league umpires' performances as they advance from rookie and instructional leagues to the Double A level, the corporation is lightly funded and only six people are assigned to evaluate umpires in all of those leagues.[31] Lopez notes that Evans' and Wendelstedt's schools have earned respect for proper classroom and field instruction, but that anyone with $3,000 and a plane ticket to Florida can get in. The top students at both schools are selected for the next step, which is an evaluation of their skills by the PBUC, which make assignments to the entry-level minor league positions, but that the minimum score necessary to be a top student is only 70 percent. Major league umpires can now take vacations during the season, where previously their off-season was the same as the players. This can lead to a situation that occurred in the first week of August 2003, when eight umpires with a total of 127 years of big-league experience were replaced by eight umpires with a total of 27 years of big-league experience. Add to what some see as a less than rigorous selection and evaluation process the other stresses on umpires and you have, in Lopez's opinion, "more bad calls than should be considered part of the 'human element' of the game and too many young umpires buckling under the pressure."

One stressor is ongoing pressure to speed up games despite the fact that pitchers increasingly tease rather than challenge hitters. "Pitchers today," Evans says, "are often more reluctant to throw strikes than their counterparts of years ago who took the position, 'Here's my best pitch, let's see your best swing.'" Another stressor is the new electronic QuesTec system that tells an umpire how many correct and incorrect calls he's made and that varies in its criteria from stadium to stadium as some call for a higher strike and some a wider zone. It's hard to be consistent when the measuring tool is inconsistent.[32]

Some, including Astros general manager Gerry Hunsicker, favor a return to recruiting former players because "they at least had a feel for the game.... Now we have a hodgepodge of people who have no feel for the game."[33]

There may be no easy answers to establishing and maintaining a high quality of umpiring, but McGowan's story may contain a few pointers in that direction. While McGowan was not a former professional player, it must be said that he had a feel for the game. McGowan, like many umpires then and now, had played organized baseball and aspired to the majors—plus his ten years as an umpire in the minor leagues no doubt combined to develop his sophisticated feel for the game before he made the majors. Through considerable practice and teaching from senior umpires, he learned how to call balls and strikes, make safe and out calls on the bases, and keep control of the game to the admiration and satisfaction of players, manager, and fans alike — no small feat. And he, and many of his fellow umpires, did it without the benefit of an umpires' school or a systematic development program. And while he was becoming competent, he developed a style all his own that was, as Bob Addie and others reported, a joy to watch.

What might we learn about umpire selection and training from McGowan's experience? One lesson is that commitment, or that experiencing umpiring as a calling, as Jim Evans put it, is a must. You need to have your heart in it to generate the necessary hustle, focus, and determination to give it your all. No one questioned McGowan's heart. In talking about what an umpire needs, McGowan wrote about his students: "They must have knowledge of the rules. If they don't, we try to give it to them. They must also have good character. We can give them everything but the heart after a class of five weeks."[34]

A feel for the game, heart, and good character would make a good foundation for any umpire. While these traits can't be taught, they can serve as selection criteria. There are a range of assessment and selection processes that could be adapted to discerning those aspirants with heart and a feel for the game from those without these traits, be they former ball players or not.

It's interesting to note that both Jim Evans and McGowan were athletically inclined, started umpiring in their teens, developed a love for it, and applied themselves to learning the profession. Their experience suggests that having a feel for the game, however acquired, may be a necessary foundation from which one learns the tools of the trade, either at a school or from a senior umpire, needed to control games and earn respect. "Respect," Jim Evans said, "does not come with the uniform. All that comes with the uniform is responsibility and cleaning bills."[35]

Skills to Be Taught

An umpire, of course, needs more than heart. An umpire also needs to be proficient in calling balls and strikes, making out and safe decisions on the bases, and applying the rules to game situations. These skills can be taught, better earlier in life than later. "I want," Evans said, "to get more people interested at an early age. I can teach them the principles they need to know, but they need more time to practice using their eyes, getting themselves in the right position, and handling complex situations." Evans notes that previous experience of umpiring among his students is not always a plus. "Many come to the school after umpiring a few years bringing with them some bad habits. So, in a five-week course, it often takes me two to three weeks to get them back to ground zero so they can start the process of building the proper skills."

Three skills are particularly important. One, Evans, says, is "learning to use your eyes correctly." To call balls and strikes, Evans advises umpires to track the ball all the way from the pitcher's hand into the catcher's mitt. "Some umpires," he said, "have tunnel vision and focus only on the pitcher. That way a ball can get in 'under their eyes' so that the ball that looks good in front of the plate, be it a curve, slider, forkball—whatever—may not look so good when it gets over the plate."

A second skill is getting yourself in the right position when you're on the base paths. Like a player, the umpire watches the ball off the bat. The umpire wants to anticipate where the ball will be coming from so that he knows where to be to have a clear view of the ball before it arrives. One difference between then and now that Evans noted is that umpires in McGowan's days were often hustling to get to a play as it was developing and they were taught to get set to make their call—in other words, take it all in, make sure the ball isn't dropped, and then give a strong signal. Today's umpires are taught to get set for the play so they're not in motion at that critical time while the play is happening. That's why you see today's umpires down on one knee or with their hands on their knees. "This way," Evans said, "your eyes, which you want to treat as a camera lens, aren't moving."

The third skill is applying rules and standards to situations as they unfold. One challenging situation is the ejection. "Here," Evans said, "standards are important. If a player says, 'Son of a bitch, you missed another one,' that's not objectionable. If the player begins his sentence with the pronoun 'you,' it is and he's history. Same thing if a player says to me 'you motherfucker,' or 'you cocksucker.' I love it when a player does that because he's just thrown himself out of the game. It's so clear-cut it makes my job easy, as is the case when a player bumps me or kicks dirt at me. Other times you have to exercise your judgment, as in the case of a player being on the field too long while arguing. You use ejections only to control the game by not allowing anyone to abuse you. You let one player abuse you and they'll all do it, and you've lost control of the game."

John Rice, who was promoted to the American League in 1955 to fill the vacancy created by McGowan's death, thinks umpires today throw players out a game more quickly than was the case in the earlier days. "Then," Rice said, 'it was more man-to-man. You'd each cuss each other out, forget about it and keep on playing. You didn't want to spoil the game for the customer." The language used in the arguments between umpires and players has also changed. "You heard 'S.O.B.' and 'bastard' all the time but you didn't hear the 'm.f.' words as much as you do today."[36]

Jimmy Piersall (former center fielder for the Red Sox, Indians, Senators, Mets, and Angels) also said there was a lot of room for give and take between umpires and players in McGowan's day. "He'd say," said Piersall, "you got two minutes to talk, and then we're playing, whether you're still in the game or not. Today's umpires are more arrogant and will toss a player very quickly."[37]

Evans acknowledged that McGowan had these and other umpiring skills in abundance but that he was "what I'd consider a natural and worked a lot on instinct. He probably had an uncanny ability to track the pitch to the mitt. Many may have been more technically schooled than he was and knew the rules better, but he had the ability to sell himself."

There were those at the time who agreed with Evans' assessment of McGowan.

Cal Hubbard once characterized McGowan as a "super umpire who works by instinct and is seldom challenged."

"I hope," Hubbard continued, "Bill never gets into arguments over the rules, because I don't think he owns a rule book — but he gets by because his instincts are great."[38]

Franklin Lewis, sportswriter for the *Cleveland Press*, discovered firsthand McGowan's disdain for relying on the rulebook to make decisions. "I insulted Bill McGowan once," Lewis said. "A fan had written a letter to me, asking for a ruling on a particularly delicate and involved play. I walked into the umpires' dressing room, rulebook in one hand, and the problem in the other. Innocently, I proffered the rulebook to Bill. He snarled, 'What the hell do I need with a rulebook? What's the problem?'"[39]

He of course did own a rulebook, though he was adamant about never brandishing it during a game. "To do so," he thought, "would just confuse the situation. Bring a rulebook on the field and they'll have you pawin' through it 'til you're dizzy. I tell my students: 'leave the rulebook in your uniform bag. When you get out there on the field you should know the rules. And if a situation isn't covered in the rules, use your judgment.'"[40]

Today, the teaching methods have been refined to the point where umpires need not rely on instinct or having to sell oneself as they are better schooled and practiced before making the majors and have the support of their union. Bob Addie, sportswriter for *The Washington Post*, commented on this change in umpiring with perhaps a tinge of lament by saying, "They [umpires] are all fading into a pattern now, and few arrogate to themselves the supreme power the old-timers used as their badge of office."[41]

Whether they're better umpires—that is, make a higher percentage of correct calls behind the plate and on the bases than did McGowan and his fellow umps—is open to question. What we do know is that the style of umpiring has changed forever.

Epilogue

How is McGowan remembered?

Baseball was his life. He contributed to it in many ways—founding a school for umpires, authoring numerous articles, speaking at baseball events too numerous to count, encouraging players and umpires to give their best — but he will, of course, be best remembered for his performances on the field.

In the words of sportswriter Francis Stann: "McGowan may be the last [of the umpires] who made his name strictly off his umpiring. He has that touch of personality that set him apart from the others. It never hurt an umpire to flash a little pomp and strut, as long as he knew his business, which McGowan did and does."[1]

"Precious few," wrote Morrie Siegel in 1979, "disagreed with him twice; not just in the same season but also in a career. During McGowan's reign of terror he was all law and order — his own law and order. When his decision was rendered, ball or strike, fair or foul, safe or out, it was like a Supreme Court judgment: irreversible. 'I just call 'em, I don't explain 'em,' he said testily."[2]

His chief instructor, Al Somers, stressed the importance of "not explaining 'em" to his students. "We never," Somers said, "let a student call: 'Ball — high!' or 'Ball — low!' You just call it and let it go at that. Don't give 'em a chance to question your judgment."[3]

Jim Fridley (an outfielder for the Indians, Orioles, and Reds) noted that McGowan would use verbal retorts, as well as icy stares, if a player disagreed with a call. "McGowan," Fridley said, "would turn against the pitcher if he bitched or showed him up. He'd call the next pitch a ball even if it was right down the middle of the plate." In the same interview, Fridley also said that McGowan didn't like calling a game pitched by Cubans because they were too deliberate and took too long. He had bad legs and feet, so he hated pitchers he thought "were fooling around on the mound."[4]

In addition to being dictatorial, McGowan was also known for being a class act. In 1944, after 20 years of major league umpiring, sportswriter Vincent X. Flaherty wrote that McGowan earned the sobriquet of "The Number One Man" from senior umpire Billy Evans. "McGowan," Flaherty continued, "possesses that indefinable something called, for lack of a better word, class. No umpire in the game commands greater respect among the players than does McGowan — not even the patriarchal Bill Klem of the National League. As is usually the case with any master in any line of endeavor, McGowan has set an umpiring style. Incoming rookie umpires, as well as some of the veterans, pattern themselves after McGowan. They gesture like him; try to imitate the jerky but positive movements that are Bill's, and they even walk like him and try to talk like him."[5]

Imitation is the highest form of flattery.

He enjoyed his work immensely. Part of his enjoyment came from the pride in knowing he was Number 1. He also appreciated the occasional praise for his work from players. "An odd case in umpiring," he noted, "is that while the man in blue is never the star in any game, occasionally he is cited for good work."[6]

McGowan accepted the fact that the star role is for players. The umpire is the disciplinarian. "We know," he said, "that when we go on a ball field our job as umpires is to maintain discipline and to do it we've got to be the villains.... An umpire has got to consider lots of angles. The fans don't pay money to see an umpire. They pay to see the players play. We want to keep the players in the game, but at the same time we must have discipline. And there is no excuse for foul language. The player who uses it is not just offending us. He's hurting the game, and offending the ladies in the crowd."[7]

Part of his enjoyment also came from his relationships with players, which he was successful in nurturing even though his official role was that of the stern taskmaster. He recalled the time in 1914 when he was umpiring in a small Delmarva league that had teams in Seaford and Milford, Delaware, and Cambridge and Salisbury, Maryland. The teams traveled by cars, and the umpires had to ride with the players. "On one of these trips," McGowan wrote, "I was riding in the same car with Jimmy Dykes, Eddie Rommel, and Joe Boley when Rommel said, 'Well, fellows, we're not making much money now — but never mind, the four of us will be up there in the big leagues some day!'"

Then 17 years later in the World Series between the Cardinals and the Athletics, McGowan was umpiring the Series, and Dykes, Rommel, and Boley were playing for the A's. "This association with ball players from the minor leagues up to the majors is one of the little intimate personal touches to an umpire's job the sentiment of which gets under your skin. It is in keeping this sentiment out of his decisions that the umpire has his hard-est job."[8]

In the same article he recounted how in 1920 he recommended Goose Goslin, "a raw, green farmer boy who had never been away from home," to Zinn Beck, manager of the Columbia Comers, a Class C team in South Carolina. Then in 1935 McGowan was one of the umpires in the ninth inning of the sixth and final game of the World Series between the Cubs and the Tigers when Goslin, a Tiger, won the game and the Series with a clean base hit to right field after telling his teammates he was going to do just that.

"Don't you think I got a thrill out of that, and that my mind raced back fifteen years to the day in 1920 when I had put a green farmer boy on a train and shipped him off to his first baseball job? I'll say I did!" McGowan wrote.

While enjoying these and other relationships with players, McGowan made a point of not being "buddy-buddy" with players. In the interest of promoting an aura of dignity and majesty for the umpire role, McGowan believed umpires should never fraternize with players. "Of course," he added, "that doesn't mean we cross the street to avoid a ball player. It's all right to be friendly. You can stop and chew the fat with them on the street, but no running around with them as if buddy-buddy."[9]

His stance on umpire-player relationships was not lost on the play-ers. Billy Werber remembered that "McGowan would never drop into the dugout and visit with you before the game, tell a few jokes, and slap you on the knee like Beans Reardon would."[10]

McGowan ended this article by saying, "I like my job. I've liked it ever since the first wild-eyed fans down on the lots started to call me 'robber' and 'blind bum,' and I'll continue to like it until they cut this blue suit off me and cart me away to the junk pile. And, as Tim Hurst used to say, 'Yez can't beat them hours.'"[11]

Maybe he even relished being called "robber," "blind bum," or worse because he was ready for such brickbats. "With an even temper, a sense of humor, and aptness at quick repartee," he said, "even an ump can get a lot of fun out of his job, and I like my job. Come up and see me some-time and bring your insult."[12]

And what about the baseball he gave me 50 years ago saying I could sell it for a hundred bucks at a church bazaar? I still have it. It's a little toned with age, and protected in a plastic cube. I think McGowan would have preferred it this way.

A Word for Collectors

McGowan's autograph is highly prized among baseball memorabilia collectors because of its rarity. Just as fans rarely ask, "who will be umpiring today's game," so also is it rare that fans ask umpires for their autograph. Induction into the Hall of Fame increases the value of the autograph, especially in cases like McGowan's, when the induction occurs nearly four decades after the inductee's death.

A McGowan signature alone on a clean baseball is quite rare and can command $5,000 or more. More often seen are baseballs that he signed with umpires who worked a World Series with him; a baseball like the one he gave me that he signed with players; and paper memorabilia that he signed, including one of the letters that he banged off on his Smith-Corona, picture postcards of himself that he would often inscribe and sign, a signed copy of the textbook he published for his students; or his signature on a slip of paper.

I found three variations of his signature. One is his "autograph" signature. You can easily recognize this one by the three downward strokes forming the "M."

The other two variations are work-related. The first is the rarest variation of his signature. He used it, according to Bill Jr., only to sign his employment contracts with the American

Bill McGowan's "autograph" signature. It is this signature that is most seen on baseballs, photographs, postcards and other McGowan signed memorabilia.

This contract fully sets forth all understandings and agreements between the parties, and no other understandings or agreements, whether heretofore or hereafter made, shall be valid, recognizable or of any effect whatsoever, unless expressly set forth in a new or supplemental contract executed by the Umpire and the League (acting by its President), complying with all agreements and rules to which this contract is subject.

Signed in duplicate this ....**16th**.... day of ....**JANUARY**........, A. D. 19..**52**..

AMERICAN LEAGUE OF PROFESSIONAL BASEBALL CLUBS,

By _____
President

_____
Umpire

Bill McGowan's signature as it appeared on his 1952 American League contract (from Bill Jr.'s album).

League president. The one above is from his 1952 contract with William Harridge. Note his use of the more formal "Wm. A."

The last variation is how he signed letters. The one below was taken from a letter he sent to a prospective student for his school.

Hope to have you with us.

Sincerely,

Bill McGowan's signature as it appeared on letters he wrote (author's collection).

Appendix: The Text Book Used at McGowan's Umpiring School

Note

Each student attending Bill McGowan's School for Umpires received a copy of this textbook that he had written. McGowan would print as many copies as he needed for each session of his school. While the pagination has been altered to fit *Dean of Umpires,* and the original page numbers removed from the Table of Contents, the text and pictures have been reproduced exactly as they appeared in the original.

TEXT BOOK

Bill McGowan's School for Umpires

Daytona Beach, Florida

Jan.— Feb. 1949

APPROVED BY THE VETERAN'S ADMINISTRATION
UNDER G. I. BILL OF RIGHTS

"Babe" Ruth, on a visit to school at West Palm Beach
1948 Class — with Bill McGowan

Top: Lou and Babe, Lou Gehrig Day — Yankee Stadium. *Right*: Happy Chandler, Commissioner of Base Ball, and Bill McGowan, 1948.

The "Yankee Clipper" acting as instructor
McGowan's School, W. Palm Beach, Fla.
1948

McGowan and Al Somers instructing proper positions on pitching
rubber.

INDEX

FOREWORD
INSTRUCTION NO. 1
    Appearance and Equipment
    Batting Order and Ground Rules
INSTRUCTION NO. 2
    Stance Behind the Plate
    Calling Balls and Strikes
    The Called Strike Gestures
INSTRUCTION NO. 3
    Sweeping off the Plate
    Relaxation
    Fair and Foul Balls
INSTRUCTION NO. 4
    "Don'ts" for Umpires
INSTRUCTION NO. 5
    Umpire-in-Chief
    Fitness of Field for Play
    Single Umpire System
    Base Umpire — Double System
INSTRUCTION NO. 6
    Every Day Problems
INSTRUCTION NO. 7
    Aces for Umpires
    Every Day Problems
INSTRUCTION NO. 8
    Triple Umpire System
    Flashes
    On the Bases
INSTRUCTION NO. 9
    Position Sketches
INSTRUCTION NO. 10
    Follow the Ten Little Umpires
        Honesty
        Common Sense
        Loyalty
        Courage
        Ability

Character
Honor
Fair Play
Intelligence
Hustle
ANSWERS TO QUESTIONS — EVERYDAY PROBLEMS IN
    INSTRUCTIONS 6 AND 7

STAFF

DIRECTOR OF SCHOOL

BILL McGOWAN, AMERICAN LEAGUE

CHIEF INSTRUCTOR

AL SOMERS, PACIFIC COAST LEAGUE

WITHOUT DOUBT, THE FOREMOST INSTRUCTOR
IN ALL BASEBALL

INSTRUCTORS

ROCKY FLAMMIA, WESTERN INTERNATIONAL LEAGUE

NICK REVIELLE, SOUTHERN ASSOCIATION

JAMES (RED) MC CUTCHEON, SOUTHERN ASSOCIATION

AUGIE DONATELLI, NATIONAL LEAGUE

BILL HUSBAND, CENTRAL LEAGUE

LES SANDERS, CENTRAL LEAGUE

PETE DONETT, PIONEER LEAGUE

EDDIE CARNEY, EASTERN SHORE LEAGUE

JOHN FERRY, GEORGIA STATE LEAGUE

FOREWORD

The three greatest umpires of my time were Tommy Connolly and Billy Evans of the American League and Bill Klem of the National League.

I was fortunate on my way to the majors in having teamed with these umpires on occasion and were it not for their generous help and instructions, in all probability I would still be a minor league arbiter. I took something from each of these masters and moulded it into my own style of work. Later, after arriving in the majors I worked with Connolly and Evans in the American League, and with Klem in World's Series competition. Today I still seek their advice on matters pertaining to umpiring.

Brother umpires, let us dedicate these instructions to three of the greatest umpires of all time. Men of whom our grand old National Game might well be proud — and to all sand-lot umpires.

Remember that the game is what the umpire makes it. You have it in your power to make or break baseball as it comes under your influence. You are part of the game. You are important to the game. But you are not more important than the game.

Bill McGowan
American League Umpire

INSTRUCTION NO. 1

Appearance and Equipment

An umpire must consider his appearance on the field. A blue uniform. Have it pressed frequently.

Have your baseball shoes polished before every game. They will become soiled and dusty a minute or so after the game is started. It is that flash of a minute at the home plate that counts.

Clean white linens—Your shirt and handkerchief.

Always a dark blue or black tie. A black bow tie preferably.

A dark blue cap to match the uniform. Make it a point to get a fresh cap when the old one becomes shabby. Six and eight new caps during the season is a regular custom.

Now we are ready to start for home plate and get the game under way.

-o-

"The second step" is the umpire's paraphenalia. Tommy Connolly, chief of umpires for the American League years ago made the remark to me. "Show me an umpire with a good kit of tools and I'll show you a good workman."

Protect yourself from injuries. Use a strong mask, well padded. The chest protector I use is an inflated one and offers the utmost in protection from foul tips.

Good shinguards and shoes with the padded tongue and box toe for use behind the plate are essential. Remember you are not of much value to your President or league if sent to the side lines often by injuries caused by poor working paraphenalia.

If a sandlot umpire can afford two pairs of shoes, the regulation shoes for behind the plate and the simple baseball shoe for the bases, he is getting away to a good start.

Don't forget your indicator, watch, cup, whiskbroom, and, most important of all, your rule book.

Sandlot umpires are called upon in most cases to make announcement of the batteries, and in some cities announce each player and his position his first time at bat.

Always take off your cap. Make your battery announcement in a loud clear tone of voice, facing the grandstand. Stand about 15 feet to the left of home plate the first time, then take position about 15 feet to the right of home plate and repeat the announcement.

When giving the players' names and their positions as they step to the batter's box the first time around, just turn toward the stands and make the announcement once.

(You will always find hecklers in every ball park. When they yell "Who" after you have made known a player's name, ignore them. Don't repeat.)

Batting Order and Ground Rules

The umpire behind the plate will have charge of the batting orders. Insist that each manager or captain give you, in writing, his batting order with names of players and their positions.

After the batting-order cards are presented to the umpire-in-chief, the line-ups for that day are official. Do not allow the two official batting orders to leave your possession.

In the American League — Each manager or Captain of the contending clubs presents the umpire behind the plate, the chief umpire for that day's game, two batting orders, showing the line-ups and including the manager's or captain's signature. We compare first the line-up (names and positions) of the home team. Place one card in your pocket for ready reference, in case of batting-out-of-order situations. The other card we hand to the visiting manager. Take the two batting orders *which must be identical* from the visiting manager and compare them. Place one in your pocket and hand the other to the manager of the home club.

Make ground rules covering every place a ball could possibly go out of play. When the managers disagree on any ground rule, the umpire should step in and make an arbitrary ground rule.

If working double, be sure the base umpire is standing by to offer the chief umpire his assistance, in case anything has been overlooked.

Hold down the ground rules to a minimum. Too many ground rules cause complicated discussions, arguments and quarrels that hold up the game. Fans everywhere resent this practice.

In the American League — a drive is either a two-base hit or a home run, regardless of whether or not the two-base hit was a longer drive than the homer. We do not have any *ground rule singles* or three-base hits.

I strongly urge umpires to take this matter up with their League Presidents, or the managers of teams competing in games which you umpire.

Keep your Field Clean — You are the Boss — Run Your Ball Game

At the start of every inning —
Do not allow players warming up in the bull pen to lay their sweaters,

wind-breakers, etc. on the field. This is courting trouble. If necessary, call time and have the sweater or equipment removed by the players.

Insist upon players being seated on benches, throughout the game. The bats should be kept in order, not all over the field and around the bench in careless fashion.

Always insist on the bat and ball bags being closed and out of the way.

Insist upon these matters being carried out. If not done they can only cause the umpire plenty of worry.

Never Lose Sight of the Ball —

They call this the first rule of the book. It is vastly important. Keep your eye on the ball if you desire to avoid trouble.

Instructors at McGowan Umpire and Jack Rossiter Baseball Schools
Left to right — Buddy Lewis — Washington "Nats"; Bill McGowan — American League; Travis Jackson — New York Giants; Gus Donatelli — New National League Umpire; Jake Early — Washington "Nats"; Art Passarella — American League Umpire; Andy Semimick — Phillies.

INSTRUCTION NO. 2

Stance Behind the Plate

There are two distinct forms used by umpires working behind the plate. One style finds the arbiter with his left foot extended about 12 inches in front of his right foot, when a right-handed batsman is in the box. The umpire peers over the left shoulder of the catcher. With a left-handed batter up, the stance is reversed — the umpire places his right foot forward and the left foot in the rear and looks over the catcher's right shoulder. We will call this style A.

Style B finds the umpire placing his feet almost on a straight line, and about 22- to 26-inches apart. He straddles with catcher. The umpire's left foot is directly behind the catcher's left, his right is directly behind the catcher's right.

Regardless of whether or not the batsman is right- or left-handed, this style calls for the umpire to look directly over the catcher's head — not over his shoulders.

-o-

Since entering the American League I have always found Style B gives me a better opportunity to focus both eyes on the ball. It affords the best vision for those tough curve balls that break across the outside corner of the plate about knee high.

Size up your pitch by looking straight at the pitcher.

No matter how tall a catcher is he must take a low stance in order to catch the low ball. If the catcher is the bobbing, jumping type, ask him to get down and stop prancing around so much. POINT OUT THE ADVANTAGES FOR HIS PITCHER BY KEEPING DOWN.

Don't work too close to the catcher. You may interfere with him when he turns sharply to chase a fly ball. If he bumps you as he is about to go into a play of any kind, it is a most embarrassing situation for an umpire. Stand about a foot and a half behind the catcher. When he shifts or turns to the left or right in going after a foul fly, shift the same way he does. *Move fast. Get out of his way.* Working too close behind the catcher affords too many chances for a collision.

Calling Balls and Strikes

First set yourself by placing both feet on a direct line, with a spread between your feet about 24 inches. This is called "Straddling." As the pitcher steps on the rubber for his sign from the catcher, bend your body slightly forward. Look straight over the catcher's head, and line up the pitcher. If it comes over low, crouch and go down with the ball.

Don't crouch low if the pitch is high.

It is wise to bring that low ball up. This has been a war cry from the benches or dugouts for years. When you call a ball that has crossed the plate an inch or so below the batter's knees a strike, it appears to the players on the benches and the spectators on the right and left sides of the playing field, as a ball in the dirt.

The same may be said for the ball around the batter's shoulders. It is true that the rule says "Any ball that passes over the plate between the shoulder and the knee is a strike." However, if you make it a point to guide yourself using the top of the player's shirt front letters as a line of demarcation, you will become more proficient behind the plate in the calling of balls and strikes.

Call your balls and strikes in a clear tone of voice. (My advice is not too loud.) If you "blow" one while calling strikes and balls at the top of your voice, everybody in the park catches on. On the other hand, the fellow who works more smoothly in this department, not attracting too much attention, now and then gets away with one of those questionable decisions unnoticed.

However — if you must call them in a thunderous voice, and really want to make a hit with the players and fans. "Save it for the pinches." Then give it all you have. Your rating will scoot skyward.

The Called Strike Gestures

To signal a called strike. Adopt a certain motion of your own and stick to it. I would strongly advise one complete motion. Some umpires have their own individuality.

There are many ways to signify a called strike.

a. One umpire might raise his hand high above his head pointing toward the sky (A la Red Ormsby.)

b. Another may use the inimitable Klem style by raising his arm, then crossing it in front of his body in the general direction of the third base coaching box for strike number one. For strike number two Klem raises his arm and then points toward first base coaching box.

c. Bill Summers raises his arms and snaps off a strike in the direction of first base.

d. The writer uses a closed fist, held about four inches above his head.

Don't use the left arm at all. In the old days, an umpire waved his left arm for called balls.

Cultivate a deeper toned voice for balls than you carry for strikes. Ball players tell umpires they don't mind if you miss a first or second strike, *but be sure you call that third one right.*

I have always made a practice of putting more emphasis on that called third strike. You will get more alibis, more kicks and more howls, when the third strike is called. Therefore, make sure you are right, then full speed ahead. Crack down on that third strike with some action!

Bill McGowan
26 years — Umpire, American League

INSTRUCTION NO. 3

Sweeping Off Home Plate

Always, in sweeping off the home plate, turn your back to the pitcher. Face the stands. You will note in watching major league umpires that there is more significance to sweeping off the plate, than just cleaning off the dust.

It is a trick of the trade and a smart move, if nothing else. It is a gesture of respect to the patrons of the game.

-o-

Relaxation

After setting yourself, keep in mind to watch every move of the pitcher. The slightest turn of your head may cause you to lose a balk motion.

Do not work too fast. Take a good look at the ball, follow its course, then make up your mind and call it a strike or a ball. Now step back one or two paces, relax and say to yourself, "Am I calling 'em too fast?"

Get ready as the pitcher is about to step on the rubber. When he takes his sign and prepares to pitch, then get set. Give your decision, and relax again by stepping away a few feet.

Keep on relaxing after each pitched ball. It is a good habit to acquire and naturally tends to make an umpire loosen up. Don't be tense.

The closer the competition, the more you relax. In this way you soon have the happy faculty of controlling your game in a more thorough manner.

While the pitch is on its way plateward, bear down hard. Concentrate on the ball and if it's below the belt line crouch low and follow its course.

-o-

Never stand directly behind the catcher on a throw to the plate to get a runner. Watch the throw-in. Line up your play and get into the proper position. Your angle on the play is everything. Stand to either side of the plate. Keep the ball always in sight.

Do not allow the catcher's body to come between you and the runner's foot, thus blocking your view of the play.

The runner will as a rule slide into the plate on one side or the other. His intention is to give the catcher the least part of his body to tag. For instance, a runner on third base attempts to score on a single to right field; if the catcher goes forward to meet the throw, the runner will naturally slide away from the plate toward the third the third base side of the field. He will give the catcher his left foot to touch.

On such a play I usually place myself about 15 feet up the line toward third base in foul ground as the runner passes me and hits the dirt I follow him a step or two. As the catcher turns and dives for his foot, I have complete vision of the play in front of me. The plate, the runner's left foot, the catcher's glove, hand and ball.

In sizing up a play after a ball is hit to left field I see the catcher will be pulled to his left. I take my position accordingly, keeping in clear view the plate, the runner's right foot (in this instance), and the touch of the catcher.

Sometimes, an umpire is forced to change his position at the last second. There isn't any certain spot in which to stand. The main idea is to get the proper angle of the play and not allow either the runner or the catcher's body to block your view.

The best way to learn these angles is by umpiring ball games. It will come to you naturally if you are alert and observing the field.

Fair and Foul Balls

In the American League the umpire behind the plate calls all fair or foul balls over or near the bag. He also decides a ball that goes over the fence or into the stands, fair or foul, as to where the ball left the playing field.

Any fly ball that comes down near the foul line that the first baseman and second baseman are attempting to catch (between the regular position of the base umpire and the fence in right field) the base umpire will call it fair or foul.

The same thing goes when the shortstop and third baseman go after a fly ball near the foul line. The umpire working at third will decide it fair or foul.

The regular position of the umpires at first and third bases is about twenty feet beyond the bag in foul ground.

Balls that are topped by the batsman often strike the ground in the batter's box, sometimes hitting the home plate, and seem to confuse umpires and players alike.

If a ball struck by the bat settles on home plate without having touched the person of the batsman, catcher or umpire, it is a fair ball. If the ball had touched the batter still in his box, it is a foul ball. If it touched the catcher or umpire, it is a foul ball.

You must be alert on these plays. In a glance you can tell whether the ball touched the batter or catcher. In the event no one touches the ball, disregard where it struck the ground. It could hit the ground ten feet behind the catcher and will roll into the diamond to become a fair ball. The umpire, batter and catcher are in foul ground. If the ball doesn't touch them or some other object and then settles in fair ground, it is a fair ball.

It is where the ball settles between home and first and home and third base.

Where it hits the ground doesn't matter until after it has passed first or third base. It is where the ball settles on the infield.

Of course if touched by a player or umpire in fair ground it is a fair ball, if touched in foul ground it is a foul ball. If the ball touches a glove, mask, or a bat in foul ground, before having been touched by a fielder in fair territory, it is a foul ball.

By consistently having in mind what takes place on these balls that hit the ground around the plate, or on it, you will not find making decisions such a hard task.

I strongly advise, however, that once the ball strikes the ground around the box then touches the batter or the catcher, you wave your hands high in the air and declare it a foul ball immediately. Do not hesitate. Call it quickly and make a demonstration.

In working the double umpire system — always have a sign with your brother umpire. If the batsman takes a half cut at the ball, and the plate umpire due to some action on the part of the catcher is partially blocked from view, take a quick glance at your partner. If he thinks the batter went around, took the bat across the plate, he will nod his head once...Yes.

If he saw it that the batter did not go all the way round or across the plate, he will shake his head from side to side, quickly, and just the one time...No.

The umpire-in-chief will then indicate the count by raising his fingers over his head — "One and one" or "Two and one," whatever the count.

You do not call the half swing a ball or strike when you did not see it. Simply hesitate a second, look to your partner for the sign. Then give the decision and the count with fingers.

-o-

The same sign works on a play whereby the base umpire calls a runner out but unfortunately turned away before the play was completed. The ball was dropped. The players are ready to swarm the umpire. The base umpire immediately looks in the direction of his partner behind the plate.

He in turn answers the question — was the ball dropped? With a nod of the head...Yes, or with a shake of the head...No, — whatever was the correct ruling on the play. The base umpire then rides through with the decision given by his partner.

Any time a play in the making, such as a dropped ball, a half swing, or the foot off the bag, comes up and you are blocked out of the play by some action of a player, always look sharp and direct to your partner.

He knows your glance means that you want help. You are asking him by that glance, without using words...Did he drop the ball? Did he take a full swing? Was his foot off the bag?

By shaking or nodding the head...Yes or No...the problem has been solved.

On all batted balls with a runner on first base. The plate umpire must go down to third base for a possible decision. Make it a practice to break toward third and going about half way down the line when the batter connects, with first base occupied. If the runner on first base comes around to third, you are a couple of steps ahead of him. If he holds up at second you at least were hustling and anticipating the play. Always be ready for that third base decision when working behind the plate. Keep moving around. Step out into the diamond. Don't let the ball players say you are a stationary umpire. Don't let 'em out-hustle you.

Al. Somers,
Chief Instructor

INSTRUCTION NO. 4

Don'ts for Umpires

1. Don't take your eye off the ball.
   (This is the first rule of baseball and in the long run, one of the most important. Frank Crosetti of the Yankees successfully pulled the hidden ball trick eleven times in two seasons. If you are in the habit of taking your eye off the ball, make certain there isn't a ball player named Crosetti in the park.)

2. Don't take anything for granted in baseball.
   (Never say "I figured he would touch the bag," or "I felt sure he would make the catch," or, "if he wasn't out, he should have been out." Be positive. Always wait until the play is completed and see it through to the finish.)

3. Don't call your plays too quickly.
   (At first base particularly, take your time. At the last particle of a second a foot off the bag, or a juggled ball, may cause you to reverse yourself, and on this sort of a play the umpire is generally criticized. The players will yell "You always have that thumb in the air"—and plenty more.)

4. Don't explain your decisions.
   (Simply call the plays as you see 'em. That's the best anybody can do. Explaining why you called a runner out or safe, in many cases signifies a weakness on the part of the umpire.)

5. Don't argue with the ball players or managers.
   (A manager or player, on a close play, will make a kick. If it is a legitimate protest, listen to their complaint for a brief period. Tell them you called the play as you saw it, and then walk away. When they follow you, you might repeat that it was your judgment. Walk away with a warning finger. If they continue protesting, go through with your threat. Get somebody out of there.)

6. Don't carry a chip on your shoulder.
   (Nothing disturbs a manager or player more than a chesty umpire. When a player tells you a ball was low in a sarcastic manner, reply by saying , "Well, Joe, it looked high enough to me." Suppose you did call one a ball that you later thought you might have called a strike. If the catcher puts up a squawk and raises a rumpus in protesting your deci-

sion; under the circumstances, you might possibly say, "It might have been." You will catch more flies with sugar than you will with vinegar.)

7. Don't look for trouble.
(As far as the "man in blue" is concerned, trouble comes uninvited. For instance, you have called a third strike on a batter, as he walks away from the plate, he grumbles something about your eye sight or your Aunt Kate. Forget it. Umpires make the mistake of yelling what was that remark. *That is looking for trouble.*)

8. Don't be a grinner.
(It is tactful to smile once in a while on the ball field, but to be out there with a grin on your face almost through an entire game is ridiculous. If you are going to be smiling and grinning most of the game, don't forget the boys are expecting you to keep smiling in those real tough spots. Hence, you are not kidding anyone but yourself.)

9. Don't challenge ball players.
(Yes, I'll see you under the stands any time, etc. You know the type. Some day you are going to challenge the wrong guy, "No runs, No hits, No errors.")

10. Don't talk back to the fans.
(While it is a shame that some of those grandstand managers and grandstand umpires are allowed to get away with so much, still it goes with the job. You have to take a lot of things right on the chin for the good of the game. Pay no attention to the jibes, put cotton in your ears if necessary, but go right on doing your work. After all, those babies are sending the groceries to your home.)

11. Don't make decisions for your partner.
(The best of us are not too good. It's a tough job at times, and you've got to love it to succeed as an umpire. If shortstop Brown says "Gee, your partner behind the plate has missed a lot of them today," ignore the remark. If you ever agree with Mr. Brown you are not an umpire at heart.)

12. Don't be vindictive.
(No matter how much trouble you have with a team or player today, tomorrow is a new day and a new baseball game. Wipe the slate clean. Never carry a grudge. Remember ball players are fighting to win. They say things on the spur of the moment that they regret an hour later. Better than 95 percent of the players with whom I've had run-ins have later apologized in their own way.)

13. Don't let coaches call your plays.

(Speak to them in a nice way about it. Don't be sarcastic. Inject a little humor with your warning if you wish. He knows the golden rule. Earl Combs is as fine a gentleman as you'll ever meet. Once in a while he becomes excited, and with palms downward will signal a runner (naturally, a Yankee) is safe. I always manage to get a laugh, and at the same time an apology from the former great ball player by saying something to this effect: "You will be on our staff next year, Earl, if you keep improving on those close decisions!")

14. Don't take your eyes off the pitcher once he steps on that rubber.

(The very moment you turn your head for the first time during a game, that's the time a pitcher will make a false move and the opposing team swarms on the field, crying, "Balk! Balk! Balk!" Well, if you've never been in hot water, this will be the turning point.)

15. Don't clown on the field.

(No matter what a player has done to draw a laugh, stay out of the picture if you happen to be wearing a blue suit and carrying an umpire's indicator. Umpires are hired to render decisions in baseball — without a doubt the greatest game on God's green earth. If you are a comedian on the field, I strongly advise taking up show business. They will surely take care of you, providing you have the goods.)

16. Don't turn away from a play too quickly.

(Something may happen. On an attempted double play, the second baseman may fail to tag the bag with his foot; he may drop the ball before he gets a firm hold on it, or he may drop the ball in the act of throwing it to first base, which under the rules is not construed as a dropped ball. I repeat…take nothing for granted in baseball — wait until the play is completed at second base before turning your head.)

17. Don't attract too much attention.

(It's all right to have a little color. Hustle your head off! Move around! Be alert! Be alive! Concentrate on every pitched ball regardless of whether you are behind the plate or on the bases. If you are going to wave out a runner who is out by fifteen feet with a great demonstration of arm motion, make sure you go through the same gestures when the going is toughest. The boys who toss that little white pill around will love you for that.)

18. Don't work without proper equipment.

(Make sure you are well protected from all possible injuries. A foul tip could ruin an umpire's career and possibly his life.)

19. Don't hold idle conversations with players or coaches.
    (Anybody can talk a good game. It is the umpire who umpires a good game who goes up the ladder. Besides after listening to your chatter, the coach or player invariably goes back to the bench and remarks, "What a barber that guy is.")

20. Don't stand on a dime.
    (Try to be a step ahead of the players on every play. Be on top of your plays. Keep the ball game moving by hustling the players but keep hustling yourself.)

21. Don't call your plays on the run.
    (Hustle over to a base on a play — take up a stationary position when giving your decision. But get over to the right spot in a hurry.)

22. Don't fail to call interference plays immediately.
    (When you call a runner out for running more than three feet from a direct line to avoid being touched by the ball in the hands of a fielder, call it quickly and don't keep it a secret. You will be in a predicament if you wait for a team to protest and then decide the runner ran out of line. *BEAT 'EM ALL TO THE PUNCH.*)

23. Don't fail to expect the unexpected.
    (Figure out plays in advance. What might happen? What could happen? Keep your head out of the stands. Regardless of the score, stay in that ball game.)

24. Don't forget you represent America's National Game.
    (This goes for on and off the ball field. Remember, despite the jibes, the mob scenes or the unkind things they say about the "Boys in Blue," despite the thankless job it is, all umpires are proud to the core of their jobs and their 100 years' record for honesty and integrity.)

25. Don't kid yourself.
    (And I'll leave that one to you.)

INSTRUCTION NO. 5

Umpire in Chief

The umpire behind the plate has the sole power to forfeit a game. He is responsible largely for the conduct of the game. He shall rule on batting out-of-order plays. The plate umpire shall see to it that ground rules are covered before the game starts. He shall call all infield flies. He also calls all interference calls at the plate. He decides whether or not a runner remains within the three foot line in running the last half of the distance to first base.

The umpire working behind the plate when two umpires are teamed or when three men are working a game, is the chief umpire for that particular game.

In organized baseball, all umpires alternate in working behind the plate. For instance, when three men are working together, Umpire Jones is behind the plate in the game of Monday, he will work at third base on Tuesday and at first base on Wednesday. Umpire Smith who worked at third base on Monday, goes to first base on Tuesday, and behind the plate on Wednesday. Umpire Brown who worked at first base on Monday goes to the plate on Tuesday and to third base on Wednesday. With the double umpire system, the umpires work the same way, simply alternating each game.

When rain or darkness is the cause of time being called. The plate umpire shall be the judge, as to the fitness of the grounds for play, once the game has been started.

Fitness of Field for Play

If it is raining before the start of a game: The home manager or captain shall be the sole judge of the fitness of the field for starting a game. The umpire or visiting manager has no vote in the matter. However, once the game has started, and play has been called by the umpire, the latter becomes the sole judge as to whether or not the ground is fit to continue playing.

When it has been raining during the first game of a double header, and the question arises as to whom falls the authority of starting the second game regarding the fitness of the field for play, there are many who are of the belief the home manager has the matter in his hands.

The chief umpire for the second game determines whether the field is fit for play or not.

You will hear it said hundreds of times, "You cannot start a game in the rain." Disregard the remark entirely, for it may be raining pretty hard when the game is about to start. The home manager decides the fitness of the field of play. If he says, "the grounds are all right, let's start the game," play begins. Then the chief umpire has full charge from that point.

Single Umpire System

With a lone umpire handling the game it is a difficult job. He is called upon to be all over the field. Certainly he cannot be in two different parts of the diamond at the same time. He simply is compelled to do his best.

He starts off behind the plate. If the batter hits a fly ball, move into the infield, watch fielder complete the catch. Take a look at the runner rounding first base to see that he touches the bag.

If there is a possibility, he might continue on to second base on a dropped fly ball. When you come into the infield continue toward second base until you come to a spot about half way between the pitcher's box and the bag.

When working behind the plate, and the batter hits safely to the outfield it is wise to run between the pitcher's box and first base to a spot about twenty feet to the home plate side of second base. In this manner you watch the runner tag first base, and are ahead of him if he continues on to second.

In the event the batter hits for extra bases, get out into the center of the diamond, watch him tag the bases, and then hustle to the base where the play is finally made. From fifteen to twenty feet from the base is a dandy position to take on base plays.

Don't get too close to a base when a runner is sliding into a bag or the plate. The dust in many cases could hide the play from your view. Get the proper angle and the dust will not bother you in the least.

With a runner on first base only, stand behind the pitcher. You will then be in a good position for an attempted steal of second base.

In practically every other situation it is best to stand behind the plate, if the bases are filled, or with runners on first and third or second and third. Behind the plate is the spot.

If you happen to be working behind the pitcher and the batter hits a ball over the first or third base bag. To begin with you are out of position. Do the best you can. Scamper over to the foul line as near as possible, line up the play, call it as you see it.

If you are behind the plate and the batter hits a long drive to right field that may fall near the foul line, go down the line on the run to get as close to the place where the ball strikes the ground as you possibly can. The closer you are the better. Besides giving you a better vision it shows that you are hustling, trying to get them right.

Base Umpire — Double System

At the beginning of an inning the base umpire takes his position about twenty feet beyond first base, and about two feet in foul ground. American League umpires try to place themselves on all plays in fair territory.

The first batter hits a ground ball to the third baseman. Starting from your position 15 to 20 feet beyond the bag in foul ground, dash into the diamond. Take up the position that gives you the best angle on the play.

Keep your eye on the third baseman until he releases the throw to first. Allow the ball to come in direction over your right shoulder. Make sure you are not in line of the throw. Watch the feet of the first baseman, if he comes off the bag or not. Watch for the runner's feet. Listen to the thud of the ball as it strikes the first baseman's glove. If you hear the sound of the ball contacting the glove before the runner's foot touches the base, you know he is out. This plan works wonders when the play is close.

Watch for the juggled ball. See that the runner's foot actually gets to the bag.

On balls hit to the shortstop, take up your position the same way, and make sure you do not come in line of the throw.

In other words don't go into the diamond quite as far as you do on the play — third to first.

On balls hit over the bag and fielded by the second baseman, or balls hit directly at the second baseman, take up your position in the same manner. Do not go into the diamond too far. Keep out of the line of the throw, but call the play from the infield.

When the second baseman comes over near first base for a ground ball and it is apparent you may be struck by the ball on his throw, keep out of the diamond. Move up the line in foul ground about five feet beyond the bag. The right field side of the bag.

On all batted balls to the outfield. Start running from your original position toward second base, keeping well ahead of the runner, at the same time watching to see if he touches the bag or not. If he continues on to second, head for the best possible place to judge the play.

After each runner has rounded first base and it is apparent he might stretch the hit into a triple; as he goes into second, the umpire should cut short and head for third base. Be ahead of the runner by about twenty feet, on the infield side of the base line, so that you will not obstruct the runner in any way. Take up a stationary position about 20 feet from the bag in fair ground.

In working double, and a runner on second base. The base umpire should stand about half way between the pitchers' box and second base. Of course not in a direct line, because the pitcher might make a snap throw to pick the runner off, and hit you with the ball.

If a left-hand pitcher is on the rubber with a runner on second, stand about ten feet to the right of the box, or almost in front of the runner in the crouched position.

With a right-hand pitcher working take your place about ten feet to the left of the box.

The reason you move to the right side or the left side when a righthander or southpaw is on the rubber, is to keep out of the batter's line of vision. Otherwise, the pitcher would actually be pitching out of your white shirt, which greatly hampers a batter. The background means the utmost in importance to a hitter.

Roman Bentz, Pacific Coast League Umpire lifting
"Johnny" of Phillip Morris.

INSTRUCTION NO. 6

There are some umpires, when discussing their vocation, who are referred to as "trick play crazy". These fellows seem to dwell upon digging up weird, unusual plays that seldom come up in a ball game. For that reason many novice umpires come to the conclusion that knowing the answer to near impossible plays is the prime factor in being a good umpire. While it is essential to be able to meet any situation that may develop on a ball field, knowing the answers to this type of problem does not necessarily indicate the caliber of an umpire.

Thomas H. Connolly, chief umpire of the American League, and a former "comrade in blue," never had a superior when it came to technicalities in the rules of baseball. Billy Evans, my choice of the nearest to perfect umpire, was another marvel on tearing the rules apart and putting them together, but both Connolly and Evans years ago discovered the fact that the majority of widely discussed "tough decisions" seldom, if ever, happen. They learned that those plays, which the "smart alecs" concocted, never happened on the playing field, but were conceived at some "fireside league" meeting during the winter. As Connolly often has discussed this matter, I will try to give you his version of the umpire: "The man in blue is called upon to render decisions by the thousands, giving his answers instantly, with a snap judgment that must be correct, for close plays, as a rule, are vital and play a major part in deciding a ball game. When a technical point of rules is involved the umpire is expected to give his decision in the twinkling of an eyelash. As a matter of contrast, consider the learned Judge, with a brilliant mind, sitting on the bench of his court, when the facts and the evidence have been summed up, has been known to proclaim: 'I will take the evidence and facts under advisement, and I will render my decision Tuesday of next week.'"

Every Day Problems

The point I am trying to put over with the young and inexperienced umpires is this—concentrate on your rules and the fundamentals of umpiring.

It's good for the umpire's soul if he knows all the answers to knotty problems, but remember, he could know all the rules in the book and all trick-play answers, and still not be recognized as a good umpire.

I have never known an arbiter who was "trick play crazy" who has ever reached the major leagues. Do not misunderstand — master the rules, and dope out the solutions to unusual plays but, when they border on the ridiculous, ignore them.

I have prepared a list of problems that could happen in any ball game. To the regular umpire, these are known as "Every Day Problems."

Let's go.

1. Runner on third base and one out. Batter lifts a fly ball to the centerfield. Runner on third tags up and starts for home as the ball touches the fielder's hands. The fielder, however, allowed the ball to pop out of his hands but recovered it before striking the ground. The ball was thrown to third base where a claim was made to the umpire that runner left the bag too soon. Runner left the bag we will say while fielder was recovering the ball.
   (Give your decision and reason for same.)

2. Home team is leading 6 to 4 at end of 8th inning. In the first half of the ninth, the visiting team made three runs, to take a lead of 7 to 6. In last half of the ninth the home team has scored one run, and one man is retired, when rain falls. The umpire waited thirty minutes then called the game.
   (What was the final score?)

3. In the same situation, suppose the home team failed to score and two men had been retired when umpire called the game.
   (What was the final score?)

4. Batter hits a ball that strikes the ground six inches to the rear of home plate which is foul territory and rebounds into fair territory. The pitcher fielded the ball in fair ground and threw to first base, and the base umpire declared the runner out at the bag.
   (Was it a fair or foul ball? Why?)

5. With a runner on second base batter hits a ground ball which is fielded by the first baseman, who walks toward the plate to tag the runner coming down the line, at same time keeping his eye on the runner who is on second base. The runner going to first base stops and retraces his steps, the first baseman follows him with the ball in his hands.
   (How shall runner be retired other than being tagged, the ball being thrown to first base, or by running around the first baseman?)

6. Batsman hits ball over the left field fence. Just prior to the ball leaving the playing field, the left fielder threw his glove at the ball, hit it, but ball continued over the fence.
   (What is the proper decision?)

7. On the same play, suppose the ball when deflected by the glove did not go over the fence but was picked up by the outfielder and returned to the infield, holding the runner at second base.
   (Give correct ruling.)

8. A manager sends a pinch hitter up to the plate with two runners on the bases and he hits for three bases. Neither the manager nor the pinch hitter announced the substitution to the umpire.
   (What happens?)

9. A runner on first starts to steal second base. The catcher's throw to second was high. The second baseman throws his glove and strikes the ball.
   (What ruling?)

10. Runner on first base. Batter hits a long fly ball to left centerfield. Runner on first rounded second base and went half way to third. Center fielder made a great catch and wonderful return throw. Before the runner could get back to second base the shortstop took the throw-in and stepped on the bag.
    (Give correct ruling.)

11. Runner on third base — one out. Batter hits a fly ball to the right fielder. Runner tags up. Third baseman places himself in direct line of vision and before the catch is made deliberately sways his body from side to side, thus in great measure blocking the runner's view.
    (What action should umpire take?)

12. Runners on second and third. Catcher picks runner off third and rundown play follows between third and home. Finally, catcher chases runner back to third base. In the meantime runner from second comes over and both runners are standing on third base.
    (How should play be executed for umpire to declare an out?)

13. Same play — with both runners are standing on third base, catcher tagged the man whom he ran back to third base.
    (Which runner is out?)

14. Same play — while both runners are standing on the bag, the catcher tags the runner who came over from second base.
    (Who is out?)

15. Same play — catcher tags both runners while they are standing on third base.
    (Which runner is out?)

16. Same play — catcher tags both runners standing on third base. The

runner whom he chased back to third base then walks off the bag and catcher tags him a second time.
(What is proper decision?)

17. One out — runner on third base comes home on a fly ball to left field after properly tagging up. He failed to touch home plate, missing it by several inches. The catcher being alert noticed what happened.
(What should be done by catcher if runner had continued to dugout?)

18. Runners on first and second bases. Pitcher makes a balk. Base umpire called the balk and advanced both runners one base.
(Was ruling correct?)

19. Runners on first and third. Pitcher steps toward third base coming off rubber, then quickly turns and picks the runner off first base, for the second out of an inning.
(A balk or not a balk?)

20. With first and second bases occupied and one out, the batter bunts a short fly ball to the second baseman, who dropped the ball all three runners advancing to fill the bases.
(What should be the correct ruling?)

Bill McGowan and Tommy Richardson, President, Eastern League

INSTRUCTION NO. 7

Aces for Umpires

Always keep the Golden Rule in mind. If a manager or player wants to give you his version of some technical point that may be involved in a ruling, lend an ear. As long as he doesn't abuse you, show him the courtesy of listening to his side of the matter. However, that does not mean that you are to allow a manager or player to hold up the game while he tries to convince you that you erred in your ruling.

If a player or manager becomes nasty in his remarks while arguing his point, warn him, and if he continues to show you up or abuse you with his remarks, oust him from the game.

Don't be too quick on the trigger. Give the boys a chance, a reasonable chance, to present their arguments. After all, if there were no kicks registered, there wouldn't be need for umpires.

Umpires are necessary evils. If the game could be played with the same spirit by players and fans, without umpires, you can readily see that it would be done.

Naturally, the fellow with the most ability, common sense and good judgment goes to the top. (Of course a good background and character are vital factors.)

No matter what league you are working in at present, don't become too intimate with the players. It is fine to have them like you; in fact, it is the players who either make or break an umpire. But the umpire who can make them like you and still respect you, is the man who succeeds in the art of umpiring. Make them respect and like you by showing you have the courage of your convictions, your hustling attitude on the field, your knowledge of the rules, by using good judgment, and by giving civil replies to their questions concerning different points of the game.

Remember, the umpire whose main forte is smiling or grinning his way through, or by constantly jabbering with players, or by pulling gags and "yessing" them out there, isn't kidding anybody but himself.

You can't kid the ball players. It's my personal opinion that ball players are one of the smartest groups of men when it comes to knowing their profession.

Everyday Problems

These questions pertaining to positions of umpires in reference to double umpire system.

-o-

21. Runner on first base. Batter singles to right field. Runner on first goes all the way to third. Man who hit the ball tries for second base on throw to third.
(Place umpires in position.)

22. Runners on first and second. Batter hit to shortstop who pegged to third baseman, the latter stepped on the bag and then threw to first base.
(Place umpires in position.)

23. Runners on first and second. Batter singles to right field. Runner who was on second came home standing up as fielder threw to third base. The runner who was on first base went to third and man who hit the ball went to second.
(Place umpires in position.)

24. Runners on first and second. Batter singles to right field. Fielder throws home but throw is late and catcher taking the throw pegs down to third in attempt to get runner who came around from first base.
(Place umpires in position.)

25. Runners on first and third. One man out. Batter hits fly ball to centerfield. Both runners tag up and try to advance.
(Place umpires in position.)

26. Runners on first and second. Batter hits fly ball to right fielder with one man out. Both runners tag up and try to advance.
(Place umpires in position.)

27. Runner on third base and one out. Score 3 to 2 in favor of team on defense. Batter lifts fly ball to left fielder. Infield plays half-way.
(Place umpires in position.)

28. Runner on third base and one out. Score 10 to 1 in favor of defensive team. This situation calls for defense to play in their regular spots. In other words they play back in regular positions.
(Place umpires in position.)

29. Runner on third base — one out. Score 2 to 1 in favor of defensive team. Infield in to cut off run at plate. Batter hits to third baseman who picks up the ball and throws home. Runner going home pulls up half way home. Run down play takes place.
(Name proper way to handle the situation.)

30. Runners on first and second. Batter singles to centerfield. Runner on second misses third base on way to the plate. Ball is thrown to third base and claim is made to umpires.
(Well, what about it? Sure, but which Umpire?)

31. Runners on first and second. Batter singles to centerfield. As runner who was on second is rounding third base, he is bumped by third baseman, knocking him off his stride.
(How would you rule the play? Which umpire should call the play?)

32. Let's say Gehrig is the batter and Lary is on first base. Two out. Gehrig hits a long drive into the centerfield bleachers but ball rebounds into the field of play, and centerfielder Rice caught ball on the rebound. Lary thinking the ball did not go into the bleachers, takes a look as he rounds third base, and sees Rice catch the ball and throw back to infield. Lary then almost half way home, runs direct to his dugout, which is on the third base side. Gehrig rounds bases and touches the plate.
(What happens?)

33. Batter hits a line drive to second baseman with a runner on first base and one out. Second baseman takes ball cleanly at his belt line, but seeing batter has given up, he takes the ball to his ankles and then spreads his hands letting it drop to ground. Picking up ball quickly, he tosses to the shortstop who steps on second and throws to first base.
(Would you allow the double play or call the batter out on legal catch?)

34. Runners on first and third. Pitcher standing on the rubber turns to throw to first base but does not throw the ball. The base umpire called a balk and advanced the man on third home, and sent the runner on first to second base.
(Was decision correct?)

35. With runners on first and second. Nobody out. Batter bunts a pop fly to the pitcher who was under it, but dropped the ball. Picking it up he threw to first base but too late to get runner. First baseman then threw home to catch runner who was on second attempting to score.
(What about it?)

36. With the pitcher standing on the rubber Gehrig, a left hand batsman, turns around right-handed style. He changed from one batter's box to the other before pitcher threw a ball.
(What's your ruling?)

37. We will say Ruffing starts the fourth inning by walking the batter. A heavy left-handed hitter is now at the plate. Gomez comes in to relieve

Ruffing. He pitched one ball, then picked the runner off first base for the first out of the inning. At this point it is decided to pitch Pearson. (Is this permissible under the rules?)

38. DiMaggio on third base one out and Rolfe flashed the squeeze play sign. On the pitch DiMaggio was off for the plate. Catcher Hemsley jumps in front of the plate preventing the batter from hitting ball. Hemsley caught the ball and tagged DiMaggio sliding into the plate. (Make decision — explain reason for same.)

39. Runner on third and one out. Runner attempts to steal home, batter interferes with catcher, preventing him from tagging the runner as he slides around and reaches the plate with his hand. (Make decision.)

40. Base umpire calls runner out sliding into second on attempted steal. Runner jumps up and pushed umpire. Umpire ordered player out of the game. Player refuses to leave playing field. Argument continues for three or four minutes. After warnings to the manager of offensive team, the base umpire forfeited the game to defensive team. (Was situation handled correctly or incorrectly? Explain how you would handle the situation.)

41. Runner attempts to steal second base. Umpire decides he is out on close play. Runner throws his cap on the ground. (What action would you take?)

42. Runner on first, batter bunts toward third base. Third baseman fields ball and throws to second where play was close. Field umpire calls runner safe. Shortstop who took the throw, hollers on decision and throws the ball on the ground. (What action would you take?)

43. Bases are loaded. One out. Score tied. Infield playing half way. (Place umpire on bases in position.)

44. Bases loaded. One out. Infield playing back. Right hand pitcher on mound. (Where does field umpire stand?)

45. Bases loaded one out. Infield playing back. Left hand pitcher on rubber. (Where would you stand?)

46. Runners on second and third. One out. Score tied. Infield playing half way. (Where would you stand?)

47. Gomez pitching. First man up walks.
(Place field umpire in position.)

48. Gomez pitching with runner on first base. Second man up singles. Runners are now on first and third.
(Place field umpire in position.)

49. Ruffing pitching. First man up walks.
(Place field umpire in position.)

50. Ruffing pitching. Runner on first base. Next batter singles advancing runner on first to second base.
(Place field umpire in position.)

51. Grove pitching. Gehringer on first. Greenberg hits swinging bunt down first base line. Grove runs over picks up ball and stabs at Hank on his way to first.
(Who makes decision and what should alert umpire watch for in this case?)

52. Newsom pitching. Foxx at bat. Cramer on second base. Count on Foxx is 3 to 2. Cramer starts to steal third base but Newsom makes a balk, so declared by umpire.
(What happens?)

53. Runner on third base. Pitcher on rubber takes sign from catcher then starts his windup. Runner on third makes bluff to go home, confusing the pitcher, who drops his arms and steps back off the rubber?
(What's what?)

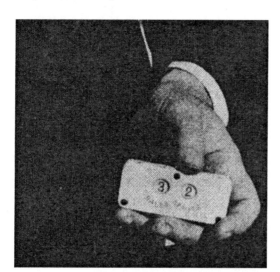

Umpire's indicator for balls and strikes

INSTRUCTION NO. 8

Triple Umpire System

Many sandlot umpires have never worked a game with three umpires on the job. In fact, there are some who have never seen three umpires in a ball game.

In the American League, we start off with the chief umpire for the day behind home plate. The two assistants take up their positions at first and third bases. At the beginning of a series of games, the three umpires go to home plate for the conference on ground rules. We allow the chief umpire to do the talking, his assistants stand by and listen. After the first day of a series has gone by, the three umpires walk to home plate as a sort of a reporting station, but do not hang around but go direct to their positions at first and third bases from that spot.

If the first batter up gets on, the umpire working at third base moves over to a spot about twenty-five feet beyond second base and toward right center field. This keeps him out of the outfield, and prevents in a measure his chances of becoming mixed up in a play, giving the players more opportunity to move around in the vicinity of the bag. The umpire working at first base, simply comes up the line from his regular position about ten feet. You are then in perfect position for those pick off plays at first base. If the second batter also gets on, placing men on first and second, the umpire at second moves over to third base, while the first base umpire moves to a spot behind the pitcher. In case a right-hand pitcher is working, the spot is about 30 feet or a trifle more behind the pitcher on the left side. You will be standing almost on a direct line between the second baseman and the pitcher. If a left-hander is on the mound, you shift to the other side, standing almost in front of the runner after he takes his lead. If the third man gets on filling the bases, you only shift position behind the pitcher according to whether he is left-handed or right-handed. With three men on and the infield plays in close, move to a spot behind the shortstop, get out of the infield.

Flashes

Don't pull your rule book out of your pocket on the ball field. Leave the rule book in your grip or bag in the dressing room. The ball players will run you crazy reaching for that book on every other play. You're running the game, make 'em abide by your decisions. The manager always has the privilege of entering a protest of the game, when a rule is violated. However, a game cannot be protested on a decision of judgment.

Don't be pulling your watch every other argument either. That is poor policy. Most of it is bluff on the umpire's part, and it doesn't bring the desired effect, nine times out of ten.

Every time a runner reaches first base — the umpire behind the plate should repeat the rule to himself, "If first base be occupied with less than two out, and the catcher drops the third strike, the umpire shall immediately declare the batter out."

By continually repeating this rule to yourself every time a man reaches first base, it will eventually come to your mind all in a flash. Thereafter you do not have to repeat the rule, the flash in your mind covers the situation.

Every time runners reach first and second bases, repeat to yourself the rule, covering the infield fly.

The same principle applies here. By continually repeating the rule, your mind becomes so accustomed to it, that after awhile, you simply see that first and second are occupied, "the flash" and everything is under control.

On the Bases

When working the bases. Try and develop your own mannerisms.

Strike on a motion for indicating a runner is "out."

Some umpires call runners out by pointing skyward. Some use the closed fist with the thumb extended and wave the arm over the right shoulder. Others close the fist and sort of punch the out.

At any rate on plays that are close, be emphatic, make your motion in a decisive manner that leaves no doubt as to the correctness of your judgment.

An umpire who calls a runner out on a tight play, by meekly waving a finger or two, or by slight wave of the hand, immediately places a doubt in the ball player's mind. The fans incidentally get the same impression.

Of course, when a runner is out by ten to twenty feet, everybody knows he's out, and the calisthenics do not count for much.

The correct motion for calling a player safe, is to extend the arms, palms down.

Never call a runner safe by using one hand. This gives the impression you are tired, lazy, and possibly in doubt.

On close plays, hustle over to the bag, get the proper angle, be ahead of the play. Crouch down and spread those palms as though you would stake life on that decision.

When calling a decision on a runner at the plate, always snap off your mask. The same idea is a good one on outfield drives or flies that fall near the foul line.

The umpire in chief determines if an infield fly can be handled by an infielder.

In the American League the umpires do not call an infield fly, when the infielder runs toward the outfield with his back to home plate.

Be alive out there on the field. When changing your position, jump around, run, don't walk.

Put a little color in your work. But not too much color.

Joe DiMaggio with instructors, 1948 class
West Palm Beach, Fla.

INSTRUCTION NO. 9

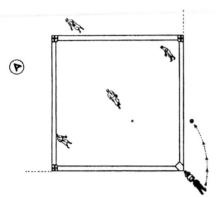

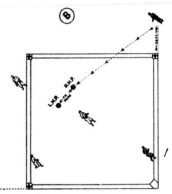

Between innings the umpire should move to a spot about 20 feet to the right of the catcher if the opposing batman is coming up from the third base side, or dugout. In the next change of sides, he should go to a spot about 20 feet to the left of the catcher. This eliminates the unnecessary gabbing with the batters.

As soon as the warm up is completed, sweep off the home plate, and take up your position behind the catcher.

Beginning an inning or with bases occupied the base umpire should take up his position about 20 feet beyond first base and about two feet in foul ground.

If the batter reaches first base. The umpire should stand about thirty feet behind the pitcher, and from 5 to 10 feet either to his right or left.

With left hand pitcher he stands on the shortstop side. With right hand pitcher he stands on second baseman side.

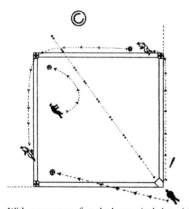

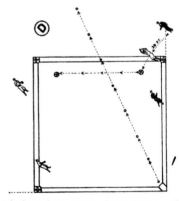

With a runner on first the batter singled to right field. The runner on first went to third and on the throw in to third base, the man who hit the ball tried for second. The plate umpire should cover the play at third. The base umpire watches the runner touch first base, then cuts into position for a play at second base.

Nobody on base. Batman hits safely to outfield. Umpire should cut into the diamond about 30 feet watch runner touch first base, and keep eyes open for interference. He should continue ahead of the runner for his position at second base, in the event the runner tries to stretch hit into a double.

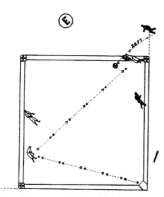

Batter hits ground ball to third baseman or short-stop. The umpire should dash into the infield to a spot about 15 or 20 feet away from the bag. Allowing the thrown ball to come over his right shoulder. The umpire of course shall not place himself in line with the throw by any means.

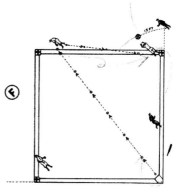

Batter hits to right of second baseman near the bag, or directly at the second baseman in his position. The umpire should not go in so far this time. He must not place himself in line of the throw. He can very nicely take his position and have perfect angle on the play, by cutting into fair gound between 15 and 20 feet.

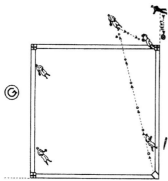

When second baseman comes over close to first base to field the ball, the umpire should under the circumstances, come up the line about 12 to 15 feet. Standing about four or five feet in foul ground.

His chances of being struck by the thrown ball are cut down considerably. Were he to take this play in fair ground the second baseman might possibly collide with the umpire.

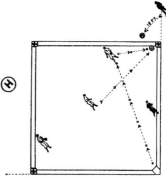

Batter drag bunts or pushes ball to right of first baseman, who fields the ball. The pitcher runs to cover the bag.

The umpire so as not to interfere with the pitcher nor the toss from the first baseman to the pitcher, should go into fair ground about 15 feet. This keeps him in the clear, and gives him a perfect view of the play.

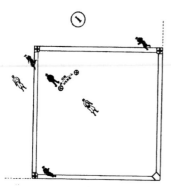

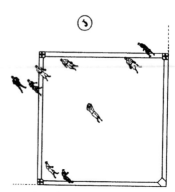

With runner on first — runners on first and second — or runners on first, second and third. Umpire should stand about thirty feet behind the pitcher, ten or fifteen feet to either side, according to right or left hand pitcher.

With bases filled, infield playing in, or playing half way, umpire should take up position behind the runner on second and the shortstop.

With runners on second and third, the infield playing in to cut off the run at the plate, the umpire should take the same position behind the shortstop.

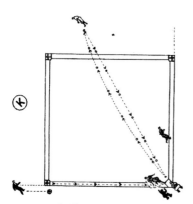

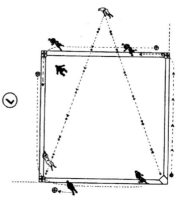

Runner on third base less than two out. Batter hits fly ball to right field. Runner on third tags up and goes home.

Third base umpire standing in regular position 15 to 20 feet beyond third base and two feet in foul ground, moves up to a spot even with the bag in foul ground, where he lines up play.

Had batter hit ground ball to an infielder instead of to outfield and play was made to first base, the umpire from his regular position beyond third would be forced to hustle through the diamond for play at first.

Runners on first and second. Batter singles to right field. Runner on second scores standing up as play was made to third base.

Plate umpire hustles down to third, watches the runner from second touch third base and also home plate, and gives decision on runner who went from first to third.

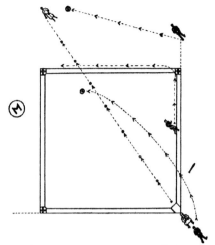

Batter hits line drive up right centerfield. Outfielder makes attempt at shoestring catch. Base umpire should run into outfield, get proper angle, to see if ball was trapped or caught cleanly.

Plate umpire should watch batter touch first base, and he should dash down to second base for possible play while his partner is hustling in the outfield.

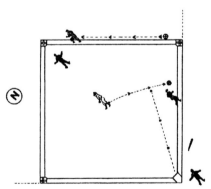

With base umpire forced to work from behind the pitcher it is utterly impossible for him to see pitcher field bunt and attempt touching the runner with the ball going down to first base.

The plate umpire should take command of this situation. He can determine whether pitcher tagged the runner, whether runner avoided the touch. Whether runner ran more than three feet out of direct line to avoid being touched, or for interference. Plate umpire should make decision on such plays with demonstration.

INSTRUCTION NO. 10

Follow the Ten Little Umpires

The question is often asked, "What are the requirements of a good umpire?"

In baseball circles they say, "all the good umpires are dead ones."

Be that as it may, there have been great umpires and there will be more great umpires.

There are ten important essentials that make up a good umpire. Without these characteristics an umpire will not go far toward success.

Always keep close with these "ten little umpires." Have them by your side and on your mind, constantly, and by making them your pals, and being able to carry out their plans you hardly can miss making the grade to the top.

1st Little Umpire
Honesty

In the history of baseball the finger of suspicion has never been pointed at an umpire. We are very proud of that fact. Woe to the man who ever enters the profession and falters.

There isn't an umpire in organized baseball, past or present, since the game began 100 years ago, who cannot stand the acid test of honesty, one hundred percent. There are a great number of them who would willingly give up their lives rather than go the other way.

That has always been the tradition of the men in blue. Remember well, it should always be thus.

2nd Little Umpire
Common Sense

The successful umpire must apply sound common sense. Sound judgment. Practical baseball "horse sense."

In other words, umpiring a game is more than just reading the rules and throwing your hands to indicate safe or out. There are scores of plays which demand a common sense ruling, and under these conditions the rule book is not of much help.

Remember, don't go on the field with *rabbit ears*. If you hear every remark they holler at you from the bench you will be in hot water constantly.

3rd Little Umpire
Loyalty

When you step out in that ball field, always keep in mind you owe the game of baseball your utmost loyalty. You must be loyal to your position, and also your partners. At any cost never let them down.

Keep in mind the remark passed by the famous Bill Klem that he doesn't umpire for the National League or the American League although he has spent 38 years in the majors as an umpire. "He umpires for that little white pill, the great American apple."

When the inimitable Klem was presented with a placque at the New York Sporting Writers' banquet, in 1938, tribute was paid to his being one of the greatest umpires who ever lived.

Klem accepted the honor with the statement that is was on behalf of all arbiters.

He closed his remarks with another vital statement, "Umpiring is a religion with me."

4th Little Umpire
Courage

For courageous umpires, they broke the mould after they made George Moriarty. Take a leaf from Moriarty's book. Another great umpire to follow.

There never was a successful umpire without courage.

Regardless of how these plays look to players, fans or the press box, it is absolutely necessary that the umpire call 'em as he sees 'em.

As for the tough spots. When the followers of the home team are howling and threatening, when that close play pops in the pinch, "call it as you see it." You must have the courage of your convictions, or you won't stand up.

The umpire who "evens up on a decision," seldom goes beyond the first year out.

The fellow known to the trade as a "homer", (deciding the close ones in favor of the home team) is the most unpopular umpire, and he will not make the grade.

5th Little Umpire
Ability

Without ability to use good judgment and common sense the road will be hard and long, and this kind of umpire should not make an attempt at organized baseball.

Study the rules, master them. Learn the fundamentals of umpiring. Apply them on the field. Some fellows are major league umpires in the corner drug store or in a hotel lobby.

Boys if there is one job in this good country that demands a person to stand on his own feet, it is the man in blue in baseball.

To secure the necessary experience, you must umpire ball games. Get all the work you can. Keep trying to improve.

Take good care of *your eyes.*

6th Little Umpire
Character

A good character is essential to all professions, and in practically all walks of life. In the umpiring profession, it is paramount.

Avoid all places of gambling, and all forms of gambling, (we do not refer to a friendly fame of cards.)

Watch your associates. You can never live down that past.

They never hire men as umpires with a poor background.

7th Little Umpire
Honor

You are always on your honor twenty four hours a day when you once don that blue uniform. Be honorable to your profession. Be proud of it every minute!

Never carry a grudge from one game to another. If you have a feud with a player or manager today, be honorable enough to consider his cause. "He was fighting to win." You are big enough to take it. You are compelled to take the bitter with the sweet.

If you want the ball players to respect you, treat them with respect.

Never pan a brother umpire.

8th Little Umpire
Fair Play

Billy Evans, and there never was a better umpire in my estimation, told me years ago, that I should always bear in mind that baseball is built on two words, "Common sense and fair play."

Whenever you are stumped on a technical point, and rules do not cover the play thoroughly, base your decision on common sense and fair play. You won't go far wrong.

9th Little Umpire
Intelligence

An umpire must have the intelligence to interpret the rules properly and execute them.

He is expected to make out reports of serious incidents, that arise on the ball field, and relate them to his League President in a clear, sensible manner.

Your League President does not see all the games. Consequently, "you are his eyes." You must place the picture before him of the trouble on the field, as it happened.

You should not be hard on the players one day and easy the next. Cultivate an even disposition.

Remember a courteous remark will take you out of a lot of trouble on the ball field. The wise retort, as a rule puts you in deeper.

10th Little Umpire
Hustle

Always try to be a step ahead of the players. Hustle is the most valuable word in baseball. It is the least expensive.

With the first pitch of the ball game, get in there and bear down. Be on top of your plays, make your decisions with determination. Be alert. Take nothing for granted.

Whenever possible watch major league umpires in action.

The ball players make or break an umpire. If you are a hustler, they will love you for it, and hustling covers a multitude of sins.

Among the American League umpires, three of the best hustlers I've seen in more than ten years are Johnny Quinn, Bill Grieve, and Cal Hubbard. Their main forte is hustle.

Here's hoping you fellows will always hustle.

ANSWERS TO QUESTIONS — EVERY DAY PROBLEMS IN INSTRUCTIONS 6 AND 7

(These answers are listed numerically to correspond with questions.)

1. The runner must of course tag up and the instant the ball touches the fielder's hands, he may advance. In case the ball is juggled or pops from one fielder's hands to the hands of another fielder, the runner goes the moment ball touches hands of the fielder the first time, or touches the person of the fielder.

2. The final score was 7 to 7. Because when the team second at bat scored in the incompleted inning, the same number of runs.

3. The game reverts back to the last equal inning played. The correct score would be 6 to 4, in favor of the home team.

4. It was a fair ball. Because it settled on fair ground between home and first or home and third, without having struck an object in foul ground.

5. The runner can be retired if he runs more than three feet out of a direct line, to avoid being touched by the ball in the hands of a fielder. He may also be retired by the first baseman, if he, the runner, in retracing his steps goes back over the plate one step, (which is more than three feet.)

6. It is a home run. We shall not take anything away from the batsman, on a ball that has been driven out of the playing field.

7. In this instance, the umpire waits until the play is completed. He then awards the runner three bases, which would place the man who hit the ball on third base.

8. The play goes as made. The manager who failed to make announcement to the umpire, shall be fined $25.00 in league baseball.

9. The runner who was on first when the pitch was made is entitled to third base when the fielder threw his glove and struck the ball.

10. The runner is safe. The ball must be thrown to first base, the base the runner originally occupied, tagged with the ball.

11. The umpire shall award the runner on third base the right to score. (This act is seldom pulled in baseball, but now and then it occurs. It

has been called in the American League three times by the writer.) The third baseman is obstructing the runner from advancing. Consequently should be penalized.

12. While both runners are standing on third base. The catcher should tag the runner who came from second base, or touch them both, while they are standing on the bag. The man from behind is always out.

13. Neither runner is out. Catcher tagged wrong man.

14. The runner who came from second base is out, when tagged by catcher, if both were standing on the bag at same time.

15. The man who came from second base is out.

16. Both runners are out.

17. The catcher should appeal to the umpire and touch home plate with the ball in his possession. The umpire should immediately declare the runner out.

18. The decision was correct. Base umpire has equal authority in calling balks with the chief umpire.

19. It is not a balk. He doesn't have to complete his throw to third base. Once off the rubber, he is in the same category as an infielder.

20. The three men are safe. A bunted ball is never an infield fly.

21. Plate umpire runs down to position within twenty feet of third base. Field umpire covers play at second base.

22. Field umpire calls both plays. Sizing up the play as it is made he should not move too close to third base.

23. The plate umpire runs down to within twenty feet of third base to make possible decision, on the runner coming from first base. Field umpire covers play at second base. (Plate umpire while making his move to third base, should watch the runner touch home plate.)

24. In this instance, field umpire must take the play at third base, as plate umpire cannot leave his station while a play is on.

25. Plate umpire moves half way down toward third to get proper angle on runner leaving bag with the catch. He then makes a quick move to get into position for play at the plate. Field umpire watches runner tagging up at first base, and takes possible play at second base.

26. Plate umpire comes out into the infield and toward third base to watch runner on second tag up, and then make possible decision at third base. Base umpire covers the runner on first base.

27. Base umpire moves up from his regular position 15 or 20 feet beyond the bag, to a spot in foul ground behind the runner, so as to line up proper angle of the play. The base umpire watches runner leave the bag with the catch. Plate umpire remains in regular position.

28. The base umpire under these conditions, whereby the defensive team is giving their opponents the run, and have elected to try for the out at first base, should take up his position behind the pitcher.

29. After the ball is thrown home, catcher naturally starts running toward the runner. Plate umpire should be right at catcher's heels, taking the play all the way, while the base umpire covers the runner going into first and possibly into second base.

30. The umpire behind the plate shall make the decision on this play. Whenever more than one runner is traveling the bases, the plate umpire should move into the infield or toward third base, to watch runners rounding the bag.

31. The plate umpire again decides the play. He allows the runner to score.

32. Gehrig is declared out for passing a preceding baserunner. No runs score.

33. Batter is out. It was a purposely dropped ball. Umpire declares same at once.

34. Again the base umpire has right to call a balk. He advanced the runners properly.

35. Never an infield fly on a bunted ball. All hands are safe.

36. Gehrig is out. Because he stepped from one batsman's box to the other while the pitcher was in position ready to pitch.

37. Gomez must continue to pitch to the batsman until he has been retired, or he has reached first base.

38. This is a balk and an interference — DiMaggio scores on the balk, and Rolfe goes to first base on the interference.

39. The runner on third is out if interference took place with less than two out. If two men are out, the batsman is declared out.

40. The umpire was wrong. The chief umpire has the sole power to forfeit a game.

41. Simply ignore the cap throwing. Walk away.

42. Use good judgment, and do not be too quick on the trigger. You do not have to expel a player when he throws a ball in the dirt. It all depends on how he does it. If he shows you up to the crowd and his actions indicate

he is covering himself up, at your expense, than you should chase him. However, most of these acts on the part of the player are done on the spur of the moment. A smart umpire is usually looking the other way.

43. Base umpire behind the shortstop.

44. Base umpire takes regular position behind the pitcher on the second baseman's side.

45. Behind the pitcher on the shortstop's side.

46. Behind the shortstop.

47. Behind the pitcher on the shortstop's side.

48. Same position.

49. Behind the pitcher on the second baseman's side.

50. If two men are out. Base umpire should stand behind the pitcher on the second baseman's side. With less than two out, and when a bunt is anticipated, stand behind the pitcher on the short stop's side.

51. The plate umpire follows through all the way. He watches for the fielder touching the runner, he watches for the runner avoiding the touch. He also watches for the runner going more than two or three feet out of the line to avoid being touched. The plate umpire also watches for the runner interfering with the fielder making his play on the ball.

52. Cramer is entitled to third base on the balk, and the count remains 3 to 2 on Foxx. If it was an illegally pitched ball and no runners on base, it would be a ball four for Foxx.

53. It is a balk and the runner on third scores.

Instructor and Students — Class 1949

THE STUDENTS' FIRST ASSIGNMENT

"THE WHIP"

CALISTHENICS

THE NEW STUDENT GETS HIS FIELD INSTRUCTIONS FROM "AUGIE"

LOBBY HOBBY

"MAC", DURING ONE OF HIS
FAMOUS STORIES.

Chapter Notes

Preface

1. Bob Luke, "Hall of Famer—Bill McGowan Umpired with Vigor and Style," *Baseball Digest*, February 2002, vol. 61, no. 2, pp. 72–75. Robert Luke, "Remembering Bill McGowan," *The Diamond Angle Quarterly*, Fall 1997, p. 51.
2. E-mail correspondence, November 23, 2003.
3. Interview with Walter Masterson, November 25, 2002.
4. In 2002, the system used video cameras in four locations at a number of ballparks, including Shea Stadium. Operators set the strike zone on the computer based on each batter's approach to hitting the ball. The umpire's union issued a statement expressing concerns about the system because "the apparatus appears to have difficulty tracking certain types of breaking pitches, and there is unacceptable consistency as to where the QuesTec operators draw the top and bottom lines of the strike zone." As an indication of the complexity that the use of computers in calling balls and strikes can engender, the union employed scientists to help compile a list of 50 questions they wanted answered by Sandy Alderson, executive vice president for baseball operation. One of the questions was, "Does the extrapolation of the final path of the ball based on the measured positions, velocity and acceleration assume constant accelerations?" (Chas. Murray, "Umps Oppose Computer That Tracks Their Calls," *The New York Times*, July 20, 2002, p. D2.)
5. Published by Collier Books, New York, 1966.

Introduction

1. www.baseball-almanac.com/umpires/umpires-ad.shtml, accessed August 24, 2004.
2. Billy Evans. *How to Umpire*. (New York: American Sports Publishing), 1917 p. 71.
3. George Will, "A Pitcher at Bat," *The Washington Post*, October 23, 1986, p. A23.
4. Ed Pollock, "Color in Baseball Umpiring," 1934 article in *The Sporting News* from Bill McGowan, Jr.
5. Phone conversation with Joe Reeves, April 5, 2004.
6. "Fanning with Lanigan," *The Sporting News*, February 12, 1931, p. 4.
7. Bill McGowan, "Umpire Gave Johnson Short Answer About Shorter Ball Games," *The Washington Times-Herald*, 1935, no date or page # on clipping.
8. *The Sporting News*, October 5, 1939, p. 13.
9. Interview with Bill McGowan Jr.'s wife, Henrietta.
10. Ed Pollock, "Color in Baseball Umpiring," *The Sporting News*, 1934, from Bill McGowan, Jr.
11. Telephone interview with Bill Werber, May 22, 2004.
12. Interview with Walt Masterson, November 25, 2002.
13. Bill McGowan, *Text Book: Bill McGowan's School for Umpires*, p. 38.
14. "Harris Will Retain Only Seven Rookies," *The Washington Post*, March 10, 1926, p. 17.
15. Bobby Doerr telephone interview, September 9, 2003.
16. Al Cartwright, "A La Carte" (column title), October 1948, p. 22, from Bill McGowan, Jr.'s scrapbook. He was referring to the 1947 World Series.

17. Dick McCann, "The Iron Horse Ump," clipping in McGowan, Jr., scrapbook. In his article, McCann used 33,600 as Shibe Park's capacity and 42,000 as the attendance. Philip Lowry's (1993) book, *Green Cathedrals*, gives the capacity figure as 27,500. A *New York Times* article gives the attendance figure as 45,000 with 15,000 waiting outside. Regardless, it was a charged event.

18. "One Game Features 17 Future Hall of Famers," www.baseballlibrary.com/baseballlibrary/excerpts/records_registry3.stm, accessed December 19, 2003.

19. "Scribbled by Scribes," *The Sporting News*, May 15, 1941, p. 4.

20. Ed McAuley, "Bill Tense, Nervous, Liked Company," *The Sporting News*, December 22, 1954, p. 14.

21. Bob Addie, "One of the InFallible," *The Washington Post*, November 14, 1969, p. D-2.

Chapter 1

1. Telephone interview with Mickey Vernon, February 2003. McGowan often referred to himself as "Number One," and that title is on his plaque in Cooperstown. Ted Williams said of McGowan's referring to himself as "Number One," "When you say you're the best and you are the best, you're not bragging."

2. Bill Werber and C. Paul Rogers III, *Memories of a Ballplayer* (Cleveland: The Society for Baseball Research), 2001, p. 99.

3. Article in McGowan, Jr.'s scrapbook.

4. Gilbert interview.

5. www.baseball-almanac.com/legendary/lispit.shtml, accessed September 24, 2003.

6. Gilbert interview.

7. Ibid.

8. Ibid.

9. Ed Linn, *Hitter: The Life and Turmoil of Ted Williams.* (New York: Harcourt-Brace), 1993, p. 128.

10. Shirley Povich, "McGowan Walked Right In, Threw Ruth Out," *The Washington Post*, December 10, 1954.

11. "Dobson Urges Pro College Officials," *The Washington Post*, November 18, 1938, p. X 23.

12. Shirley Povich, "Chisox Beat Nats, 12-6, as Umpires Squabble," *The Washington Post*, June 9, 1950, p. SP-1.

13. Gerlach, *The Men in Blue*, p. 183.

14. Jack Herman, "Umpires Are Human," *St. Louis Globe Democrat*, May 20, 1951, p. 3-E.

15. Elden Auker interview, http://loveofthegameproductions.com/modules.php?name=News&file=article&sid=421, accessed March 24, 2004.

16. John Kieran, "Smoking Out Mr. Dykes," *New York Times*, September 17, 1937, p. 74. McGowan was chosen as the Outstanding Umpire of 1935 by a vote of the American League players. Dykes didn't have it quite right. Players, not fans, did the voting.

17. Robert Obojski, "McGowan, 7th Ump to Enter Hall of Fame," *Sports Collectors Digest*, May 1, 1992, p. 140.

18. Shirley Povich, "McGowan Walked Right In, Threw Ruth Out," *The Washington Post*, December 10, 1954. These were the children of Mrs. "Madge" McGowan's brother and his wife. Her brother, Bradford Ferry, had died of burns.

19. J.G. Taylor Spink, "Series Tops in Thrills, Low in Kicks— McGowan," *The Sporting News*, October 15, 1947, p. 11.

20. Ibid. It was during this time in the Southern Association that McGowan was pressed into service for a game between inmates at the penitentiary in Atlanta. During the game McGowan called a runner out at third base and "heard a thin voice coming from the bleachers call out, 'Say mister. I got five years for less than that.'" Bill McGowan, "The Roar of the Bleachers: Pop Bottles, Hard Words, Insults a La Carte! Here's a Brisk Look at Life as a Baseball Umpire Sees It," *Liberty Magazine*, September 25, 1937, p. 61.

21. *Spalding Sports Show* for 1947. Unpaginated magazine.

22. Letter dated November 13, 1923, from J.V. Jamison, Jr., to Wm. A. McGowan. Jamison's references to the majors and the National League are puzzling. McGowan didn't make the majors until 1925 and always worked in the American League. Jamison clearly did know to whom he was writing.

23. Jimmy Isaminger, *Philadelphia Inquirer*, as quoted in 1933 newspaper article "Connie Says M'Gowan Inspiration to Players," from McGowan, Jr.

24. "Wild Willie" was used by Kieran in his January 18, 1933, column. "Willie of Wilmington" was used by Kieran in his column of November 4, 1930. McGowan lived at the time in Wilmington, Delaware.

25. Mark C. Zeigler, "The Class D, Blue Ridge League 1920: Baseball Returns to the Blue Ridge. Class D Blue Ridge League History," www.blueridgeleagure.org/history-1920.htm, accessed November 5, 2003.

26. Ibid.

27. Bill McGowan, "Little Tales of the Diamond," *The Sporting News*, February 5, 1925, p. 6.

28. Bill McGowan, "Umpiring Under Difficulties: Interesting Experiences of the Men Who Judge the Plays of the Diamond," *The Sporting News*, November 4, 1926, p. 3. Red Smith, writing in *Baseball Digest*, July 1944, p. 50, identifies the umpire as "a little wisp of a guy named Pat Shaner" and the town as Mahoney City. Smith then tells of a game in Frederick, Maryland, in which the fans were booing Shaner's every decision. He went into the grandstand and sat between two fans who were giving him the loudest raspberries. Shaner ordered the pitcher to throw the ball and asked the fan on his left, "What was that?" The fan called it a ball to which Shaner hooted: "Would you smell on ice! It was right down the middle." Shaner returned to his usual position and finished the game "before a strangely silent gathering." Smith reports that Shaner got fired.

29. Bill McGowan, "Pop Bottle Tossing Is No Joke," *The Washington Times Herald*, no date or page number on clipping.

30. www.baseballlibrary.com/baseballlibrary/ballplayers/S/Summers, accessed January 27, 2004.

31. Bill McGowan, "St. Louis Undertaker Was Umpires' Greatest Friend," *The Washington Times-Herald*, no date or page number on clipping.

32. "Three and One. Looking Them Over with J. Taylor Spink," *The Sporting News*, March 26, 1936, p. 4.

33. Ibid.

34. John Drohan, "'Ump' McGowan Learned His Job from Detroit GM," *Boston Traveler*, December 26, 1950, no page number on clipping.

35. Letter from Bill McGowan to Bob Evans dated December 26, 1953, in the Umpires file at the Baseball Hall of Fame.

36. Bill McGowan as told to Jerry D. Lewis. "An Umpire Looks at the World Series: Big-Time Jitters!—A Close-Up of Tense Moments in "The Biggest Show on Earth," *Liberty Magazine*, October 7, 1939 (vol. 16, issue 40), p. 13.

37. Ibid., p. 13.

38 Bill McGowan, "It's Three and Tuh!: Tommy Connolly's Irish Wit Seldom Failed to Stop All Argument," from McGowan, Jr.'s scrapbook.

39. Arthur Daley, "Short Shots in Sundry Directions, *New York Times*, January 25, 1946, p. 29. Five years earlier, Shirley Povich, longtime Hall of Fame sportswriter for *The Washington Post*, gives an account of the same story but says it happened in the club car of a train. *The Washington Post*, May 11, 1941, p. S1.

40. Gerlach, *The Men in Blue*, p. 102.

41. Al Cartwright, "A La Carte" (newspaper column title), October 1948, p. 22. From Bill McGowan, Jr.'s scrapbook. A player with a "bucket foot" is often referred to as a "bucket hitter." A bucket hitter is "One who often steps back from the pitch; one who steps in the bucket" (Paul Dickson, *The New Dickson Baseball Dictionary*. New York: Harcourt & Brace, 1999, p. 88).

42. *The News Journal*, March 18, 1992, Wilmington, Delaware.

43. Other versions of McGowan's debut into umpiring exist. For instance, as Doug Gelbert tells the story, McGowan's first game was in New Castle, Delaware, and he worked the game claiming to be his brother Jack because neither team had seen either McGowan. Gelbert further states that Jack had to teach Bill the arm motions for out and safe. Gelbert says McGowan was talked into going because it was a chance to re-pay his brother a $2 debt. Doug Gelbert, "Big Shot," *The Great Delaware Sports Book* (Montcharin, DE: Manatee Books), 1995, p. 100.

Still another version of McGowan's debut was offered in *The Evening Star*'s obituary of McGowan. In that story McGowan's wanted to be a sportswriter and was working as a sportswriter for a Wilmington paper. At a Class B baseball game that he was covering at the Wilmington ballpark the umpire didn't show up, and the managers of the rival teams talked him into umpiring the game. (*Evening Star*, December 9, 1954, p. C-2.) I believe he umpired his first game in New Castle given that, in an article in the *Washington Times Herald* (Bill McGowan, "M'Gowans Relieved When Hagerstown Won Pennant" (no date or page number on clipping), McGowan says he umpired his first game in New Castle at the urging of his brother Jack. Bill Jr. also said his father's first game behind the plate took place in New Castle.

Later, McGowan would return the favor to his brother Jack by recommending Jack for a job in the Blue Ridge League in 1921. The league's president, J.V. Jamison, Jr., in a letter dated February 22, 1921, to Jack McGowan wrote, "I wrote your brother Bill that I had offered you $200.00 per month and an increase of $225.00 if you made good. He comes back at me today and insists that you are as good or better umpire than he is and that you are really worth $250.00 to this League. Consequently I am enclosing your contract for $250.00 per month plus transportation around the circuit, and will refund your transportation for reporting."

44. Don E. Basenfelder, *The Sporting News*, January 23, 1936, p. 5. The president of the Virginia League initially needed convincing. The first thing he noticed when he met McGowan was McGowan's slight build — 135 pounds. He laughed and said, "You, an umpire. You'll have to show me your credentials and prove you are the fellow Graham recommended to me." McGowan made a convincing case for himself. J.G. Taylor Spink, "Series Tops in Thrills, Low in Kicks— McGowan," *The Sporting News*, October 15, 1947, p. 11.

45. Doug Gelbert, *The Great Delaware Sports Book*, Montcharin, DE: Manatee Books, 1995, p. 100.

46. "J.G. Taylor Spink. Series Tops in Thrills, Low in Kicks— McGowan," *The Sporting News*, October 15, 1947, p. 11.

Shirley Povich gives an account of events leading up to Johnson's telegram. According to Povich, Bill Coyle, sports editor for the *Washington Herald*, saw McGowan work in the minors and touted him to Clark Griffith as "the best umpire, young or old, in baseball." Griffith encouraged McGowan to work the Nats spring training in 1925 and a month later demanded that Ban Johnson, AL president, put him on the American League staff. Shirley Povich, "The Morning Line," *The Washington Post*, December 10, 1954.

47. Bill McGowan, "Do 'Umps' Experience Thrills," *The Washington Times Herald*, no date or page number on clipping.

48. Newspaper clipping dated November 30, 1939, in McGowan's Hall of Fame file.

49. Family history paper.

50. Newspaper clipping in Hall of Fame file.

51. Telephone interview with Charlie Metro, May 3, 2004.

52. "Stamina Never Challenged," newspaper article in file of *The Sporting News*.

53. Bill McGowan, "Pitch Hittin'. On the Line for Bill Considine," *The Washington Times Herald*, no date or page number on clipping.

54. Photograph caption, *The Washington Post*, April 1, 1952, p. 18.

55. Interview with McGowan, Jr., November 22, 2003.

56. John Kieran, Sports of the Times, "Giving the Readers the Run of the Field," *New York Times*, November 4, 1930, p. 38.

57. Fred G. Lieb, "Everything's Jake with Johnny's Arm," *The Sporting News*, November 23, 1939, p. 8.

58. Jack Walsh, "McGowan Got Bad Rap, Thomas Says," *The Washington Post*, August 17, 1952, p. C-2.

59. Interview with McGowan, Jr., January 20, 2003.

60. Ibid.

61. Dave Hughes, "Ump McGowan Gets Belated Call," *Sunday News Journal*, August 2, 1992, Wilmington, DE. p. E-1.

62. "Three and One: Looking Them Over with J.G. Taylor Spink," *The Sporting News*, December 8, 1938, p. 4.

63. McGowan, Jr., interview

64. Tom Meany, "The Shrinking Strike Zone," *Colliers*, February, 1954, p. 26.

65. Bill McGowan, "Through the Eyes of an Umpire," *The Sporting News*, January 29, 1925, p. 8

66. McGowan, Jr., interview, January 20, 2003.

67. James C. Isaminger, "Pennock Toasted at Annual Spread," *The Sporting News*, November 29, 1928, p. 7.

68. Frank "Buck" O'Neill, "McQuinn, Case Face Operation to Save Careers," *The Washington Times-Herald*, 1944, no page number on clipping.

69. Bill McGowan, "Rookies Provide Laughs in Spring," *The Washington Times Herald*, no date or page number on clipping.

70. "Umpire-Magician Stumped Squawker with Card Trick," *The Sporting News*, April 14, 1948, p. 16.

71. Ralph Cannon, "Comedy from the Fields of Sport," *Esquire*, February, 1944, p. 120.

72. Shirley Povich, "Frederick Goes Wild Over Yankee Slugger," *The Washington Post*, October 12, 1939, p. 21.

73. "Eastern Branch Boys Club Honor Baseball Champs," *The Washington Post*, October 20, 1944, p. 12.

74. Bob Addie, "Hit Show Looms," *The Washington Post*, January 15, 1966, p. D-1.

75. "Touchdown Club Honors Baseball Figures Tomorrow," *The Washington Post*, October 16, 1944, p. 12.

76. "ERCO Athletic Club to Hear Bill McGowan," *The Washington Post*, February 11, 1945, P. M-6.

77. "Lefty Grove Sought for Other Team," *The Washington Post*, August 11, 1946, p. M-7.

78. "$250,000 Goal in Nats Bond Game Today," *The Washington Post*, September 9, 1943, p. 25.

79. Vincent X. Flaherty, "Vets Play Ball as If They Never Stopped Bullets," *The Washington Times-Herald*, 1945, no date or page number on clipping. McGowan frequently made gifts of baseballs signed by the stars. Nick Najjar, a graduate of his 1950 umpires' school in Cocoa Beach, Florida, recalled the time he visited McGowan at Fenway Park in the summer of 1950 after deciding not to umpire in the Kansas-Oklahoma-Missouri League where he'd been assigned. "McGowan," Najjar said, "looked at me and said, 'What are you doing here? Where did we send you?' I explained to him that I decided umpiring wasn't for me so he said, 'Wait right here.' Five minutes later he was back with two baseballs one signed by DiMaggio and one by Teddy Williams. So I guess he had no hard feelings. I gave 'em to my nephews." (In person interview, June 4, 2004.)

80. "Soldiers Play Snappy Ball Despite Loss of Leg or Arm," *The Evening Star*, April 11, 1945, Washington, D.C., no page number on clipping.

81. Fran "Buck" O'Neill, "McGowan's Vet Work Hailed; Chandler's Mistake," *The Washington Times-Herald*, May 7, 1945, p. 20.

82. "Baseball Urged to Strengthen Wartime Ties," *The Washington Post*, March 7, 1945, p. 10.

83. "Major League Note," *The Sporting News*, April 15, 1943, p. 8.

84. "Sports on Television," *The Washington Post*, October 24, 1954, p. T-10.

85. Bob Considine, "Radioed Sob Story Brings Offer of New Dog to 'Lead' M'Gowan," *The Washington Times-Herald*, no date or page number on clipping.

86. "Honor Outstanding A.L. Umpire of 1935," *The Sporting News*, July 9, 1936, p. 5.

87. "Three and One: Looking Them Over with J. Taylor Spink," *The Sporting News*, 1936, January 16, p.4.

88. "115 to Attend Phila. Sporting Writers' Event," January 28, 1936, no paper (probably from Wilmington) noted or page number on clipping.

Chapter 2

1. Shirley Povich, "This Morning," *The Washington Post*, July 22, 1948, p. 17.

2. Bob Luke, Hall of Famer—"Bill McGowan Umpired with Vigor and Style," *Baseball Digest*, February 2002, vol. 61, no. 2, pp. 72–75.

3. *The News Journal*, Wilmington, Delaware, March 18, 1992, p. C-4,

4. Bob Feller interview, February 13, 2005.

5. While Abner Doubleday did live for a time in Cooperstown, it is now well accepted that he did not discover baseball though the myth that he did persists. That honor goes to Alexander Cartwright who set down the first rules of baseball in 1845.

6. Jimmy Isaminger, *Philadelphia Inquirer*, as quoted in 1933 newspaper article "Connie Says M'Gowan Inspiration to Players," from Bill McGowan, Jr.

7. Telephone interview May 22, 2004.

8. Interview with Bill Gilbert, November 2002. Lee Allen tells the same story in his *Sporting News* column "Cooperstown Corner," March 8, 1969, p. 28, and adds that McGowan had never heard of a losing World Series pitcher complimenting the umpire-in-chief and that the compliment gave him a very warm feeling.

9. Paul Gallico, "Gallico," *The Washington Post*, October 10, 1935, p. 14.

10. Gerach, *The Men in Blue*, p. 82.

11. Hugh Trader, "Sports A La Carte: McGowan Held Greatest Command of Any Major League Umpire," Daytona Beach newspaper, December 11, 1954 (from files of *The Sporting News*).

12. Eugene V. McCaffrey and Roger A. McCaffrey, "Players' Choice: Major League Baseball Players Vote on the All-Time Greats" (New York: *Facts on File Publications*), NY, 1987, p. 178.

13. The Strike Zone: A historical timeline, http:\\mlb.mlb.com/NASApp/mlb/mlb/official_info/umpires/strike_zone.jsp, accessed December 18, 2003.

14. Meany, "Baseball's Shrinking Strike Zone," *Colliers*, February 18, 1955, p. 25

15. Telephone interview, February 22, 2003.

16. Bill McGowan, *Text Book: Bill McGowan's School for Umpires* (Cocoa, Florida) January–February 1947, p. 5

17. Ibid.

18. Meany, op. cit., p. 26.

19. "McGowan on Umpiring," *The Sporting News*, September 9, 1937, p. 2.

20. Bill McGowan, "The Umpire Talks Back," *Liberty Magazine*, September 11, 1937, p. 41.

21. Bill McGowan, "Umpiring Under Difficulties," op. cit.

22. Gene Kessler, "Billy McGowan Earned 'BIG Shot' Sobiquet," op cit.

23. Telephone interview, January 2002.

24. Telephone interview, November 25, 2002.

25. Telephone interview, December 2001.

26. Donald Honig, *The October Heroes* (New York: Simon and Schuster), 1979, p. 252.

27. Ibid.

28. Bob Luke, op. cit., p. 73.

29. *The Sporting News*, December 22, 1954, p. 14.

30. Shirley Povich, "This Morning," *The Washington Post*, May 30, 1958, p. A-21.

31. Bill McGowan, "The Umpire Talks Back," *Liberty Magazine*, September 11, 1937, p. 42.

32. Shirley Povich, "This Morning," *The Washington Post*, May 30, 1958, p. A-21.

33. Shirley Povich, "This Morning," *The Washington Post*, July 11, 1935, p. 19.

34. Bill McGowan, as told to John M. Ross, "Anything Can Happen in a World Series," *The Washington Post*, September 26, 1954, p. AW 12.

35. "Major League Flashes," *The Sporting News*, August 24, 1944, p. 14.

36. Bob Addie, "Willie on-the-spot McGowan," *Baseball Digest*, January, 1953, p. 32.

37. Glen Waggoner, Kathleen Moloney, and Hugh Howard, *Baseball by the Rules* (Dallas: Taylor Publishing Co.), 1987, pp. 202–203.

38. Art Kruger, "He Made the Umpires Raise Their Hands," *Baseball Digest*, May, 1954, p. 50.

39. Paul Dickson, *The Hidden Language of Baseball* (New York: Walker & Company), 2003. pp. 46–50.

40. Tom Simon (ed.), *Deadball Stars of The National League* (Dulles, VA: Society for American Baseball Research), 2004, p. 25.

41. Ibid. Still other accounts of the origins of umpires using signals can be found. The November 6, 1886, edition of *The Sporting News* carried a story of a former major league pitcher who was deaf, Ed Dundon, using signals to umpire a game in Mobile, Alabama, between the Acids and the Mobiles. Fingers of the right hand indicated strikes. Fingers of the left meant balls. A wave of the hand meant "out." A shake of the head meant "not out." Harry Wright, manager of the Cincinnati Red Stockings, asked, in a letter to the editor published in the March 27, 1870, *New York Sunday Mercury*, that umpires raise their hand to indicate a man is out.

42. James M. Kahn, *The Umpire Story* (New York: G.P. Putnam's Sons), 1953, p. 155. Arthur Daley tells much the same story (*New York Times*, December 10, 1954, p. 38) but says it occurred when McGowan entered the American League in 1924. McGowan actually entered the American

League in 1925 and van Graflan not until 1927 so I'm inclined to believe it did occur in their International League days.

43. Bill McGowan, *Text Book*, op. cit., p. 5.

44. Charles Einstein, *The Second Fireside Book of Baseball*, "Whitey Ford as Told to Edward Linn" (New York: Simon and Schuster), 1958, p. 144. Ford went on to add that he was sure that Parnell and Stobbs got together later that day; just not while McGowan was nearby.

45. Bob Addie, "Sports Addiction," *The Sporting News*, May 7, 1952, p. 2.

Chapter 3

1. Deron Snyder, "McGowan Remembered," *USA Today Baseball Weekly*, July 29, 1992, p. 22.

2. Bob Addie, "Sports Addition," *The Washington Post*, December 9, 1954, p. 39.

3. "More bounce to the ounce" was Pepsi-Cola's in those days.

4. Bob Addie, "Hats Off," *The Sporting News*, October 1, 1952, p. 23.

5. "Umps Who Called 'Em with Flourish," *The Sporting News*, December 13, 1961, p. 7.

6. Max Kase, "Iron Man Still," *The Sporting News*, December 22, 1954, p. 13.

7. James B. Harrison, "Ruth Hits 40th But Yanks Lose 8–4," *New York Times*, August 29, 1926, no page number.

8. Frank Graham, *Baseball Extra* (New York: A.S. Barnes), 1954, pp. 176–177.

9. Gerlach, *The Men in Blue*, p. 106.

10. Barney Krememko, "Summers Thumbs Pages of Lively Diamond Tales," *The Sporting News*, February 3, 1960, p. 8.

11. David Halberstam, *Summer of '49* (New York: Wm. Morrow), 1989, p. 87.

12. Shirley Povich, *Baseball Digest*, April 1954, p. 35.

13. Shirely Povich, "This Morning," *The Washington Post*, September 3, 1962, p. A-24.

14. Halberstam, *Summer of '49*, p. 217.

15. Telephone interview with Sid Hudson, November 23, 2002.

16. Telephone interview with Charlie Metro, May 3, 2004.

17. Mac Davis, *Lore and Legends of Baseball* (New York: Lantern Press, Inc.), 1953, p. 223.

18. Cy Peterman, "Rommel as Freshman Umpire Admitted Errors for 'Peace,'" *The Sporting News*, January 19, 1939.

19. Harridge obituary in Hall of Fame folder.

20. Bill McGowan, "It's Three and Tuh!: Hands Jim Dykes a Few Pats on the Back and Recalls a Little Spat with Chisox Manager," article in McGowan, Jr.'s scrapbook.

21. Morris Siegel, "Dykes Has a 'Fine' Time with McGowan," *The Washington Post*, July 15, 1951, p. C-2.

22. "Marrero, Hudson Win," *The Washington Post*, July 9, 1951, p. 10.

23. "Loafing Official Burns Up Pilots, Players and Fans," *The Sporting News*, January 24, 1946, p. 11.

24. "How to Win at Marbles," *Baseball Digest*, May 1954, p. 54.

25. Lawrence Keating, "Baseball's Daffy Day," *Coronet*, June 1957, p. 73.

26. Bill James, *The New Bill James Historical Baseball Abstract* (New York: The Free Press), 2001, p. 413.

27. Gerlach, *The Men in Blue*, p. 71.

28. Shirley Povich, "This Morning," *The Washington Post*, August 19, 1943, p. 16.

29. www.enel.net/beisbol/history/people/manager/mccaj101/mcca.

30. Bill McGowan, "Tris Speaker Was Master at Setting Fans on 'Umps,'" *The Washington Times-Herald*, February 19, 1935, no page number on clipping.

31. Gilbert interview.

32. Bob Addie, "Willie-on-the-Spot McGowan," *Baseball Digest*, January 1953, p. 32

33. Billy Evans, *How to Umpire* (New York: American Sports Publishing Co.), 1920, p. 24.

34. Telephone interview.

35. Louis Kaufman, Barbara Fitzgerald, Tom Sewell, *Moe Berg: Athlete, Scholar, Spy* (Boston: Little Brown), 1974, p. 66. Billy Werber, a Red Sox teammate of Berg's in 1935 and 1936, told me that "Berg could have been a great player, but what he really liked to do was sit in the bullpen

and chew the fat with the pitchers. You never saw him without the *Wall Street Journal* under his arm."

36. Davis J. Walsh, *Chicago Herald American*, October 29, 1950.

37. McGowan, Jr., interview.

38. James Carmichael, "Dean of the Men in Blue," *The Sporting News*, December 22, 1954, p. 14.

39. Bill McGowan, *Text Book*, p. 13

40. Bill McGowan, "Umpiring Under Difficulties," op. cit.

41. Carmichael, op. cit., p. 14.

42. Ibid.

43. Ibid.

44. Bill McGowan, as told to Frederick G. Lieb, "Loafing Official Burns Up Pilots, Players and Fans," *The Sporting News*, January 24, 1946, p. 11.

45. Red Smith, "Nallin Umpired with 'Animal Instinct,' McGowan Rests Eye on Some Pitches," *The Sporting News*, April 12, 1945, p. 14.

46. Telephone interviews with Bill Gilbert and Buddy Lewis, December 15, 2002.

47. www.philadelphiaathletics.org/history/joyner2.html, accessed October 30, 2004. While there is no date for the game given in the story, the game would have had to be played between 1949 and 1954 as those were the only years that Joost and Shantz were on the A's together.

48. www.pubdim.net/baseballlibrary/ballplayers/M/McGowan_Bill.stm.

49. Bill James, *The Bill James Guide to Baseball Managers from 1870 to Today* (New York: Scribner), 1997, p. 104

50. James C. Isaminger, "A's Fall Back to Z with Bats on Strike," *The Sporting News*, May 12, 1938, p. 3.

51. Roland Wenzell, "Allen Came Out Ahead on Shirt Row — McGowan," *The Sporting News*, January 28, 1953, p. 13.

52. Johnny Allen: "Rhubarber to Ump," *The Sporting News*, December 24, 1952, p. 1.

53. Gordon Cobbeldick, "Allen Changes Mind After Walkout: Vitt Won't Let Nurler Finish Game," *Cleveland Plain Dealer*, June 8, 1938, pp. 1, 15.

54. "$500 Shirt!," *The Washington Post*, June 11, 1938, p. X17.

55. "McGowan's Chin Out," *The Sporting News*, December 15, 1938, p. 2.

56. www.sptimes.com/News/101399/Sports/The_Splendid_splinter.

57. Ted Williams, as told to John Underwood, *My Turn at Bat: The Story of My Life* (New York: Simon and Schuster), 1969, pp. 85–86. There is another version of the conversation between Hayes and Williams. Ed Linn, in his book *Hitter: The Life and Times of Ted Williams* (New York: Harcourt Brace, 1993, p. 128), says the quote as stated was McGowan's version. Linn says Williams told him that Hayes said, "Mr. Mack says we're not going to make it easy for you, Ted. But we are going to pitch to you." Linn said he thinks the second quote is the correct one because Mack had decided that year to pitch to Williams with men on base rather than walk him in that situation as other managers were prone to do. Whatever Hayes said, it is not in dispute that McGowan's comments had a calming effect on Ted's nerves.

58. Daniel Okrent and Steve Wulf, *Baseball Anecdotes* (New York: Oxford University Press), 1989, p. 155.

59. Shirley Povich, "The Morning Line," *The Washington Post*, p. 57, December 10, 1954.

60. "Three and One: Looking Them Over with J.G. Taylor Spink," *The Sporting News*, January 20, 1938, p. 20,

61. Telephone interview. Though McGowan may not have passed along all his observations to Noren and other rookies, Shirley Povich noted that McGowan said, "He is overswinging and it will probably take him about six years to learn what the umpires already know about him," after watching Noren swing for the fences only to strike out. Shirley Povich, "Less Gusto, More homers," *Baseball Digest*, July 1950, p. 67.

62. Telephone interview, May 22, 2004.

63. Ira Smith, *Baseball's Famous Pitchers* (New York: A.S. Barnes), pp. 235–36.

64. Oscar Ruhl, "Rule Book," *The Sporting News*, August 32, 1944, p. 7.

65. Maury Allen, "Going by the Book," TheColumnists.com, www.the columnists.com/allen/allen2.html, accessed April 23, 2003.

66. Interview with McGowan, Jr.

67. Interview with McGowan, Jr.

68. "Goslin a Ball Player Because Dad's Cows Roamed Off Base," *The Washington Post*, December 16, 1928, p. 22.

69. Lawrence S. Ritter, *The Glory of Their Times* (New York: McMillan), 1966, pp. 252–3. It should be noted the Shirley Povich reported that Griffith didn't go immediately but waited until he learned from a Baltimore friend that the owner of the Orioles, Jack Dunn, had offered $6,000 for a South Atlantic League outfielder. Griffith boarded the first train for Columbia. Shirley Povich, "This Morning," *The Washington Post*, April 10, 1938, p. X-1.

70. Interview with Griffith in *The Evening Star*, Washington, D.C., January 9, 1954, p. C-1. Shirley Povich in his April 10, 1938, column reported that Griffith paid no heed to McGowan's tip until late in the 1921 season when the Columbia owner offered Goslin's contract to Griffith as repayment for the loan of two players. Griffith sent scout Joe Engel to appraise Goslin but, hearing nothing from Engel, forgot about Goslin but soon heard that Jack Dunn of the Orioles was willing to buy Goslin's contract for $6,000. That information got Griffith on the train to South Carolina.

71. Bill McGowan, "It's Three and Tuh!: Played Prominent Part in Getting Goslin His Start in Organized Baseball," 1936, from McGowan Jr.'s scrapbook. The ball Goslin hit is on display at the Baseball Hall of Fame.

72. "In the Press Box with Baxter," *The Washington Post*, April 3, 1924, p. S-3.

73. Baxter, op. cit.

74. Henry W. Thomas, *Walter Johnson: Baseball's Big Train* (Washington, D.C.: Phenom Press), 1995, p. 322.

75. Shirley Povich, "This Morning," *The Washington Post*, May 13, 1938, p. 21.

Chapter 4

1. The only other reference to a major league umpire being suspended for his on-field conduct that I found was National League Umpire Joe West's three-day suspension by NL president Chub Feeney for shoving Atlanta Braves manager Joe Torre during an argument after a game on June 28, 1983. (Associated Press, "National League umpire suspended," *Times Union*, Albany, N.Y. July 12, 1983.)

2. Larry Moffi, *This Side of Cooperstown* (Iowa City: University of Iowa Press), 1986, p. 242.

3. Ibid.

4. Morris Siegel, "League to Investigate Charges by Joe Kuhel," article in McGowan Jr.'s scrapbook.

5. Siegel, op. cit.

6. Shirley Povich, "McGowan, Dean of A.L. Umps, Suspended After Run-in With Senators," *The Sporting News*, July 28, 1948, p. 6.

7. From McGowan's Hall of Fame file.

8. "McGowan Is Suspended for 10 Days," *The Washington Post*, July 29, 1948, p. 18.

9. Ibid.

10. Siegel, op. cit.

11. Danny Peary, *We Played the Game* (New York: Hyperion), 1994, pp 78–79.

12. Ibid., p. 102.

13. This was the first published reference I found to his diabetes. Others would follow.

14. Arthur Daley, "A Master at His Trade," *New York Times*, December 10, 1954, p. 38.

15. "Old Story — Blaming the Umpires," *The Sporting News*, August 18, 1948, p. 12.

16. "McGowan Suspended 10 Days for Temper Display, Starts Calling 'Em Again Friday," *Washington Star*, July 29, 1948, p C-1.

17. Newspaper article in Hall of Fame file on McGowan.

18. "McGowan Ribbed by Offer of Evangeline League Post," *New York Times*, July 25, 1948, p. 38.

19. "Rabbit Chases Dog, or Something Like That," *Los Angeles Times*, July 23, 1948, p. A4.

20. Shirley Povich, "This Morning," *The Washington Post*, July 21, 1948, p. 17.

21. "Nats Beaten by Feller, 3–0; Divide Pair," *The Washington Post*, May 18, 1946, p. 12.

22. Vincent X. Flaherty, "McGowan Saluted as No. 1 Umpire," *The Washington Times-Herald*, April 13, 1944, p. 29.

23. Shirley Povich, "This Morning," *The Washington Post*, June 2, 1940, p. SP1.

24. Jack Miley, "Umpire's Wife Called Out of Line by Prexy," *New York Post*, April 16, 1940, no page number on copy in Hall of Fame file of Harridge.

25. Shirley Povich, "This Morning," *The Washington Post*, p. 8, August 18, 1945.

26. Joe Martin, "Ramblin' Round," *The Delaware Star*, no date or page number on clipping but about mid-'50s.

27. Shirley Povich, "This Morning," *The Washington Post*, July 21, 1948, p. 17.

28. Oscar Ruhl, "Ump McGowan Suspended After Clash with Writers," *The Sporting News*, August 13, 1952, p. 15.

29. "In The Dugout with Rumill: The Veeck Case," *Christian Science Monitor*, June 19, 1952, p. 10. Perhaps McGowan alone made the call at third for in another account, Harridge is quoted as saying "that it was definitely proved there was no foundation for the charge that umpire Hank Soar made one decision on the play and McGowan another. Soar made no decision." "A.L. Blasts Marion but Lifts Ban," newspaper article on file with *The Sporting News*.

30. "A.L. Blasts Marion but Lifts Ban," newspaper article on file with *The Sporting News*.

31. Oscar Ruhl, "From the Ruhl Book," *The Sporting News*, November 5, 1952, p. 13.

32. While there is no debate about McGowan being suspended, there are accounts that differ from Ruhl's in some of the details. Arthur Daley, in his *New York Times* column "Sports of the Times" tribute to McGowan on December 10, 1954, stated that the precipitating event for McGowan's action was his belief that the Tigers were unnecessarily rough in their riding of Satchel Paige. McGowan, according to Daley, furiously ordered them to stop and cleared off part of the Detroit bench, which led to the St. Louis writers asking for the details. Bob Addie's account in the January 1953 issue of *Baseball Magazine* says the precipitating event was McGowan objecting to the riding the Tigers were giving Satchel Paige (who was en route to pitching a complete game, a 12 inning, 1–0 shutout) and battery mate Clint Courtney. The account in the *St. Louis Post Dispatch* for August 7, 1952, merely says McGowan received a suspension without going into the details.

33. Jack Walsh, "McGowan Got Bad Rap, Thomas Says," *The Washington Post*, August 17, 1952, p. C-2.

Chapter 5

1. "McGowan to Tutor Umps," *The Sporting News*, November 24, 1938, p. 8.

2. Bob Considine, "On the Line with Considine," *The Washington Post*, February 10, 1941.

3. *The Sporting News*, January 5, 1939, p. 10.

4. "Green Pastures for Beavers," *The Washington Post*, December 26, 1941, p. 16.

5. Shirley Povich, "This Morning," *The Washington Post*, November 6, 1939, p. 17.

6. John C. Skipper, *Umpires* (Jefferson, NC: McFarland), 1997, p. 9.

7. "Three and One. Looking Them Over with J.G. Taylor Spink," *The Sporting News*, November 30, 1939, p. 4.

8. Al Cartwright, "A La Carte," October 1948, p. 22, from Bill McGowan, Jr.'s scrapbook.

9. Shirley Povich, "This Morning," *The Washington Post*, March 18, 1939, p. 17.

10. Gerry Hern, "Layoff No Handicap to McGowan's Sight," *The Sporting News*, December 22, 1954, p. 14.

11. Jack Herman, "Umpires Are Human Too," *St. Louis Globe Democrat*, May 20, 1951.

12. "McGowan Seeks Jobs for Student Umpires," *The Washington Post*, December 7, 1951, p. B-7.

13. John C. Skipper, op. cit., p. 26

14. Telephone interview with John Rice, October 30, 2003.

15. Bud Harvey, "Skill the Umpire," *Sports World, America's Fan Magazine*, May 1949, p. 63.

16. Gerlach, *The Men in Blue*, p. 154.

17. Frank Graham, *Baseball Extra* (New York :A. S. Barnes), 1954, p. 175.

18. Names taken from the letterhead of a September 29, 1946, letter written by McGowan to a prospective student, Roman W. Bentz.

19. Bill McGowan, *Text Book*, p. 3.

20. Ibid., pp. 3–4.

21. Telephone interview with John Rice, October 30, 2003.

22. Jimmy Burns, "Ailing Babe in Miami to Soak Up Sunshine," *The Sporting News*, February 18, 1948, p. 2.

23. *Text Book Bill McGowan's School for Umpires* 1955. Daytona Beach, Florida. 16th Year (a 16-page booklet published by McGowan for prospective students), p. 8.

23. Dink Carroll, "Playing the Field," *The Gazette*, March 11, 1954, p. 16.

24. Ibid.

25. "Specs Okayed for Umps," October 19, 1974, article in McGowan Hall of Fame file.

26. Interview with Jim Evans.

27. "Ump Closed His Eyes Then Opened the Fans," newspaper article in files of *The Sporting News*.

28. Letter from Bill McGowan's School for Umpires to Roman W. Bentz, September 29, 1946.

29. Ed Rumill, "'Jocko': Story of an Umpire," *The Christian Science Monitor*, June 29, 1967, p. 10.

30. Edward Grant Barrow with James M. Kahn, *My Fifty Years in Baseball*, p. 70.

31. Frank Eck, "What Makes a Good Umpire," *Sports Magazine*, AP News Features, March 4, 1954.

32. Ev Gardner, "How to Survive in a Blue Serge Suit," Wilmington newspaper, don't know name, February 14, 1951.

33. *Bill McGowan's School for Umpires Text Book*, Daytona Beach, Florida, 1955, p. 7.

34. "School for Umpires," *People and Places*, February 1954.

35. Edwin C. Johnson, Democrat, U.S. senator from Colorado from 1933 to 1951.

36. Telephone interview with John Rice, October 30, 2003.

37. Bill McGowan, *Text Book*, op. cit., p. 11.

38. Gordon Cobbledick, "An Ump Must Be Broken in Right," *Baseball Digest*, July 1944, p. 37.

Chapter 6

1. While there had been a few oblique references in the press over the years to the possibility of McGowan having diabetes, Bob Addie noted in his December 12, 1954, *Washington Post* article, that McGowan had diabetes since 1938.

2. Bob Addie, "Sports Addiction," *The Washington Post*, December 9, 1954, p.39.

3. Bob Addie, "Sports Addiction," *The Washington Post*, August 20, 1954, p. 31.

4. Bob Addie, "Willie on-the-spot McGowan," *Baseball Digest*, January 1953, pp 30–32.

5. "Major Flashes," *The Sporting News*, August 5, 1953, p. 17

6. Gerlach, *The Men in Blue*, pp. 183–184.

7. In the aftermath of the Pete Rose betting scandal, it's natural to ask if there is any evidence of McGowan's performance on the field being influenced by his betting. As far as could be determined, he limited his betting to horse and dog races. A search of the *Commissioner's Bulletin*, a monthly publication on file at The Baseball Hall of Fame, describing disciplinary actions taken against major league baseball personnel, yielded no mention of McGowan save for his suspensions in 1948 and 1952. The suspensions had nothing to do with gambling.

8. Gerlach, *The Men in Blue*, pp. 102–103.

9. Telephone interview, May 22, 2003.

10. Bill Werber and C. Paul Rogers III, *Memories of a BallPlayer* (Cleveland: Society for American Baseball Research), 2001, p. 100.

11. Telephone interview May 22, 2004.

12. "Bill McGowan, AL Ump Dies," United Press article in Hall of Fame file.

13. Bob Addie, "Sports Addiction," *The Washington Post*, December 12, 1954, p. C-2.

14. Bob Addie, "Still Plans Umpire School," *The Washington Post*, December 8, 1954, p. 31.

15. Shirley Povich, "McGowan Walked Right In, Threw Ruth Out," *The Washington Post*, December 10, 1954, no page number.

16. *The Washington Post*, December 10, 1954, p. 37, and December 12, p. 28.

17. Telegram in files of William A. McGowan, Jr.

18. "Touchdown Club Will Honor McGowan with Griffith Award," *The Evening Star*, December 12, 1954, no page number.

19. Telephone interview with John Rice, October 30, 2003.

20. "McGowan's School Opens," *The Washington Post*, December 16, 1954, p. 28.

21. From the files of William A. McGowan, Jr.

22. Interview with Bill McGowan, Jr., November 23, 2003.

23. Brad Wilson, "Wendelstedt to Rename Somers School," *The Sporting News*, February 25, 1978, p. 63.

24. Ibid. The Kinnamon School joined forces with Jim Evans Academy of Professional Umpiring.

25. *The News Journal*, Wilmington, Delaware, March 18, 1992, p. C-1.

26. "Vet Committee Lists Shrine Candidates," *The Sporting News*, February 7, 1976, p. 33.

27. "Mize, Foster Elected to Hall," *New York Times*, March 21, 1981, p. 23. How prominently we don't know because the committee did not issue a vote count. Since McGowan's induction, only one other umpire, Nester Chylak in 1999, has been enshrined in the hall.

28. David Hughes, "Son Feels McGowan's Honor Overdue," *The News Journal*, Wilmington, Delaware, p. D-2. We'll probably never know why Hubbard was inducted 16 years before McGowan. Hubbard umpired in the majors for 15 years compared to McGowan's 30. Perhaps Hubbard's health had something to do with the timing of his induction. He died in 1977, a year after his induction, so he had some time to enjoy the honor. McGowan, Sr. said of Hubbard, "I'll tell you another guy you don't hear much about that I think is a whale of an umpire. Cal Hubbard. He's a shark on the rules and he's got good judgment and he's got guts and he always hustles. Cobbledick, *Baseball Digest*, op. cit., p. 37.

29. Izzy Katzman, "Memo to MacPhail: Let's Elect Willis and McGowan," Wilmington paper-clipping from McGowan, Jr.'s file — same day McGowan inducted in Delaware Hall of Fame, May 7, 1977.

30. Robert Obojski, "McGowan, 7th Ump to Enter Hall of Fame," *Sports Collector's Digest*, May 1, 1992, p. 140. Willis, who died in 1947, was elected to the Hall of Fame in 1995, also by the Veterans Committee.

31. Brad Harris, "For the Cycle: June 4, 2002 Cleaning Up the Hall of Fame, Part II," www.baseballtruth.com/cycle/cycle_060402.htm, accessed November 5, 2003.

32. Telephone interview with Broeg, March 25, 2003. Broeg said he was initially opposed to McGowan's induction, preferring to see a player get the nod instead, but voted for McGowan in the end.

33. "Will Vets Elect Fox or Leo?" *The Sporting News*, February 26, 1990, p. 29.

34. Bill McGowan, *Text Book*, op. cit., p. 6.

35. "Umpire Bill McGowan Dies at 58 After Heart Attack," *The Evening Star*, December 9, 1954, p.C-1.

36. Interview with John McGowan, January 29, 2004.

37. Bob Broeg interview.

38. E-mail correspondence, May 3, 2004.

39. www.baseballhalloffame.org/hof%5Fweekend/2000/past%5Fceremony%5Froll%5Fcall.htm, accessed October 22, 2003.

40. Program for *A Celebration of the Life and Baseball Career of Vic Willis and Bill McGowan*, Delaware Stadium Corporation, August 30, 2001.

41. Max Kase, "Iron Man Still," *The Sporting News*, December 22, 1954.

42. Henry W. Thomas, *Walter John: Baseball's Big Train* (Washington, D.C.: Phenom Press), 1995, p. 173.

43. Bill McGowan as told to Bob Gordon, "The Umpire Never Sees the Plate," *Modern Mechanix*, June 1936, p. 65.

44. Max Kase, "Iron Man Still," *The Sporting News*, p. 13, December 22, 1954.

45. Bill McGowan, "Broadminded Not Enough," clipping in McGowan Jr.'s files.

46. Billy Evans, *How to Umpire*, p. 67.

47. Oscar Ruhl, "From the Ruhl Book," *The Sporting News*, December 24, 1952, p. 16.

48. Gene Kessler, "Billy McGowan Earned 'Big Shot' Sobriquet Playing Second Base with Powder Co. Team," *The Sporting News*, January 4, 1934, no page number.

49. Bill McGowan, as told to John M. Ross, "Anything Can Happen in a World Series," *The Washington Post*, September 26, 1954, p. AW 12.

50. Newspaper article, McGowan Hall of Fame file.

51. "Umpire Bill McGowan Dies at 58 After Heart Attack," *The Washington Post*, December 9, 1954, p. C-1.

52. Morris Siegel, "Joe Kuhel Even Has Pitching Woes in Family—Son Loses," *The Washington Post*, July 24, 1949, p. C-3.

53. J. Taylor Spink, "Series Tops in Thrills, Low in Kicks—McGowan," op. cit., p. 11.

Chapter 7

1. Henry Chadwick, ed., *Beadle's Dime-Base-Ball Player: Comprising the Proceedings of the Tenth Annual Base-Ball Convention, Together with the Amended Rules Adopted, Rules for the Formation of Clubs, and the Constitution and By-Laws of the National Association. Also Base-Ball Averages for 1866.* (New York: Beadle and Co.), 1867, p. 31.

2. Ibid., pp. 31–32.

3. Billy Evans, *How to Umpire* (New York: American Sports Publishing Co.), 1920, p. 72.

4. Ibid., pp. 31–32.

5. Jim Evans umpired in the American League for 28 years before retiring in 1999 and was a crew chief for 19 of those years. He umpired in four World Series, numerous postseason events and three all-star games. He has written several books and many articles on umpiring and is owner and chief instructor of the Jim Evans Academy of Professional Umpiring in Kissimmee, Florida.

6. Interview with Jim Evans, August 16, 2003.

7. History of Umpiring, www.sdabu.com/Umpire-History.htm accessed November 20, 2002.

8. Don Schlossburg, *The Baseball Almanac* (Chicago: Triumph Books), 2002, p. 27.

9. Bill McGowan, "It's Three and Tuh!: Few Big League Umpires Ever Played Ball in the Majors" from McGowan, Jr.'s scrapbook.

10. www.baseballlibrary.com/baseballlibrary/ballplayers/H/Hubbard_Cal.stm, accessed September 29, 2003.

11. Shirley Povich, "This Morning," *The Washington Post*, March 6, 1953, p. 32.

12. Bill McGowan, "It's Three and Tuh!: Bill Summers Was a Boxer Before Becoming an Umpire," Bill McGowan, Jr.'s scrapbook.

13. Bill McGowan, "It's Three and Tuh!: Too Much Harness with Job of Calling Balls and Strikes to Suit Fred Marberry," article from McGowan, Jr.'s scrapbook.

14. Shirley Povich, "This Morning," *The Washington Post*, July 11, 1935, p. 19.

15. Bill McGowan, "It's Three and Tuh!: Few Big League Umpires Ever Played Ball in the Majors," from McGowan, Jr.'s scrapbook.

16. "Calling All Umps—With Vets Teaching," *The Sporting News*, October 29, 1952, p. 10.

17. History of Umpiring, www.sdabu.com/Umpire-History.htm, accessed November 20, 2002.

18. Ibid.

19. Ibid.

20. Ibid.

21. Ibid.

22. Ibid.

23. Copy of Associated Press story, August 24, 2001, in umpires-general file at Hall of Fame.

24. Interview with Jim Evans.

25. Ibid.

26. Telephone interview with Charlie Metro, May 3, 2004.

27. Schlossberg, p. 27.

28. Draft of an article typed by McGowan in McGowan Jr.'s scrapbook.

29. Bill McGowan, "M'Gowan Says: Yankees Set Pace for 'Bench Jockeys' in American League," *The Washington-Times Herald*, February 8, 1936, no page number on clipping.

30. Interview with Jim Evans.

31. Major League Baseball supervisors scout Triple A umpires and determines who goes up on a temporary or full-time basis.

32. John P. Lopez, "Baseball Striking Out in Umpire Development," *Houston Chronicle*, from www.chron.com/cs/CDA/story.hts/sports/lopez/2042845, accessed September 30, 2003.

33. Ibid.

34. Frank Eck, "What Makes a Good Umpire," *Sport*, AP News Feature, March 4, 1954.

35. Interview with Jim Evans.

36. Telephone interview with John Rice, October 30, 2003.

37. Telephone interview, January 20, 2003.

38. Carl Lundquist, "No Introductions Needed at Induction," *USA Today Baseball News*, August 5, 1992, p. 42.

39. Gerry Hern, "Layoff No Handicap to McGowan's Sight," *The Sporting News*, December 22, 1954, p. 14.

40. Harvey, op. cit., p. 63.

41. Bob Addie, "One of the Infallible," *The Washington Post*, November 14, 1969, p. D-2.

Epilogue

1. Francis Stann, "Connolly's Motionless Call: Old-time Umps Would Have Been TV Naturals," *Baseball Digest*, April 1954, p. 63.

2. Morris Siegel, "Why, You Can Even Blame Original Sin on the Umpires," *The Evening Star*, April 29, 1979, no page number on clipping. In an article in *USA Today Baseball Weekly*, April 15–21, 1998, Larry Gerlach, a professor of sports history at the University of Utah, characterized McGowan's years as being part of "a tough era with dominant personalities who took no lip from anybody."

3. Harvey, op. cit., p. 74.

4. Danny Peary, *We Played the Game* (New York: Hyperion), 1994, p. 200.

5. Vincent X. Flaherty, "McGowan Saluted as No. 1 Umpire," *Washington Times Herald*, April 13, 1944, p. 29.

6. "Do Umpires Get Thrills? McGowan Tells You," article in McGowan Jr.'s scrapbook.

7. Bernard Kahn, "It Says Here: McGowan Was Fired Once for Defending Himself in Fight," 1952, newspaper article in files of *The Sporting News*.

8. Bill McGowan, "The Umpire Talks Back," op. cit., p. 42.

9. Harvey, op. cit., pp. 74–75.

10. Werber, telephone interview, May 22, 2004.

11. Bill McGowan, "The Umpire Talks Back," op. cit., p. 43.

12. Bill McGowan, "The Roar of the Bleachers: Pop Bottles, Hard Words, Insults a La Carte! Here's a Brisk Look at Life as a Baseball Umpire Sees It," *Liberty Magazine*, September 25, 1937, p. 62.

Bibliography

Baseball America (editorial staff). *It's Your Call! Baseball's Oddest Plays*. New York: Macmillan, 1989.
>Seventeen major and minor league umpires tell "the wildest and wackiest stories they could remember." Plus 90 hypothetical situations for the reader to make the call on.

Baum, Jay. *Umpiring Baseball*. Chicago: Contemporary Books, 1979.
>"Rules, photographs, diagrams, and examples— all showing how you can keep peace on the diamond while dispensing honest calls."

Brinkman, Joe, and Charlie Euchner. *The Umpire's Handbook: The Complete Guide to Umpiring Baseball and Softball — From Little League to Major League*, rev. ed. Lexington, MA: Stephen Greene Press, 1987.
>Brinkman is a former major league umpire.

Conlan, Jocko, and Robert W. Creamer. *JOCKO*. Philadelphia: J.B. Lippincott, 1967.
>The autobiography of National League Hall of Fame umpire Jocko Conlan.

Evans, Billy. *How to Umpire*. New York: American Sports Publishing, 1940.
>One of the best umpires of all time describes what you have to do to umpire with knowledge and confidence. American Sports published five earlier editions of this book. One, published in 1917, includes his classic "Knotty Problems."

Evans, W.G., ed. *The Toughest Decision I Ever Made as Told by the Leading Umpires*. Self-published, 1912.
>Thirty one-page accounts by some of the best-known early umps, including Bill Dinneen, Hank O'Day, Billy Klem, Jim Johnstone, Billy Evans, Silk O'Loughlin, and Bill Brennan. The only copy I could find was at the Library of Congress.

Gerlach, Larry R. *The Men in Blue: Conversations with Umpires*. Lincoln: University of Nebraska Press, 1994. Reprint of the 1980 edition published by Viking.
>An excellent oral history book on major league umpires featuring interviews with 12 umpires, including Bill McKinley, Emmett Ashford, Jim Honochick, Beans Reardon, and Ernie Stewart.

Gittlitz, Hy. *Don't Kill the Umpire*. New York: Grosby Press, 1957.
>Explains why many situations on the field look different to umpires than to spectators in the stands.

Gorman, Tom, as told to Jerome Holtzman. *Three and Two!: The Autobiography of Tom Gorman, the Greatest Major League Umpire*. New York: Charles Scribner's Sons, 1979.

Gregg, Eric, and Marty Appel. *Working the Plate: The Eric Gregg Story*. New York: William Morrow, 1990.
    Gregg became one of the most controversial umpires in major league baseball due to his weight and his large strike zone.

Gutkind, Lee. *The Best Seat in Baseball but You Have to Stand*. New York: Dial Press, 1975.
    The author accompanied a National League umpire crew throughout the 1974 season to the ball park, umpires' dressing room, homes, bars, and restaurants to portray a candid picture of their experiences in their own, unvarnished language. Southern Illinois University Press issued a reprinted edition in 1999.

Hadley, George B. *Fundamentals of Baseball Umpiring*. Fullerton, CA: Umpire Press, 1981.
    A description of umpiring mechanics including proper use of equipment, signals and communication, duties of the plate and base umpires, and handling arguments.

Johnson, Harry "Steamboat." *Standing the Gaff*. Nashville, TN: Parthenon Press, 1935.
    The autobiography of perhaps the most famous minor league umpire who never umpired in the majors. He spent the bulk of his career, 28 years, in the Southern Association. The University of Nebraska Press reprinted it in 1994 with a foreword by Larry R. Gerlach.

Kahn, James M. *The Umpire Story*. New York: G.P. Putnam's Sons, 1953.
    A history of the profession and the umpire's role from the late 1840s to 1950.

Luciano, Ron. *The Fall of the Roman Umpire*. New York: Bantam Books, 1986.
    More stories from the author of *The Umpire Strikes Back* (see below).

_____. *Remembrance of Swings Past*. New York: Bantam Books, 1988.
    More stories.

_____. *Strike Two*. New York: Bantam Books, 1984.
    More stories.

_____, and David Fisher. *The Umpire Strikes Back*. New York: Bantam Books, 1982.
    A former major league umpire known for his theatrics on the field gives the inside stories on players and umpires that you rarely see in the sports pages and on his short-lived career as the color commentator for NBC's *Game of the Week*.

Mason, Tom, ed. *Softball Umpires Manual*. Oklahoma City: Amateur Softball Association, 1977.
    "Descriptions of good umpiring techniques at the plate and on the bases, handling of unusual situations, and ... how to look, act and be, a proud professional softball umpire."

Merrill, Durwood, with Jim Dent. *You're Out and You're Ugly, Too!* New York: St. Martin's Press, 1998.
    A former major league umpire's humorously written autobiography.

Pallone, Dave, with Alan Steinberg. *Behind the Mask: My Double Life in Baseball*. New York: Viking Books, 1990.
    A revealing look at baseball through the eyes of a man with two perspectives: one as an umpire, the other the gay sensibility in forbidden straight territory.

Pinelli, Babe, as told to Joe King. *Mr. Ump*. Philadelphia: Westminster Press, 1953.

The autobiography of a minor and major league ball player turned umpire for the Pacific Coast League and the National League. Fisticuffs came naturally.

Postema, Pam, and Gene Wojciechowski. *You've Got to Have Balls to Make It in This League: My Life as an Umpire.* New York: Simon & Schuster, 1992.
An account of her 13 years as a minor league umpire and her disillusionment with Major League Baseball after being told in 1989 that she was no longer a major league umpire prospect.

Pyle, Thomas F. *Listen, Ump: 500 Knotty Problems in Baseball.* Self-published, 1948. Allied Printing issued a revised edition in 1950.

Shannon, Mike. *Everything Happens in Chillicothe: A Summer in the Frontier League with Max McLeary, the One-Eyed Umpire.* Jefferson, NC: McFarland, 2004.

Shirts, Morris A., and Kent E. Myers, with the help of Klien Rollo. *Call It Right! Umpiring in the Little League.* New York: Sterling Publishing, 1977.
The signals, positioning and responsibility, field decorum, troublesome rules and difficult calls.

Skipper, John C. *Umpires: Classic Baseball Stories from the Men Who Made the Calls.* Jefferson, NC: McFarland, 1997.
Accounts of "some of baseball's finest moments" including Don Larsen's perfect game, Roger Maris' sixty-first home run, and a Nolan Ryan no-hitter, by umpires who called the games.

Index

prepared by Skip McAfee
Bibliography Committee, Society for American Baseball Research

Numbers in *italic* represent photographs.

Abrahams, Edward, Jr. 46
Addie, Bob 58, 66, 101, 103, 125, 198
Adragna, Lou 93
Alcoser, Vince 93
Allen, Johnny 71–72
Allen, Maury 74
Altrock, Nick 14
Ambrosius, Mark 7
Aparicio, Luis 109
Appling, Luke 78, 116
Auker, Elden 25

Bagby, Jim, Jr. 69
Baker, K.O. 37–38
ball boys 26
Baltimore, Kid 38
Bancroft, Dave 52
Barlick, Al 50, 108–109
Barr, George 30, 87, 92–93, 118, 120
Barrett, Charley 43–44
Barrow, Ed 34, 95
Basenfelder, Don E. 33
Bassler, John 59
Batts, Matt 51
Beck, Zinn 75, 131
Bench, Johnny 109
Bentz, Roman 88, 95, *161*
Berg, Moe 13, 67, 195–196
Berger, Wally 49
Bergman, Arthur (Dutch) 44
Berra, Yogi 5, 67–68, 74, 81, 109

Bisher, Furman 13
Bishop, Max 112
Blue, Lu 111–112
Bluege, Ossie 105
Boley, Joe 35, 75, 130
Boston Braves 14, 23–24
Boston Red Sox 23, 54
Boudreau, Lou 57, 84
Boykin, Tyrone 121
Bradley, Alva 54, 72
Bridges, Tommy 74
Briggs, Spike 104
Broeg, Bob 108–109
Buckley, Rev. William 104
Burnes, Robert L. 85
Burns, Howard 43–44
Burt, Brig. Gen. Andrew Sheridan 56
Burt, Brig. Gen. Reynolds J. 56
Busby, Jim 6, 105, 113
Byrne, Tommy 61
Byron, Bill 67–68

Caldwell, Earl 69–70
Campanella, Roy 6
Caras, Jimmy 47
Carmichael, John 68
Carpenter, Bill 34, 96
Carrasquel, Chico 24
Cartwright, Al 17
Cerv, Bob 57
Chandler, A.B. (Happy) 96, 106, *138*

Chapman, Ben 63
Chicago White Sox 24, 54
Chylak, Nestor 2, 200
Cifrese, Frank 93
Cincinnati Reds 49
Cleveland Indians 19, 54, 71–72
Coan, Gil 73
Cobb, Ty 19, 42–43, 112
Cobbledick, Gordon 54
Cochrane, Mickey 19, 43, 49–50, 61, 76, 122
Coleman, Joseph P. 5
Collins, Eddie 19, 35
Combs, Earle 19, 67, 112, 156
Conlan, Jocko 33, 50, 95, 108, 116
Connolly, Tommy 16, 19, 30–32, 53, 84, 95, 108, 116, 118, 120, 143–144, 162
Considine, Bob 21
Cooke, Dusty 54
Corriden, Johnny (Red) 24
Courtney, Clint 198
Coyle, Bill 192
Craig, Lefty 82
Cravath, Gavvy 68
Cronin, Joe 43, 71–72, 123
Crosetti, Frank 23, 154

Daley, Arthur 82, 198
Dandridge, Ray 109
Deary, Barney 94
DeMaestri, Joe 84
Derringer, Paul 49
Detroit Tigers 59, 85, 198
Dickey, Bill 49, 51
Dickson, Paul 56
DiMaggio, Joe 22, 45, 49, 69, 93, 96, 111, 113, 139, 173, 193
Dinneen, Bill 35
Dixon, Hal 99
Doerr, Bobby 16, 109
Donatelli, Augie 59–60, 93, 99, 146
Donnelly, Arthur 29
Drennan, Mike 75
Dropo, Walt 60
Duffy, G. Thomas 85
Dundon, Ed 194
Dunn, Jack 76, 197
Durocher, Leo 14, 19
Dykes, Jimmy 13, 25, 29, 35, 61–64, 67, 75, 89–90, 118, 130

Early, Jake 24, 93, 146
Earnshaw, George 40
Ebert, Bernie 85
Egan, Ben 76
Engel, Joe 197
Engleman, George 47
Etten, Nick 55
Evans, Al 70
Evans, Billy 7, 13, 26–27, 29–31, 54, 66, 96, 108, 111, 114–116, 118, 120, 122, 130, 143, 162, 180
Evans, Bob 30
Evans, Jim 1–4, 20, 95, 115, 119, 121–127, 200–201

Fain, Ferris 63
Falk, Bibb 53
Feeney, Chub 197
Feller, Bob 5, 15, 48, 61, 72, 109
Ferguson, Robert (Death to Flying Things) 120
Ferrell, Rick 53, 109
Ferry, Bradford 38
Ferry, Carol 39
Ferry, Magdaline P. see McGowan, Magdaline (Madge)
fines 23, 80, 84–85
Fingers, Rollie 109
Flaherty, John (Red) 2, 88, 99
Flaherty, Vincent X. 130
Flammia, Rocco 93
Flanagan, Glen 38
Ford, Whitey 57
Fothergill, Bob 36
Fowler, Dick 73
Fox, Nelson 5
Foxx, Jimmie 19, 40, 45, 71
Frick, Ford 40, 108
Fridley, Jim 129
Frisch, Frankie 32, 46
Froese, Grover 99
Furillo, Carl 6

Gaffney, John 120
Gallin, John 93
Galloway, Chick 35
gambling 180
Gehrig, Lou 17, 19, 25, 43, 45, 70, 74, 111, 122–123, 138
Gehringer, Charlie 67, 109
Gelbert, Doug 191

Gerlach, Larry 7, 8, 109
Gibson, Bob 109
Gilbert, Bill 22
Giles, Warren 108, 118
Gilks, Bob 30–31
Gomez, Lefty 15, 22, 123
Goodman, Ival 49
Gordon, Joe 66
Gorman, Tom 7
Goslin, Goose 13, 75–76, 131, 197
Graham, Frank 93
Graham, George M. 34
Greenberg, Hank 16, 45, 78, 94
Grieve, Bill 16, 181
Griffith, Clark 45, 75–76, 80, 89, 103, 105–106, 192, 197
Griffith Stadium 5–6
Grove, Lefty 19, 43, 45
Guglielmo, Augie 99
Gutkind, Lee 7

Haas, Mule 112
Hall of Fame 107–110
Hall of Famers 19, 109–110
Harridge, Will 17, 24, 33, 62, 72, 80, 82–85, 104–105, 116, 118, 198
Harris, Brad 108
Harris, Bucky 13, 22–23, 35, 54, 74, 76, 105
Hartnett, Gabby 49–50
Hayes, Frankie 73, 196
Heilmann, Harry 68–69, 72
Helms, Paul 56
Hemond, Roland 94
Henrich, Tommy 22, 49
Herman, Billy 76, 109
Herman, Jack 25
Heydler, John 120
hidden-ball trick 154
Hodges, Gil 6, 118
Hoeft, Billy 85
Honochick, Jim 24–25, 102
Hoover, J. Edgar 45, 105
Hornsby, Rogers 43, 84
Hoy, William (Dummy) 55–56
Hoyt, Waite 19
Hubbard, Cal 16, 41, 104, 107–108, 116–117, 127, 181, 200
Hudson, Sid 53, 57, 61, 66, 122
Huggins, Miller 19, 40
Hughes, James Y. (Shorty) 23–24

Hulbert, William A. 116
Hunsicker, Gerry 124
Hurley, Ed 24, 90
Hurst, Tim 131

Isaminger, James 49, 71

Jackson, Travis 93, *146*
James, Jesse 55
Jamison, J.V., Jr. 27, 192
Jenkins, Ferguson 109
Johnson, Ban 30, 34, 56, 76, 116, 120, 192
Johnson, Eddie 76
Johnson, George 99
Johnson, Harry (Steamboat) 42
Johnson, Jack 42–43
Johnson, Walter 43, 45, 52, 76, 110–111
Jones, Ed 70
Joost, Ed 70
Jorgens, Arndt 64
Judge, Joe 14, 105

Kahn, James 7
Kaline, Al 109
Kase, Max 59, 110
Katzman, Izzy 108
Keenan, Tommy 42–43
Kell, George 109
Keller, Charlie 22, 44, 49
Kellner, Alex 90
Kennedy, Bob 24
Kieran, John 28, 40
Kiner, Ralph 109
Kinnamon, Bill 93, 107
Klem, Bill 16, 31–32, 43, 50, 56, 95, 108, 118, 122, 130, 143, 148, 179
knockdown pitches 22–23
Kozar, Al 80–81
Kruger, Art 56
Kryhoski, Dick 50
Kuhel, Joe 78, *79*, 81

Lajoie, Nap *104*
Landis, Kenesaw Mountain 29, 84, 102
Lary, Lyn 70
Lawry, Otis 26
Layden, Pete 81
Lazzeri, Tony 19, 74, 111
Lemon, Bob 109
Lemon, Jim 6

Leonard, Buck 109
Leonard, Emil (Dutch) 46
Lewis, Buddy 69–70, 93, 121, *146*
Lewis, Franklin 127
Lindell, Johnny 55
Longines watches 14–15
Lopat, Ed 55, 94
Lopez, Al 94, 109, 118
Lopez, John 124
Luciano, Ron 7
Luke, Don 5
Lynch, Thomas 120

Mack, Connie 19, 43, 45, 49, 73–75, 96, 196
MacPhail, Lee 110
Maddux, Greg 121
Mantle, Mickey 5, 115
Mapes, Cliff 85
Marberry, Fred (Firpo) 117–118
Marichal, Juan 109
Marion, Marty 84
Marshall, Bob 110
Martin, John D. 27
Masterson, Walt 7, 15–16, 22–23, 53
Mayburry, W.T. 106
Mays, Willie 6
McAuley, Ed 19, 72
McCaffrey, Eugene 50
McCaffrey, Roger 50
McCann, Dick 17–18, 83
McCarthy, Catharine Agnes *see* McGowan, Catharine Agnes
McCarthy, Joe 48, 60–61, 64–66
McClellan, Jim 93
McCurdy, Harry 26
McDonald, Arch 46
McGowan, Alexander (brother) 36
McGowan, Alexander (uncle) 35–36
McGowan, Bessie (aunt) 35
McGowan, Bill *35, 39, 40, 46, 59, 65, 88, 105, 137, 138, 139, 146, 149, 165*; autocratic personality 21–22; autograph of 132–133; basketball 38–40; birth of 35; blown calls 53–55; Blue Ridge League 27, 29, 34, 44; boxing 26–27, 36–38, 41–43; catcher's balk 68; childhood 36; chocolate, fondness for 15; coaching players 72–74; consecutive games streak 17–18; consistency 53; controlling the game 58–

66; cooking 41; Cuban pitchers 129; death of 101; debuts as umpire 33–35, 191–192; Delaware Sports Hall of Fame 101; diabetes 101–103; dog racing 91, 199; ego 21–22; ejection of players and managers 23–25, 61–66, 71, 84; endorsements (advertising) 14–15; fines 80, 85; fraternization rule 57; funeral of 104; gambling 102, 199; gardening 15; golf 40; half-swings 111; Hall of Fame induction 8, 107–110; health (broken toe) 17; health (general) 101; health (heart attack) 101, 103; health (heat exhaustion) 101; health (neuritis) 17; honors 25, 43, 45–47, 50, 105, 107–110; horse racing 102, 199; humor, sense of 14, 66–68; hustling 16, 49, 103, 110; International League 26–27, 34, 76; marriage 38–41; nervousness 19, 31; New York State League 34; nickname "Big Shot" 26–28; nickname "Broad-minded" 111; pension 103–104; physical conditioning 16; Piedmont League 103; players, interaction with 15–16, 19–20, 130–131; playoff game (1948) 82; quips 8, 21, 23, 54; radio 46; respected as umpire 48–50, 102, 104–106, 109, 125, 130; rules, application of 70–72, 127; rules, breaking the 68–70, 81; scouting players 74–77; selection of umpires 20, 87–100, 106–107, 118; signals 57; skills as umpire 127; softball 16, 45; South Atlantic (Sally) League 75; Southern Association 27, 34; Southern League 68; speaker 43–45, 103, 187; *The Sporting News* 42, 47; sportswriters, relationships with 85–86, 108; sportswriting 33, 42–43, 83; suspensions 26–27, 78–86, 198; teaching 33, 51, 117, 125; teetotaler 36; television 46, 103; textbook on umpiring 135–187; Touchdown Club (Washington, D.C.) 43–45, 86, 105; Tri-State Basketball League 40; Tri-State League (Pennsylvania, Delaware, New Jersey) 34; umpires, relations with 24–25, 32–33, 64, 82, 117; umpiring attitude 16, 21, 25, 58–66, 121; umpiring style 16, 57–58, 83, 110, 129–130;

Virginia League 18, 34; wedding 38; World Series (1928) 18, 31, 112; World Series (1931) 31, 130; World Series (1935) 47, 49–50, 76, 131; World Series (1939) 49; World Series (1947) 113; World War II 45–46
McGowan, Bill (Bibbs) (nephew) 39, *40*
McGowan, Bill, Jr. (son) 8, 18, *35*, 38, *39, 40,* 41–42, 46, 106–107, 110, 192
McGowan, Catharine Agnes (mother) 35–36
McGowan, Catharine M. (sister) 36
McGowan, Elizabeth (sister) 36
McGowan, Henrietta (Hetsy) (daughter-in-law) 8
McGowan, Jane F. (sister) 36
McGowan, John (grandson) 109
McGowan, John A. (Jack) (brother) 33, 36, 41, 191–192
McGowan, John Aloysius (father) 35–36
McGowan, Joseph (uncle) 35
McGowan, Magdaline (Madge) (wife) *35,* 38–41, *39, 40, 46,* 83, 101, 103, 105–106
McGowan, William (uncle) 35
McKechnie, Bill 49
McKinley, Bill 90, 92–93, 99
McNair, Eric 24
McQuinn, George 43
Meany, Tom 42, 51
Merrill, Durwood 7
Metro, Charlie 37, 61, 122
Meusel, Bob 59
Michaels, Eddie 47
Miley, Jack 83–84
Millelbuscher, C.F. (Skip) 7
Miller, Bing 31, 63
Mize, Johnny 109
Monteagudo, Rene 24
Morgan, Joe 109–110
Moriarty, George 89, 179
Murray, Ray 50
Musial, Stan 110
Mutart, Al 93

Najjar, Nick 193
Nallin, Dick 122
Napp, Larry 2, 99, 123
Naquin, Oliver F. *88*

New York Giants 19
New York Yankees 18–19, 20–23, 49, 55, 59, 112
Newcombe, Don 6
Newhouser, Hal 110
Noren, Irv 73, 196

Obojski, Robert 26
O'Loughlin, Silk 29, 120
Ormsby, Red 14, 29, 41, *59,* 87–89, 116, 143
Ott, Mel 46
Owens, Brick 54

Paige, Satchel 198
Palmer, Jim 110
Paparella, Joe 79–80
Parnell, Mel 53, 57, 78
Passarella, Art 93, 118, *146*
Pennock, Herb 43
Perry, Gaylord 110
Pesky, Johnny 123
Peters, Rusty 55
Philadelphia Athletics 18–19, 22, 34–35, 75, 112
Phillips, Dave 7
Piersall, Jimmy 113, 127
Pinelli, Babe 7, 41
Pipgras, George 50, 55, 116
Pollock, Ed 13
Potter, Nelson 117
Povich, Shirley 26, 48, 60, 81–82, 118, 192, 197
Powell, Jake 65–66
Prince, Frank 93

Queen, Mel 74
Quigley, Ernie 118
Quinn, Johnny 16, 24, 181

Radcliff, Ray (Rip) 29
Reardon, Beans 41, 131
Reese, Pee Wee 6, 110
Reeves, Joe 14
Reynolds, Allie 81, 90
Rice, Harry 70, 74
Rice, John 2, 90–91, 94, 99, 106, 127
Rice, Sam 75, 105
Richards, Paul 51, 63
Richardson, Tommy *165*
Rickey, Branch 108

Rigler, Charles (Cy) 56
Rigney, Johnny 36
Ripken, Cal, Jr. 17
Ritter, Lawrence 8
Rizzuto, Phil 5, 76
Roberts, Robin 110
Robinson, Aaron 25
Robinson, Brooks 110
Robinson, Eddie 54
Robinson, Jackie 6
Rockwell, Norman 110
Rolfe, Red 22
Rommel, Eddie 35, 75, 94, 116, 130
Rosen, Al 94
Rowland, Clarence (Pants) 59, 120
Rue, Joe 64
Ruel, Muddy 52
Ruffing, Red 22, 94
Ruhl, Oscar 85–86
Runnels, Pete 19–20
Russo, Marius 66
Ruth, Babe 19, 23, 42–43, 59, 70, 74,
    76, 88, 93–94, 108, 111–112, 137, 138

Sain, Johnny 118
St. Louis Browns 84–85, 111
St. Louis Cardinals 31–32
Scarborough, Ray 78–80, 79
Schacht, Al 35, 46, 122
Schalk, Ray 43
Schilling, Curt 3
Schoendienst, Red 110
Seaver, Tom 110
Seminick, Andy 93, 146
Sewell, Joe 53–54
Shaner, Pat 191
Shantz, Bobby 70
Shawkey, Bob 43
Shea, Spec 113
Sheridan, Jack 116, 120
Shibe Park 19
Siegel, Morrie 46, 129
Simmons, Al 19, 22, 33, 68–69, 113
Sisler, George 69
Skipper, John 7
Skowron, Bill 57
Slaughter, Enos 110
Smith, Gene 38
Smith, Ira 74
Snyder, Deron 58
Soar, Hank 2, 84, 117, 198

Somers, Al 91, 93, 105–107, 129, 139,
    153
Spahn, Warren 110
Speaker, Tris 19, 43, 65, 65, 104, 113
Spencer, Roy 63
Spink, J.G. Taylor 41, 106
spitball 22
Stahlbusch, Erik 121
Stann, Francis 129
Stengel, Casey 55, 66, 68
Stephens, Vernon, Jr. 93
Stewart, Ed 79, 79
Stewart, Ernie 33, 55, 60, 102
Stewart, Walter 87
Stobbs, Chuck 57
strike zone 50–53
Sudol, Eddie 93
Summers, Bill 29, 33, 41, 60, 64, 117,
    148

tag plays 52–53
Tebbetts, Birdie 55, 63–64
Thomas, Knocky 86
Thompson, Forrest 81
Toole, John Conway 27
Torre, Joe 197
Trade, Hugh 50
Travis, Cecil 113
Tresh, Mike 24

Umont, Frank 94
Umphlett, Tommy 60–61
umpires and umpiring: advice 154–157,
    178–181; appearance 144; arguments
    154, 166; balks 156; base umpire 160–
    161, 172, 174–177; batting order 145,
    158; becoming an umpire 2, 30–33,
    114–115; books on 7–8; calling balls
    and strikes 50–53, 147–150, 152;
    career choice 114–118; code of ethics
    120–122; common sense 178, 180–181;
    conduct of the game 158; controlling
    the game 58–66, 120, 125–126, 150;
    decisiveness 172; double umpire sys-
    tem 160–161, 167–170, 174–177, 183–
    185; dropped third strike 172; ejec-
    tions 23–25, 61–66, 71, 84, 126–127,
    166; equipment 97–98, 118, 144, 156;
    evaluation of 124; "even up" deci-
    sions 179; eye on the ball 146, 154;
    eyesight 94–95, 126, 180; fair and foul

balls 151; fans, relationships with 155; field of play 145–146; finding a job 99–100; fitness of the grounds 158–159; forfeitures 158; framing the pitch 61; ground rules 145, 158; grudges 155, 180; "homer" 179; honesty 178; hustling 16, 49, 103, 110, 153, 157, 181; impartiality 114, 116; indicator 170; infield fly rule 158, 172–173; interference 157–158; judgment 162; partner umpire 152–153; physical stature 95; players, interaction with 15–16, 19–20, 130–131, 166; positioning 126, 152–151, 172, 174–177; Professional Baseball Umpires Corp. 119, 124; protests 172; public perception of 115; quality of 118–119, 124–125; QuesTec 3, 124, 189; rabbit ears 178; rule book 171; rules, application of 70–72, 125–127, 162–165, 167–170, 182–185; salary 97; selection of 20, 87–100, 106–107, 116–118, 125; "shown up," being 66, 166; signals 55–57, 172; single umpire system 159–160; stance behind the plate 147; style 13, 57, 119–123, 128; supervision of 119; support from league 120–121; sweeping off home plate 150; triple umpire system 171; umpire in chief 158; umpire schools 30, 87–100, 106–107, 118–120, 124, 185, 186; uniforms 30, 32, 97; union benefits 123; violence, coping with 28–29, 119

Van Graflan, Roy 57
Veech, Ellie 85

Veeck, Bill 84–85
Vernon, Mickey 21, 70
Vitt, Oscar 71–72
Vitter, Jack 28–29

Walker, Dixie 105
Walker, Tom 28
Wallace, Bobby 118
Wallaesa, Jack 61
Walsh, Big Ed 118
Walsh, Francis 93
Washington Senators 14, 22–24, 34–35, 70, 75–76, 78–81, 83, 192
Wendelstedt, Harry 20, 106–107, 119, 124
Wendelstedt, Hunter 107
Werber, Billy 15, 21, 49, 73–74, 102–103, 131, 195
Wertz, Vic 6
West, Joe 197
Will, George 13
Williams, Billy 110
Williams, Ted 5, 16, 23, 48, 72–73, 106, 109–111, 113, 117, 190, 193
Willis, Vic 110, 200
Wilson, Frank 59
Wilson, Jack 23
World War II 45–46, 69
Wright, Harry 194
Wyman, Sid 102
Wynn, Early 110

Yawkey, Tom 103–104
York, Rudy 67
Yost, Eddie 5
Young, Benjamin F. 120